Thomas Campbell Finlayson

Essays, Addresses, and Lyrical Translations

Thomas Campbell Finlayson

Essays, Addresses, and Lyrical Translations

ISBN/EAN: 9783744787437

Printed in Europe, USA, Canada, Australia, Japan

Cover: Foto ©Thomas Meinert / pixelio.de

More available books at **www.hansebooks.com**

ESSAYS, ADDRESSES AND LYRICAL
TRANSLATIONS

Very sincerely yours,
T. Campbell Finlayson.

ESSAYS, ADDRESSES

AND

LYRICAL TRANSLATIONS

BY THE LATE

THOMAS CAMPBELL FINLAYSON, D.D.

MINISTER OF RUSHOLME CONGREGATIONAL CHURCH,
MANCHESTER

With a Biographical Sketch

BY

A. S. WILKINS, LL.D., Litt.D.

OWENS COLLEGE, MANCHESTER

London
MACMILLAN AND CO.
AND NEW YORK
1893

PREFACE.

ON the death of my brother, many of his friends expressed a desire for a memorial volume containing a notice of his life and some selections from his MSS. or published articles.

Professor Wilkins, who had known him in Cambridge, as well as in Manchester, kindly undertook to write a biographical sketch.

As various volumes of his sermons and expositions had already appeared, it seemed desirable, in making a selection from his writings, to present something different. During one part of his long illness, while anticipating a partial recovery, he had beguiled the time by planning, in his own mind, a possible volume of essays, to be prepared while waiting for the return of bodily strength. He had even dictated a list of those he had in view. On tracing the titles in MSS. or in magazines, it was found that some were scarcely adapted for the purpose of such a collection unless re-written: they were too much in the sermon form. No doubt the author had intended to re-write the whole of his proposed essays, condensing or expanding as occasion demanded, and recasting the form of some of them. Such revision being now impossible, the only way was to exclude those which seemed unsuitable.

The MSS., although not prepared for the press by the author, were so carefully written that they could be used, as they stood, for the present purpose. It was felt that no changes could be attempted except by the omission of certain portions to lighten the essay, or by slight verbal alterations, in accordance with the requirements of this volume. Even as regards omission, the presence of certain marks in the MSS. frequently allowed of this being done in accordance with his own ideas.

The author had not included in his list the first paper in this volume—on Tennyson's "In Memoriam." He had prepared in 1870 a somewhat elaborate series of notes as a Commentary on "In Memoriam," and he had used these in various prelections. He intended at one time to publish this Commentary, but on the appearance of Dean Gatty's volume he hesitated and postponed. The notes referred to seem of too detailed a character to be suitable for any but close students of the poem, and so they have not been included in this volume; his more popular essay, however, on the same subject, is here given. The Commentary may yet appear by itself if this is desired.

Nor had the author named the translations of the German lyrics which appear in this volume. These were made, for the most part, about the year 1875, when the issue of the first edition of the "Deutsche Lyrik," in the *Golden Treasury Series*, had directed his attention to them. They were carefully copied into a book kept for the purpose, and my brother had often thought of submitting them in some form to the public, but his desire to improve them, or other reasons, kept him from doing so. It seemed a pity, when this chance of a miscellaneous collection of papers arose, to deprive his friends of the result of so much care. Although many verses of his own poetry exist in his MSS. or in magazines, it appeared best to limit the selection of poetry to the translations from celebrated German lyrics. The rendering of Heine's pieces into English verse is confessedly difficult, and any serious attempts in this direction are likely to prove interesting.

The selections from the author's printed articles include some of his earliest as well as his latest. The group of essays on the "Imagination" begins with one dated 1858: the same group contains his latest public address, which he used, on an emergency, as an Ordination Charge in 1891.

The portrait prefixed to this volume is from a negative kindly supplied by Mr. Warwick Brookes, Manchester.

For those friends who may have heard or read certain addresses or papers not included in this volume, or who may desire to recall or consult them, the following list has been prepared. It is as complete as it can be made with the materials at hand: it probably omits nothing important, except a few letters of a controversial character, which were published in newspapers and magazines; although some of these were on important questions, they seemed too ephemeral for reference here.

The author's various published volumes are enumerated in the biographical sketch, pp. xxxvii., xxxviii.

JAMES FINLAYSON, M.D.

2 WOODSIDE PLACE,
GLASGOW, *August*, 1893.

LIST OF PAPERS.

"The Real and the Ideal," *The Christian Spectator*, 1858. "The Earth's Future," *The Christian Spectator*, 1861. "The Conversion of Children"; read at a meeting of the Cambridge Sunday School Union: *Union Magazine*, 1861. "The Athanasian Creed and The Burial Service," *The Christian Spectator*, 1863. "The Absolution of the Prayer Book," *The Christian Spectator*, 1863. "On the Use of a Liturgy," *The Christian Spectator*, 1863. "Propriety," *The Christian Spectator*, 1864. "The Songs of Degrees," *The Christian Spectator*, 1865. "The Spirit of Cynicism," *The Christian World Pulpit*, Dec. 6th, 1876. "The Dangers of Sentimentalism," *The Christian World Pulpit*, Jan. 10th, 1877. "The Worship of the Net," *The Christian World Pulpit*, March 14th, 1877. "Law, Miracle, and Prayer; a Parable for the Times," *The Congregationalist*, Feb., 1877, and *The Expositor*, March, 1877. "The Father's Drawing," *The Christian World Pulpit*, May 2nd, 1877. "Imputed Righteousness," *The Christian World Pulpit*, May 30th, 1877. "The Garden of the Soul," *The Christian World Pulpit*, Aug. 1st, 1877. "The Blunt Axe," *The Congregationalist*, Oct., 1877. "The Loving Discipline of God," *The Christian World Pulpit*, April 18th, 1877. "Personal Immortality," *The Christian World Pulpit*, Jan. 31st, 1877. "Golden Texts," *The Congregationalist*, Jan. 6th, Feb. 3rd, March 3rd, April 7th, May 5th, June 2nd, 1878. "Christ outside of the Inn," *The Homiletic Quarterly*, Oct., 1878. "The Irrevocable," *The Homiletic Quarterly*, Oct., 1878. "The Joy of Harvest and Victory," *The Homiletic Quarterly*, Oct., 1878. "The Practical Uses of the Imagination," *The Congregationalist*, July, 1878. "The Power of Christ's Resurrection," *The Homiletic Quarterly*, 1879. "The Concealing Power of Light," *The Manchester, Salford and District Congregational Magazine*, Nov., 1879. "Slippery Places," *The Homiletic Quarterly*, April, 1879. "Growth in Grace," *The Homiletic Quarterly*, 1879. "Christ Demanding Hatred," *The Expositor*, June, 1879. "The Healing Waters from the Temple," *The Homiletic Quarterly*, 1879. "To Him that Overcometh," *The Homiletic Quarterly*, Oct., 1879. "The Spirit, the Water, and the Blood," *The Christian World Pulpit*, Sept. 29th, 1880. "On Shirking Duty," *The Homiletic Quarterly*, Jan., 1880. "The Apotheosis of Atheism," *The Manchester, Salford and District Congregational Magazine*, Feb., 1881. "On the Duty of Giving Pleasure," *The Christian Leader*, Feb., 1882. "The Relief of Constraint," *The Manchester, Salford and District Congregational Magazine*, July, 1882. "Expectations Unexpectedly Fulfilled," *The Homiletic Magazine*, Feb., 1882. "Our Nursery Rhymes," *The Christian Leader*, Jan. 4th, 1883. "Vashti," *The Manchester, Salford and District Congregational Magazine*, July, 1883. "The Coleridgian Theory of Church and State," *The Congregationalist*, Jan. and Feb., 1884. "Unwashen Hands," *The Manchester, Salford and District Congregational Magazine*, Jan., 1884. "Ministerial Success," the Chairman's Address to the Ministers' and Deacons' Association, *The Manchester, Salford and District Congregational Magazine*, July, 1885. "Servant-Friends"; read at a devotional meeting held in connection with the Cheshire Congregational Union at Middlewich, April 6th, 1886, *Sun and Shield*, May, 1886. "The Discipline of Chance," *The Congregationalist*, August, 1886. "The Dangers of Experience," *The Manchester, Salford and District Congregational Magazine*, Oct., 1887. "The Rebel Island; a Parable for the Young," *The Congregational Monthly*, Oct., 1888. "The Evangelistic Power of Christian Character," Chairman's Address to the Lancashire Congregational Union, March 6th, 1869, *The Lancashire Congregational Calendar*, 1889. "The Importance of Discipline in the Sunday School," an Address delivered at the Manchester Sunday School Union, April, 1890, *The Congregational Monthly*, June, 1890: also *Brook & Chrystal*, 11 Market Street, Manchester, 1890. "The Beauty and Music of God's Laws," *The Christian Leader*, July 16th, 1891. "Browning's 'Pippa Passes,'" *The Christian Leader*, July 23rd, 1891. "Tested by Praise," *The Christian Leader*, Dec. 10th, 1891.

CONTENTS.

	PAGE
BIOGRAPHICAL SKETCH,	xiii
TENNYSON'S "IN MEMORIAM,"	1
CHRISTIANITY AND "THE RELIGION OF THE FUTURE,"	36
TRANSLATIONS FROM HEINE,	76
PROPRIETY AND POLITENESS,	93
THE REAL AND THE IDEAL,	111
THE PRACTICAL USES OF THE IMAGINATION,	128
THE USES OF THE IMAGINATION IN THE CHRISTIAN MINISTRY,	154
BROWNING'S "PIPPA PASSES,"	168
VASHTI,	175
STOICISM,	184
CYNICISM,	194
SENTIMENTALISM,	203
MEEKNESS,	212
THE DANGERS OF EXPERIENCE,	223
THE CONCEALING POWER OF LIGHT,	230

	PAGE
THE EVANGELISTIC POWER OF CHRISTIAN CHARACTER,	236
ON THE DUTY OF GIVING PLEASURE,	256
UNWASHEN HANDS,	260
CHRISTIAN HOSPITALITY,	266
MINISTERIAL SUCCESS, I.,	276
MINISTERIAL SUCCESS, II.,	289
THE RELIEF OF CONSTRAINT,	296
SERVANT-FRIENDS,	302
LAW, MIRACLE, AND PRAYER,	310
TRANSLATIONS FROM GOETHE,	316
TRANSLATIONS FROM SCHILLER,	323
GERMAN LYRICS—MISCELLANEOUS,	329

BIOGRAPHICAL SKETCH.

THE attempt to offer some sketch of the character and work of the author of the Literary Remains, published in this volume, need not involve much biographical detail. His life was simple and uneventful. Its incidents were, for the most part, such as were of interest and significance for few beyond a narrow circle. It would be in harmony neither with the tenor of his own life, one of singular reserve and reticence, nor with the feelings of those who are most directly concerned themselves, and most able to judge of his own wishes, to encumber the picture of his public work with the trivial details which are too often allowed to overload biographies. But the leading facts of his life may be fitly given, to suggest the forces by which that character was shaped, and the circumstances under which that work was done. And one or two critical periods may be dwelt upon somewhat more fully, as being not of merely personal interest, but as also throwing no little light upon features in the history of the Christian church on either side of the Border, which many at the present day probably fail to realize.

Thomas Campbell Finlayson was born in Glasgow on 5th February, 1836. His father, Thomas Finlayson, was a manufacturer in that city, subsequently residing at Southcroft, some three miles away in the country. His mother (Georgina Campbell before her marriage) was a woman of simple piety. As the firstborn, he was named after his parents, though not perhaps without remembrance of the Glasgow poet, Thomas Campbell. Both were members of the United Presbyterian Church, and were attracted to the ministry of the Rev. Dr. William Anderson, of the John Street Church, partly by his fame as a preacher of much power, but not less by his liberal views on questions of election and predestination. A certain repugnance to the rigid Calvinism of the Confession permeated the household, and had already led a brother of Mr. Finlayson, sen., to withdraw from the University, which he had entered with a view to the ministry.

Mr. Finlayson's education was begun at the St. Enoch's Parish School, where he was soon the leading scholar, and continued in classics and mathematics at the Glasgow High School, under Dr. Low and Dr. Bryce, where he had a tough struggle with the future Professor J. W. Hales for the Greek medal. But according to the custom of the time, not wholly abandoned even yet, at the age of fourteen and a half he proceeded to the University of Glasgow, where he was a student for five sessions (1850-1855). He appears to have made his mark from the first among an unusually brilliant group of undergraduates. Among his classmates were three who were afterwards to be eminent professors of their own University, Edward Caird, John Nichol, and William Jack; the present Provost of Oriel College, Oxford, and eminent Homeric scholar, D. B. Monro; his schoolfellow, Professor Hales; Professor J. D. Everett, F.R.S., of Belfast;

two with whom he was to be closely associated in later life, the Rev. Dr. Macfadyen of Manchester and the Rev. Dr. Mackennal of Bowdon; and others who gained distinction in various walks of life. His professors during his earlier years were, that most finished and graceful of scholars, who has unfortunately preferred to live in the memory of many generations of almost adoring students rather than in the gratitude of readers, E. L. Lushington; that prince of teachers and soundest of writers, William Ramsay; and for a session the substitute of the latter, W. Y. Sellar, for so many years the illustrious professor at Edinburgh. The prelections of the last, with his admirable criticisms of the Latin poets, and not less admirable illustrations of them from the stores of English literature, were greatly appreciated by his young pupil, and he set much store by the prize which he gained in this class. Later on he passed into the classes of Hugh Blackburn, the professor of mathematics, and of the present Lord Kelvin (the only one of his professors who is still a member of the Senate), in both of which he gained prizes; and also in the logic class of Professor Buchanan, and especially in that of moral philosophy of Dr. Fleming, he highly distinguished himself. Of the students with whom, to judge from the correspondence which has been preserved, he was on the most intimate terms, may be mentioned J. W. Hales (until he proceeded to Durham Grammar School, on his way to Christ's College, Cambridge); J. M. Ross, the sub-editor of *Chambers's Cyclopaedia*, editor of the *Globe Cyclopaedia*, and author of *Early Scottish History and Literature;* James Brown, afterwards minister in Paisley; J. D. Everett; George

Palmer, who perished in the wreck of the *London*; A. G. Fleming, the U.P. minister, who married his sister; and Tiyo Soga, the first native Kaffir missionary. Besides the work of the University classes, which he followed with the greatest regularity and diligence, though this often implied a walk of three miles in from the country before 7.30 A.M. on a dark winter's morning, he took an active part in the young men's societies both at Dr. Anderson's church and, occasionally, at the Greyfriars' Church; and there are still some who remember his clear and effective speaking, and his passionate love of debate. At the "Southcroft Club," which met on Saturday evenings at his father's house, literary, political, and philosophical questions were in the winter discussed with not less eagerness, and his circle of University friends was increased by the addition of others, of whom Dr. R. Giffen, C.B., was afterwards the best known. But in the summer the club devoted itself rather to athletic sports, into which Finlayson, with his spare, active frame, threw himself with great enthusiasm. During this period some time was also spent in his father's office, where he developed those habits of methodical accuracy which marked his writing and his conduct.

From an early age he was destined, alike by his parents' wishes and by his own predilections, for the work of the Christian ministry; and mainly through the influence of his pastor, Dr. Anderson, he decided to apply for admission to the United Presbyterian Theological Hall in Edinburgh, which he entered for the session August—September, 1854. But it was not long before he found his position there becoming untenable. He was already a deeply interested student of F. D. Maurice, though it was only at a later date that J. M. Ross introduced him to the fountain-head of much of Maurice's teaching in the theological works of Coleridge. On some points the doctrines of Dr. James Morison would have attracted him, but on others, he would have found these at least as repellent. His standpoint at this time cannot be better stated than by some extracts from a letter which he sent early in 1856 to Dr. Anderson:—

"So long as the formula put to young men at license and ordination requires them to signify an *unqualified* adherence to the doctrines of the Westminster Confession of Faith, I feel that I cannot conscientiously become a licentiate or a minister of our church. Nor so long as that Confession teaches the doctrine that God for His own glory passed an unconditional decree of reprobation upon some men and angels—that Christ died for the some who are elected, and for them alone—that there are *elect* infants—that the heathen world and all those to whom the light of the gospel never came, are inevitably and endlessly damned, etc.—I feel that I could not signify my adherence, even generally, to that Confession, because these doctrines appear to me to spring directly from the *root* of its theology, and not merely to be accidental blemishes upon it."

He goes on to reject emphatically the pleas that this subscription is a matter of form, or of historic interest, or that there is a tacit understanding that the assent is merely general. He makes a characteristically frank and earnest appeal to Dr. Anderson to use his influence, for the sake of the many whom his preaching and his books had brought to convictions directly at variance with the obvious meaning of the standards of the church, to get such a tacit understanding put into plain honest English. But he repeats that for his own part he could not give even a general assent. Dr. Anderson, in a sympathetic but not very helpful reply, recognises the extreme difficulty of his position, and evidently feels that it can only have one result. But it is worth while observing precisely what this was, especially as it has been misunderstood. It was not a question of being *required* to withdraw from the Theological Hall. No test was demanded, if I am rightly informed, of students as such. But the question was whether he should continue to travel along a road—not very attractive to him, it may be remarked, in itself—knowing all the time that he would find an insuperable barrier at the end on applying for license.

Even at this stage strong pressure was put upon Mr. Finlayson to enter the Church of England, rather than join the Independents, to whose ideal he felt himself much attracted. In March, 1856, Dr. A. Macleod, at this time joint pastor with Dr. Anderson, afterwards of Birkenhead, and to the end a much loved friend of Finlayson, dissuaded him from the latter course, advising in preference the temporary abandonment of the ministry; and his intimate friend J. M. Ross enforced the same view very strongly:—
"The unwritten creed of their churches, the motley crowd of passions, prejudices and ignorances which so frequently are opposed to a high-minded minister, render his position almost intolerable. True, if the Congregationalists accept you, you are free from the perjury attending your entrance into the United Presbyterian

Church, and you can leave when you disagree; but even when you are not at issue with your many-mouthed session in vital questions, you are almost sure to be subjected to petty annoyances arising from the contemptible spite of your counsellors darkening wisdom." Happily the experience of thirty-three years of untroubled peace on the one hand, and of the most loyal support and devotion on the other, was destined to prove to the recipient of these warnings on what narrow and partial views they were founded. But it cannot be wondered that at the time they caused much hesitation, and Finlayson finally decided to return to the Theological Hall for another autumn session, though conscious, as he acknowledged, that he had no hope left of ever being a minister in the United Presbyterian Church.

But events moved on, and Finlayson's lack of sympathy with the methods and the doctrines of the U.P. Hall became still more complete. "What think you," he writes to his friend J. G. Whyte, " of our sometimes having *four* sermons and *ten* prayers within the space of five hours? We had in one of our lectures to-day a thorough exposition of the doctrine of 'original sin,' in which it was attempted to be shown that we are treated *as if* we had been partakers of Adam's sin, and that believers are treated by God *as if* the righteousness of Christ were their own! Think of a new-born infant being liable to everlasting damnation because of a sin committed thousands of years ago! Such a doctrine is not in the Bible, or, if it is, the Bible should be shut."

Early in September he writes: "On Wednesday an essay was due to one of the professors on 'The Imputation of Adam's Sin.' The essay which I gave in very plainly denied the doctrine of imputation, although admitting all the facts of depravity and suffering. [Three other students] have given in essays to the very same effect, so that in all probability a crisis is approaching."

Shortly afterwards he preached a sermon before the students of the Hall and one of the professors, which seems to have led to severe criticisms, and there was even some talk of expulsion. Some of his friends were desirous that it should come to this. George Palmer wrote to him, giving him the judgment of Nichol and himself that he should by no means resign. "To be expelled is an ugly word, but in this case it is as honourable as resignation," whereas expulsion might result in an inquiry as to the conditions on which students were to be allowed to remain in the Hall. Mr. Finlayson did not stand alone. His friend Ross (who completed his course, but never took license) and two other students, who afterwards held important positions in the United Presbyterian Church, shared his views to some extent. An interview which each of the four had with two of the professors led only to a recognition of the extent of the divergence, although both expressed themselves as satisfied with Finlayson's frankness and candour, and as admiring the integrity of the resolution to which he had come, and early in October 1856, his resignation was sent in. He hoped it would have been accepted without further notice. But the Glasgow Presbytery also thought it necessary to take notice of the young student's heresies. After some discussion it was decided that a committee should be appointed to examine into the matter, although some held that such a course was below the dignity of the Presbytery, and one minister contended that though God Himself at times condescended to convert a sinner from the error of his ways, it was not the mission of a Presbytery, as such, to convert sinners. Mr. Finlayson felt the notoriety very keenly, but was resolved that if it came to be a matter of discipline and "session," he would be bound to carry it to the Synod. Yet he had none but grateful feelings for the courtesy and kindliness of the committee. The course of the proceedings may be best described in an extract from a letter to the lady who afterwards became his wife:—

"The committee consisted of Dr. Robertson and Messrs. Edmond, Macgill, Maclaren, and Macleod. Dr. Robertson occupied the chair, and explained to me the reason why the committee had met. The Presbytery had still a fatherly interest in me as a young man who had been under their care for some time, and they had appointed the committee in order to hear an account of the points on which I differed from the Confession of Faith. I thanked the Presbytery through them for the courtesy which had been shown me, and explained that I did not wish the conversation reported by them to the Presbytery, because, although they might report it correctly, there was a danger that afterwards it would be entirely mis-stated. To this they assented. Whereupon I commenced immediately to mention the principal points on which I differ from the Confession. . . . The whole tenor of the Confession, I said, is that Christ died for the elect alone: it is never *once* said that He died for the world, for all men. I believe that He died for all and each: this is my principal difference. I then went on to the other questions of 'imputation' and the entire damnation of the heathen world, and explained to them why I could not accept these doctrines. We then came to converse about the nature of the atonement. . . . I said I was seeking yet more light on this great subject. I told them that I knew it to be a fact that there are ministers in our Church who do not agree in their views as to the nature of the atonement, and gave it as my decided opinion that belief in the *fact* of an atonement is the *root* of the Christian life."

The report of the committee was of a vaguely exculpatory character. They were glad to be able to report that his views were not so wide of the truth as from hearsay they had been led to expect. They had to express their admiration of the conscientiousness which had led him to take this step, and were decidedly of opinion that with the views of Divine truth which he held, that step was the right and honest one to take —and so on. The report was read to the Presbytery on November 11th, when several members expressed themselves as dissatisfied with the report and with the conduct of the committee. All manner of misconceptions and misrepresentations had been rife, and the Presbytery seems to have desired more explicit statements as to the heresies of the young student. Anticipating some such possibility, Mr. Finlayson had written a letter to his friend and pastor, Mr. Macleod, claiming that they would do him the justice —in view, doubtless, of his probable future—of stating clearly that it was no question as to the nature of the atonement, but simply as to its extent, and as to the dogma of unconditional reprobation, which led to his resignation. After some discussion, the court was cleared of strangers, the letter was read, and Finlayson was suffered without further ado to cease to be a student of the United Presbyterian Church. The real point at issue could not have been put more clearly than it was by him in his interview with the committee:—

"I asked Mr. —— distinctly, whether he thought I had a right to say to *each* person in particular: 'Christ died for thee.' He answered 'No.' I care not to preach the gospel at all if it is not a gospel for *each* brother and sister whom I meet, unless I can say to *every* one, from the Queen on the throne to the humblest beggar in the land: 'My sister! my brother! Christ lived and died to redeem *thee!* thy heavenly Father has a purpose of love towards *thee!*' And, God helping me, I will preach no other gospel. . . . Surely if it be true that God willeth *all men* to be saved and to come to the knowledge of His truth, He will open up some way for me to preach this gospel of His love to my brethren. Who knows but that all these difficulties may be steps in the preparation?"

And so he went forth resolved on two things—that he would preach nothing as truth but that which commended itself to his heart and conscience, and that he would never buy the right to do so from the pulpits of his own Church by any unworthy trick or evasion in the matter of subscription. I wish here to give facts rather than comments, but it is impossible not to be struck, as one goes over the correspondence relating to this period, with the self-possession, the dignity, and the prudence of the young student not yet quite of age, as well as with the strength of his convictions. There is at times a buoyancy, almost a sportiveness, to be detected in his more familiar letters, but nowhere a touch of vanity or of love of notoriety. He is sacrificing the purpose which has guided his life so far, assuredly not with a light heart, but without hesitation, because he felt it simply impossible to do otherwise.

But the path was by no means clear. Several of his friends renewed their urgency that he should enter the Church of England. Dr. Macleod Campbell, whose discourses to the small congregation which he had gathered in Glasgow he often heard at this time, advised him to this course. His father would also have been glad if he could adopt it. His old pastor, Dr. Anderson, told him that he would be miserable in an Independent church; his other pastor, Mr. Macleod, assured him that he could find no rest there. "And yet I have always liked the idea of Independency; the principle of it seems so just, and liberal, and catholic." But he was told that in practice Independency did not fulfil its professions. Doubtless some of his counsellors had seen examples of what always is, and what always ought to be, a failure—the endeavour to work a Christian institution by un-Christian men. The ideal which Christ laid down for His disciples can hardly be suited to those who have only the name and not the heart of disciples. But it is a little surprising to find the most emphatic of warnings coming from one who held office in an Independent college. Mr. Finlayson wrote a very clear and full statement of his theological position to Dr. Samuel Davidson, then a professor in the Lancashire Independent College, and still very lovingly remembered by many of his former students. The central point, as before, was the universal extent of the atonement. As to its nature, he would be content to acquiesce in such views as those expressed in Mr. Newman Hall's popular book on *Sacrifice*, though he finds himself in fuller sympathy with Maurice, Coleridge, and Robertson of Brighton. On inspiration, too, he looks for guidance to Maurice and Coleridge, while accepting the Bible as containing a revelation of the mind of God. Imputation, whether of sin or of righteousness, he believes to be most real, and not imaginary or fictitious. And he asks whether these views would exclude him from an Independent college either in Scotland or in England. The principle of church establishments he cannot accept.

It requires us to raise again the dust of quarrels long since laid, if we are to understand how the letter which was sent in reply could possibly have been written by a member of the staff of an Independent college. Dr. Davidson was doubtless feeling keenly the suspicious injustice of the treatment which, so deeply to the regret of many of the best supporters of the college, he was then receiving; and was hardly able with all his sympathy to judge the situation aright. "I cannot encourage you," he wrote "to seek admission into any of our colleges, nor do I think you would find it easy to become the minister of an Independent church. As a friend, I would not advise you to do so. With your views and feelings, the Church of England is the only church where you would be free and unmolested. You should therefore search and try whether you could not join that communion. There may be quite as objectionable things in Dissenting bodies as the principle of an establishment." The best comment on this letter, is that, without the slightest change in his theological views, Dr. Finlayson was for years one of the most honoured and influential of the governing committee of this very college, that he acted as a most welcome occasional lecturer there, that its students often attended his ministry, that the Principal, Dr. Scott, was one of his dearest and most admiring friends, and that nowhere was the loss of his wise counsel and inspiring presence more profoundly lamented. In any case the Church of England was impossible for him. After breaking off a career of high promise in the church of his fathers by his refusal to palter with his sense of truth and honesty in subscription, he was not likely to creep in to an alien church through a gate barred at that time with a 'hearty and *ex animo* assent and consent,' involving not less strain upon his conscience than that which he had declined.[1]

In vain did Hales write from Cambridge, dwelling on the incomparable attractions of Trinity College. In vain did Ross, who had withdrawn from the Theological Hall shortly after Finlayson, express his earnest hope that he would yet see his way clear to that "asylum of earnest and liberal souls—a place of refuge both from bigotry and from unbelief." It was indeed plain enough that in Scotland there was no resting-place for him. It is happily needless to describe at any length the wide-spread distrust, fed by the most reckless calumnies, which beset him at this time.

---

[1] How strong were his conscientious objections to what he regarded as the plain and obvious teachings of the Anglican Prayer Book, came out clearly in a series of articles on the subject contributed to the *Christian Spectator* in 1863.

One specimen may be enough. No one had met him with more tender sympathy, which by no means meant agreement with his views, than Mr. James Culross, afterwards the Principal of the Baptist College at Bristol, and one of his most honoured friends. But even he tells a friend, "Our people, from servant maids to coal agents and Baptist preachers, are positively alarmed at the danger with which our orthodoxy is threatened from Mr. Finlayson's German [1] tendencies." And though he ascribes this to the action of busybodies and alarmists, he feels it is quite impossible to ask him to appear in his pulpit.

But it was not to join the English Church that Finlayson crossed the Border. For a time he seems to have cherished the plan which had been more than once previously suggested to him, of studying in Germany. But he finally decided to go to London, so as to get some insight in England into the workings of Independency, and to study at University College, London, while waiting for some way to open out for him. What he hoped for (as he says in September, 1857) was that for some four or five years, as pastor of some quiet country congregation, he might be fitting himself for more arduous and energetic work. The wrench from a much-loved home and all his Glasgow friends, and the plunge into the loneliness of London life were keenly felt; but he was convinced that it would be a wholesome discipline to be thrown

---

[1] It may be worth noting that this is only used as an indefinite term to connote suspicion and dislike. Mr. Finlayson at this time knew no German, and there is not a trace of the influence of German writers even in translation. Indeed he was never a great student of German theology.

entirely on his own resources, and so to learn the nature and the limits of his powers. He took introductions to the Rev. E. S. Pryce of Gravesend, and the Rev. J. Baldwin Brown of Claylands Chapel, Clapham. The latter had not yet begun the issue of that series of volumes which was to place him foremost among the leaders of the more liberal Independents, but he made no secret of the direction of his sympathies, and he gave the young Scotchman the heartiest of welcomes. Finlayson found also a truly congenial spirit in the Rev. T. T. Lynch, about this time so discreditably assailed and so strenuously defended in what was known as the "Rivulet" controversy, with whose little congregation, then meeting in Grafton Street, he connected himself while attending classes in German and English literature at University College. But, as it happened, it was Mr. Pryce who was able, after giving him opportunities of preaching in his church at Gravesend, to do him the greatest service by introducing him to the Congregational Church at Cambridge.

It almost requires an effort nowadays to realize the position of Nonconformity in the Universities thirty-five years ago. At Oxford, Dissenters were virtually unknown; at Cambridge they were very few and scattered. The abolition of University tests, the effect of which was destined to be so far-reaching, indirectly much more than directly, was still in the future; and although the legislation of 1856 had begun to make the higher education more easily accessible to all classes, in 1858 its beneficent effects were only just beginning to be felt. Indeed, it was in that very year that, for the first time, a Nonconformist by conviction, Mr. H. M. Bompas (now Q.C.), won a place in the mathematical tripos, which established a claim to a fellowship, and so headed the list of the "army of martyrs" whose loyalty to conscience opened the Universities to the nation. Two years previously the attempt of Mr. James Heywood to abolish compulsory attendance at College chapels had failed to gain the approval even of the House of Commons. I remember, from personal experience, the summary and even scornful manner in which a request to be allowed to attend the morning service at the Independent chapel was refused a few years later by the authorities of my own college. And owing to the circumstances of the time, it was the Baptist Chapel, of which the Rev. W. Robinson was then the minister, that furnished the meeting-point for most of the Nonconformists then in residence. The small congregation of Independents met in an old-fashioned and far from attractive little building hidden away in a back street, where its very existence was probably unknown to the great majority of the University. A letter from one who knew the church well, describes it (a little unfairly) as containing "no people of real culture and refinement, and but very few young men," but as "kind and considerate." Mr. Finlayson's chief desire, after all the warnings which he had received, some of which the experiences of his time of waiting had shown not to be wholly baseless, was to find a pulpit from which he could speak freely, and his best friends counselled him to go to Cambridge, at first purely as an experiment. After preaching for two Sundays, and leaving a very favourable impression of his genuineness and sincerity, as well as of his personal charm, he was offered an engagement for three months, covering the latter part of 1858, which he accepted. The outcome of this was a very hearty invitation to the pastorate, and he entered on his settled work on the first Sunday of March, 1859, when he was just 23 years of age. In the notes of a speech which he made two years afterwards, looking back upon this time, I find frank expression given to the anxieties with which he entered on his task, anxieties arising partly from his own inexperience of pastoral work, partly from the forebodings of his friends as to the restrictions under which he might find himself in an Independent Church, and partly, too, from the memories of divisions and discords which had not been unknown at Cambridge. But he acknowledges heartily that these anxieties had not been justified, and that nothing could have exceeded the freedom and the peace which he had enjoyed. The emoluments of his post were not large, but they were sufficient to justify him, without neglect of that prudence in money matters which always seemed to him inseparable from self-respect, to take upon himself further responsibilities. On September 15th, 1859, he married Miss Helen Rankine, of Kilsyth, a lady to whom he had been for some years engaged. It is not seemly to say more of one who is still living than that in her devoted and unfailing sympathy he found the supreme blessing of his life. One son and five daughters were born of the marriage, all of whom survived him.

Into his work as preacher and pastor at Cambridge Mr. Finlayson threw himself with an energy which overflowed the bounds of prudence. It may well have been that his want of experience, and the lack of that training as assistant to some older minister, which many of our younger men are now finding so helpful, made the burden heavier, but, in any case, the task of writing two or often three carefully-prepared discourses each week was a serious one; and he was never reluctant to meet additional claims, such, for instance, as the course of lectures on the Prayer Book, the substance of which appeared in the articles already referred to. He drew almost recklessly on the physical strength, which had never as yet failed him. Late hours, hard study, and the pressure of family anxieties—his father's circumstances about this time changing seriously for the worse—told upon him heavily, and in 1864 led to a nervous breakdown, which lasted for many months. Even when he appeared to have recovered, it left its permanent effects. In his early manhood he had been singularly cool and self-possessed. Though he was not lacking in modesty, his self-command and personal dignity had never failed him in the most trying circumstances; but from this time forward he was destined to suffer from a permanent repugnance to publicity, and a self-distrust and shyness, which, if at times all but overcome, were on other occasions absolutely paralysing. When but 23 years old, he had preached, at Dr. Anderson's request, to a congregation which filled the City Hall at Glasgow, with composure and self-control under very trying circumstances: in later life, he was at times utterly unable to address even a couple of hundred sympathetic hearers. It was no wonder that some of his friends were urging a change of pastorate. As he justly said himself, no mercantile considerations had ever entered into his relations with his church at Cambridge. As he came to be better known, various larger and wealthier churches had endeavoured to secure him. Leicester, Halifax, and Birmingham had all tempted him away; and in each case his pecuniary position would have been much improved, but he had met them with a prompt and decided refusal. But the period which he had marked out for his preliminary pastorate had more than passed: the needs of a rapidly growing family could not be overlooked, and he felt that the relief that might be gained by a respite from the duty of writing so many fresh sermons ought not to be refused.

In October, 1864, he was invited at the suggestion of his old college friend, Dr. Macfadyen, to preach in the new church which had just been erected (as an outcome of the bi-centenary movement) in Rusholme, then a suburb, and now a part of the city of Manchester. He at once declined, saying, "I am still only recovering strength after an illness of some months' duration, and, although greatly better, have not yet resumed my full work in Cambridge. I feel, therefore, that my own people here, having been deprived of my services during the summer and autumn, are fully entitled, throughout the winter months, to all the strength that is in me." But eight months later the pulpit was still vacant, and the application was renewed. Dr. Macfadyen, with his usual strong common-sense, put all the attractions and the disadvantages of Rusholme very fully and clearly before his friend, and bade him come and judge for himself, and let the people judge for themselves. He came in August, 1865, and preached twice. The morning sermon was on the text which now stands engraved on his memorial tablet, as of all words those most appropriate to his life: " Blessed are the pure in heart, for they shall see God." The evening discourse was that entitled, "Furnished, but vacant," afterwards printed in his first volume of sermons. No second visit was needed: it was a case of love at first sight. The force, the freshness, the spiritual power, and the intense practical earnestness of the preaching carried it at once to the hearts of the people. A very hearty invitation was sent and was accepted. Two points may be noted here in his letters and address of acceptance as especially characteristic. One is the frankness with which Mr. Finlayson warned the church that they were not inviting a man of very robust health, and that the hope of more vigorous service in a more bracing climate was the only motive that could have justified him in parting from his attached people at Cambridge. The second is the emphasis which he laid upon the character of the Christian minister as the first requisite for success. He was above all things to be a witness for God in his daily life. "He is called to look at all men—as much as he possibly can—in the light of God; to be no respecter of persons; to regard the spirit of faith and devoutness and brotherliness as the standard of highest excellence." How he had tried to live up to this himself may be seen from some words written by one who knew him well at Cambridge: "One beauty of our dear friend's character lay in simply ignoring social distinctions in his intercourse with members of his church and congregation. He would join a pic-nic party of domestic servants and journeymen tailors and little tradesmen as readily and as happily as the most well-to-do folks in our connection.[1] The congregation caught the tone of his tender loving spirit, and through his influence we cared more for each other than we had ever done before his coming." It is perhaps also worth while observing that the inquiries which he made before accepting the invitation, indicated the prudence and insight which added so much to the significance of his absolute subordination of material interests to higher claims. It was not from any ignorance or recklessness that pecuniary considerations held so little place in his mind, it was because they were so entirely outweighed by the claims of duty. Of his creed nothing more need be added here. Undoubtedly it had gained a depth and maturity during his six years' pastorate, with all its experience of teaching and of suffering; but in substance it was that same doctrine of the Universal Love of God in Christ, which he had been debarred from preaching in the United Presbyterian Church, that he came to declare in Rusholme.

And so in October, 1865, began the pastorate which was to continue without a break for the twenty-seven remaining years of his life. Of incidents there are few to be recorded. The story is one of deepening attachment within the limits of his own congregation, and of widening influence and recognition outside of it. The growth in numbers was not great or rapid. Dr. Macfadyen had already pointed to a hindrance which was likely to arise from the nearness of Union Chapel, which the eloquence, genius, and spiritual

[1] It is touching to remember that the last social gathering which he was able to have at his Rusholme home was one of the maid-servants of the congregation.

force of Alexander Maclaren was already crowding to the doors. He thought that the distance was sufficient to exclude unseemly rivalry, and certainly of unseemliness there was never a trace. No two neighbours were ever more closely united by brotherly sympathy and mutual respect, deepening on both sides into something like reverence, than Finlayson and Maclaren. None the less it was a fact, all the more evident after the congregation of Union Chapel moved to a much more spacious and attractive building considerably nearer to Rusholme, that each Sunday hundreds of persons, who might have naturally found a home at the Rusholme Church, were drawn past its doors by the magnetism of the famous preacher half a mile further townwards. Nor did Rusholme remain wholly unaffected by the streaming of the population into the remoter suburbs, which has tried so severely all our town churches. The young especially, as they settled in homes of their own, commonly found these in parts from which the country fields and lanes were more easily accessible. But in spite of this, the church at Rusholme continued to prosper, and the number of its members, which had been less than forty, increased to more than four times that number. Their only anxiety arose from the minister's frequent lack of strength. At one time his state of nervous depression and weakness was such that it was evident that something must be done. As early as 1876 or 1877 he had consulted his brother James Finlayson, M.D., of Glasgow, as to the wisdom of escaping the strain of preaching, which was trying his general health severely, by taking up literary work. At this time a way was found to relieve him, which proved most helpful and acceptable. Provision was made by the congregation for the appointment, for a time, of an assistant minister of his own selection. Mr. Finlayson was happy enough to find one after his own heart in Mr. J. A. Mitchell, B.A., of New College, London, who came to him in April, 1877, and for more than eighteen months worked with him "as a son with a father in the gospel." The feeling that there was always some one ready to take any part of the service (sermon included) to which he might not at the time feel equal, was an inexpressible relief to Mr. Finlayson; and often his mere presence freed him from nervous apprehensions which otherwise would have been quite disabling. When Mr. Mitchell was invited to the church over which he still is pastor at Nottingham, Mr. Finlayson had regained sufficient strength to take up full work again, but not without much shrinking self-distrust. In 1879 the question of literary work was raised again, at a time when he was stronger physically than he had been, but not less distressed nervously. His brother then wrote, "If you had a change from the constant anxiety about preaching, which assumes the character of a '-phobia,' I would expect you to recover, even as to preaching, just as you have done as regards walking." A professorship in a small college was regarded as highly desirable; and in some subjects Mr. Finlayson, with his clearness and consistency of thought, and his faculty of exposition, would have made an admirable teacher, but no opening of the kind offered itself, and so he went bravely on with his pastorate. It may be remarked that the want of a degree would have proved no barrier to an academical appointment with any who knew the facts of the case. His University distinctions pointed to attainments much above the standard of the ordinary M.A.; and that he did not happen to take his degree was due to causes familiar enough to all who are interested in the history of the Scottish Universities forty years ago.

With the exception of the time of break-down, the only incidents that marked this stage of his ministry were the publication of various books. A volume of sermons—*The Divine Gentleness and other Sermons*—was issued in 1874, reaching a second edition (now also exhausted) in 1884. *The Christian Voyage*, published by the Religious Tract Society, followed in 1877. It is interesting to know that this has been translated into Samoan, and has been found attractive to natives of the South Sea Islands. A little volume on *Nehemiah, his Character and Work*, was issued by the same society in 1880. In 1885 there was published *Biological Religion: an Essay on "Natural Law in the Spiritual World"*—the substance of a course of lectures on Prof. Drummond's extraordinarily popular book, delivered in the previous winter. This is not the proper place to offer any criticism of this essay, and any remarks upon it had better be postponed; but it may be observed that, small as was its compass, no previous publication had done so much to extend and heighten Mr. Finlayson's reputation for exact thinking, clear expression, and perfectly courteous but most effective polemic. A second edition was quickly called for, and this in its turn went rapidly out of print. In this same year Mr. Finlayson received and declined a tempting invitation to go out to Sydney, N.S.W. In 1886 the twenty-first anniversary of his settlement at Rusholme was celebrated by the presentation of a testimonial, including a purse of three hundred guineas. The meeting was one of those quiet gatherings at which, without formality or fuss, friends have a chance of saying out what is in their hearts, and the keynote set by Mr. Finlayson's dignified simplicity and frankness was happily sustained throughout. In 1887 he published what is, on the whole, the maturest and most continuous of his works—*The Meditations and Maxims of Koheleth, a practical Exposition of Ecclesiastes.* This is also now out of print and scarce.

The difficulty which he often felt in discharging even his regular duties made him very reluctant to accept engagements elsewhere, and it was rarely that he would either preach or speak at meetings at other churches—never, indeed, except when the claim upon him was exceptional; but by degrees he rose to a prominent position in the esteem of his brother ministers in Manchester, and indeed in Lancashire, as much by his character as by the strength of his convictions, and the dialectical powers which he showed at their fraternal meetings. In 1884 his name came out at the head of the ballot for the chairmanship of the Lancashire Congregational Union. This office is entirely honorary, the sole duty being to give the address at the annual meeting of the Union, and it is conferred simply as a mark of general respect, or as an acknowledgment of conspicuous services. But Mr. Finlayson shrank from undertaking even this duty, and declined to serve. Four years afterwards, in 1888, he was again elected. This time he accepted the position, but only on condition that a friend of his would read his address if he should find himself unable to deliver it himself. The promise was lightly given, with little thought that its fulfilment would be called for; but when the day of the annual meeting came in 1889, Mr. Finlayson, though not in worse health than was common with him, felt unequal to the ordeal, and the address, which is reprinted in this volume, was delivered by his substitute. It was very touching to see how wide-spread was the regret that physical weakness shut out from his proper place one to whom all would so gladly have done honour.

In 1891, to the great gratification of many friends, both in Lancashire and in Scotland, who had earnestly desired some such public acknowledgment of his varied attainments, his old Alma Mater of Glasgow conferred upon him the degree of D.D. The letters of congratulation which he received showed how well the distinction was felt to have been deserved. It was a source of hardly less pleasure when Dr. Finlayson was selected by the Church Aid Society to be one of its delegates to the International Congregational Council, which met in London in July of the same year. As the total number of English delegates, lay and ministerial together, was limited to one hundred, the compliment to one so retiring was felt to be a high one. He was further one of the first to be invited, and indeed strongly urged, to read a paper before the Council, but he could not be induced to consent. At the meetings of the Council he was a regular and a deeply interested attendant, though he took no part in the discussions. But while he was in London it suddenly appeared that he was far from well. Distressing symptoms of numbness in the feet and fingers and of general weakness called for medical advice, and during the latter part of that year he was frequently suffering. The exact cause of his distress was obscure. The Manchester physician whom he consulted was of opinion that there was no indication of the paralysis which he dreaded; but agreed with his brother that a long rest and change would be required to remove the nervous weakness. It was decided by his church that provision should be made for his pulpit duties for as long a time as might be needed. The Rev. W. J. Wilkins placed his much-valued services at the command of the church whenever they might be needed, and neighbouring ministers—Baptist, Wesleyan, and Presbyterian, as well as Congregational—cheerfully responded to every request for assistance. Dr. Finlayson preached for the last time on Sunday, January 10th, 1892. While the arrangements for the regular supply of his pulpit were still pending, an alarming disturbance of the digestive system threw the more purely nervous symptoms for a time into the shade, and brought him to the brink of death. From this, however, he rallied, and when able to be moved, on February 29th, he was taken to his brother's house in Glasgow, where his wife and two daughters, in concert with his brother and his sister, nursed him with the most unremitting care. His condition rapidly improved, and his powers of locomotion and of writing returned to such an extent that it seemed as if he might again be fit for at least partial duty. But early in the summer a recurrence of the digestive disorder brought him very low again, and about midsummer the loss of power and the nervous prostration seemed likely to be fatal. Again, however, he was rescued from immediate danger, but only to oscillate between recovery and relapse. About this time anxiety, which might have distressed him, was happily much relieved by the thoughtful generosity of an old member of his congregation (Mr. J. G. Silkenstädt), who bequeathed to him an annuity for his own life and that of his wife, which provided for their needs. Late in the autumn the physicians in attendance still allowed the hope that he might return to his people, and resume at least some part of his work. Unwilling to try any longer a generous patience, which he always very gratefully acknowledged, Dr. Finlayson placed himself unreservedly in the hands of his deacons, but the church, on their advice, unanimously declined to consider the possibility of a resignation, and instructed them to seek for some suitable assistant minister who might bear the whole burden of the pastorate, while leaving to Dr. Finlayson an adequate share of its emoluments, and such portion of his duties as he might be able at any time to discharge. It was a happy experience that one, who had been so repeatedly and emphatically warned at the outset of the difficulties and trials of an Independent minister, should have so slight an experience of them himself, and that the congregation which gathered around him—never more than 300 or 400 in number, and including few if any men of wealth—should have held to him to the very last with loyalty, self-sacrifice, and unfailing confidence.

But the end was now very near. The weakness rapidly increased, reducing terribly his physical strength, but hardly clouding to the end his mental powers or troubling the peace of his spirit. Five days before his death he was eager to learn the contents of the Queen's speech, and to hear what measures were to be proposed by the statesman whose return to power he had welcomed with deep satisfaction, as a triumph of the forces that make for righteousness, peace and goodwill among nations. He awaited his end with wonderful composure, surrounded by all the members of his family. Once when death was supposed to be near at hand, he asked his brother what time it was. On being told it was midnight, he quoted (with the author's name) the line of Keats—

> To cease upon the midnight with no pain—

evidently hoping that this might be his lot.[1] Other more sacred and personal utterances of these hours may be more fitly left among the hallowed memories of those who watched in the room of the husband, the father or the brother. He just survived to complete his 57th year, and two days after his birthday, on Feb. 7th, 1893, he entered peacefully on the life of the higher world. It was ascertained after death that the entire train of symptoms from which he had suffered was due to a lesion of the spinal cord, technically known as posterior and lateral sclerosis. By the wish of his family, in order to avoid a transference of the body, he was interred in the Glasgow Necropolis on Feb. 10th, services being conducted by his brother-in-law, Rev. A. G. Fleming, and the Rev. Dr. John Hunter.

---

[1] His thoughts may have been carrying him back to the Glasgow University class-room, in which, more than forty years before, Sellar had given out this passage (as Dr. Mackennal informs me) to be turned into Latin verse, reading it with his own admirable expressiveness.

A memorial service was held at the same hour in the Rusholme Congregational Church, conducted by the oldest (in standing) of the neighbouring Independent ministers, the Rev. Thos. Willis; and by Rev. Dr. Goodrich, the successor of Dr. Finlayson's old friend, Dr. Macfadyen: an address was also delivered by the writer of the present sketch, some part of which is reproduced in the following pages. The attendance was a remarkable one. The church was crowded, not only by the members of his congregation, and many who had formerly belonged to it, but also by almost all the leading Nonconformist ministers of Manchester and the neighbourhood, and not a few members and clergymen of the Church of England. The sense of loss was universal. But almost transcending the sense of loss was that of thankfulness that such a man had been known, and such a life lived. After the funeral, when letters and resolutions of condolence kept coming in from friends or public bodies, what was most striking in them all was the tone of thorough genuineness. It seemed to have been felt instinctively that terms of conventional eulogy were out of place, and that he who was lost was not only a man of singularly high ideal, but also one who lived up to his ideal, as few had ever done; one whose work had been bravely and faithfully done, but whose character was more than his work.

The task of portraying a character with adequacy and truthfulness is not an easy one, especially in a case where mutual friendship, though long and unbroken, never developed into a special or confidential intimacy. Yet with Dr. Finlayson, the transparent simplicity of the man may perhaps be allowed to acquit the attempt of the charge of presumption.

The quality which rises first to the minds of his friends, as it was that which first shaped his destiny in life, was his sensitive highmindedness. The love of truthfulness in word and deed was a passion with him. A story is still current of the emphatic protest which he made in one of the classes of the University of Glasgow, when a prize was nearly being awarded under circumstances which seemed to him forbidden by the regulations. The details are not after this lapse of time worth recording: it is quite possible that his action was somewhat ill-judged. What is certain is, that he deliberately took up a line which he knew would inevitably bring him great unpopularity, because he thought that justice required it. And so it was throughout his life. It was open to question whether an act of his was the wisest possible, for he was happily described, by an old fellow-student, as "the man who didn't make allowance for friction": it was never a matter of doubt that if Finlayson thought it to be his duty, he would do it. It was hard for him at times to realize that it was not always the same with others. I remember how, nearly thirty years ago, we were talking once on the question whether a common acquaintance would become a candidate for a fellowship, and give his assent to the doctrine of the Thirty-nine Articles and the Book of Common Prayer. "Impossible!" said Finlayson. "He couldn't do it! He doesn't believe in them!" I felt, and probably expressed, some doubt whether under the circumstances of the time, that would have anything to do with the question. But such an attitude was almost inconceivable to him. It has already been observed how he refused to give even a *general* assent to the Confession of Faith, because this would have implied far more agreement than he was prepared to express. This absolute assurance of truthfulness was one of the main sources of his power as a preacher. His teaching was felt to be no glib repetition of familiar phrases: it expressed exactly and clearly the convictions of his heart. His faith, firm and unwavering as it was, had been given him as the 'reward of the strictest fidelity to his intellectual conscience. No man was less open to the charge of sentimentalism, as no man would have felt such a charge more acutely. Beliefs with him were not wishes or feelings; they rested upon assured historic facts, or the primary intuitions, not less certain in his philosophical creed, of our moral and spiritual nature. To him the death and resurrection of the Lord Jesus were, as he often loved to call them, the historic pledge and assurance of all that he held most dear. And the paramount love for truthfulness gave him his remarkable fairness, and therefore his power, as a controversialist. He possessed to the full the love of argument, which seems native to his countrymen, and as it was said of him "positively revelled in a metaphysical discussion." But he never argued for victory rather than for truth. He always seemed to be thinking and speaking in the spirit of Butler's memorable words: "Things and actions are what they are; and the consequences of them will be what they will be; why then should we desire to be deceived." If he argued, with a force which few men rivalled, against agnosticism and materialism, it was not merely from fear of their results, but because he was convinced that they ignored the facts and the experience of life. He showed very early in his career that he would be hindered by no authority from following the evidence, whithersoever it led. Only it must be *all* the evidence, and not a part of it, chosen by prejudice. All that was *proved* by modern science or the higher criticism, he accepted unflinchingly; but he would always have the critics and the physicists remember that there were facts outside of their special spheres, which had also to be taken into account. A distinguished Q.C., who often heard him preach, wrote after his death: "I never heard any one who could reason more clearly or so fairly to establish his results as Finlayson did." This was of course in part the result of well-trained natural gifts; but the controlling power was a moral one, the sense of the supreme obligation of truthfulness.[1]

But even his most argumentative discourses were never in danger of becoming mere intellectual combats. If truth was first and foremost with him, next, and next only because it was of necessity based upon it, and drawing from it all its binding force, was duty. The truths which he most certainly believed were such as to awaken the strongest emotions; but on these emotions he dwelt but little. Perhaps it would have been better for the popularity, if not for the wholesomeness of his teaching, if he had dwelt upon them more effusively; but nothing was more alien to his intellectual constitution or to the habits of his life

---

[1] He once gave memorable expression to his conviction of the duty of exact carefulness in the use of words in a sermon on Deut. xxii. 8: "When thou buildest a new house, then thou shalt make a battlement for thy roof."

than anything approaching to "gush." He spoke far less of the religious emotions than of the basis of facts on which they should rest, or of the life which they would, if genuine, inspire. A liberal theology has at times been charged with leading to a lax morality. The narrowest prejudice could not have found an excuse for saying this of Dr. Finlayson. Much rather, as with the teaching of his honoured master, F. D. Maurice, the feeling may have been that his ideals of duty were too high for the daily life; that he called men to live upon the heights where the air was too pure and bracing for the weakness of humanity. But no such thought was ever allowed to weaken the force of his appeals, or to lighten the weight of his charges. For the shams and conventions of life, in which men are apt to enwrap themselves from the sight of the simplicity of duty, he had the most thorough contempt. In some measure this may have been quickened by his study of Carlyle, for whom on some points he had a profound admiration. But in substance it came rather from the very essence of his creed. The primary belief in the revelation of the fatherhood of God brought with it a permanent sense of the brotherhood of man. The phrase is commonly current: I have known no one who made it so constantly and thoroughly the keynote of his thought. To Dr. Finlayson differences in wealth or social position were, not as a form of speech, but really and in habitual consciousness, accidents of the time; the equality and the brotherhood were eternal. To be discourteous or inconsiderate, far more to be indifferent or unkind, to a brother who happened to have a little less gold in his pocket would have been to him simply impossible.

There was something in the nature of the questions most commonly present to his mind, and perhaps in the language in which he naturally clothed his thoughts, which made him less attractive than others, far inferior in power and in genuine sympathy, to the uneducated classes. But he was unwearied in his efforts to come into closer relations with the working people in the neighbourhood of his church, and not a few, especially of those who had known him in times of trouble, learnt to esteem and to love him greatly.

As a preacher he was clear and forcible, and at times strikingly eloquent. No man was ever less inclined to degrade the dignity of the pulpit by buffoonery; but not uncommonly, especially in the earlier part of his career, when the influence of Dr. William Anderson was still powerful with him, his scathing satire raised a smile, though when the smile had passed away, the wholesome sting remained. His sermons were always carefully written, but were delivered with much energy and freedom. It was probably due partly to conscientiousness, partly to self-distrust, after his health had begun to fail, that he adhered to the practice of writing, for in occasional speeches and in debate he had a quite remarkable power of strong, clear, and stirring speech. His appearances on the platform were but rare. He had little love of publicity, and when the need for husbanding his strength was obvious, he preferred to reserve it for his duties to his own congregation. But occasionally he spoke very effectively in his own district in support of the Liberal candidate for Parliament, his neighbour Sir Henry Roscoe, and of the representatives of unsectarian education on the School Board.

It was but natural, with Dr. Finlayson's firm belief in abstract principles, that, though always most willing to co-operate with others in all good works, he should be a strong supporter of the policy of Disestablishment. The considerations drawn from historical development, which still hinder some, though probably a diminishing number, of Nonconformists from accepting it, carried little weight to one whose intellectual tendencies were logical rather than historical and aesthetic, and those derived from expediency influenced him still less. Indeed, no man was ever less inclined to give expediency a place in any of his thoughts. That which was just and right was the thing to be done, whatever the immediate results. But he was no slave to party cries; and one of his most forcible letters was that written to the local committee of the Liberation Society, in protest against a resolution which had been passed in favour of allowing Mr. Bradlaugh to go through the form of taking an oath in the House of Commons.

As a pastor Dr. Finlayson did not possess the aptitudes which distinguished such men as his old friend and neighbour, Dr. Macfadyen. He had no special gift for organization; his nervous sensitiveness made him shrink from those social engagements which may be made to add so much to a minister's influence; nor do I think that he had the faculty of discovering the work which each member of his church had the capacity of doing, and setting him at once to do it. But he was never without interest in the various activities of the church. In his addresses at its meetings he was always genial and happy, and in the Literary Society his presence was greatly valued.

There he gave free play to a sense of humour that was usually confined to his intimate associates, and a series of papers which he wrote for this society were very delightful of their kind. "The Troubles of a Translator," "Tithenasmatiosophy," "An Interesting Album," and "My Comedy," are brimming over with a sense of fun and a sportive wit which probably came as a surprise to many of his hearers. Of the duty of hospitality he had a very strong conviction, and frequent friendly gatherings offered a bright welcome and a pleasant hour to such visitors especially as were strangers and friendless in the great city. And however reluctant he was to intrude uninvited on the privacies of family life, the call of duty was always strong enough to break through the barrier of reserve. Whenever he was aware of the presence of trouble or bereavement, no one could have been more assiduous in his visits, more genuine or more tender in his sympathy. It was on such occasions that many first learnt to know their minister, and to understand the power of those eternal realities in the presence of which he habitually lived.

As a student, he was acute and scholarly rather than learned, and his interests lay in the direction of poetry and philosophy, not of erudition. He never seemed to read, as so many do, to accumulate knowledge, still less for the sake of fashion or ostentation. Of much ephemeral literature he was well content to be ignorant; but books of value he studied carefully and critically, and it was always a great delight to hear his suggestive and outspoken opinions upon them. He attached much importance to the systematic exposition of books of Scripture, and always kept this well abreast of the best and most recent authorities, without sacrificing his own independence of judgment. A good but by no means unique specimen of his work in this direction is furnished by the volume which he was induced to publish on *Koheleth*. But perhaps he was most at home in the region where the results of science or philosophical speculation seem to touch upon religion. Hence he was peculiarly fitted to deal the *coup de grace*—as I think all qualified critics admitted that he did—to Professor Drummond's fascinating but fantastic theories of *Natural Law in the Spiritual World*. The very title of his essay, " Biological Religion," struck at the heart of the fallacy, pointing out, as it did, the dangerous delusion of " making God's action in the world of matter the measure of His action on and towards the spirits who are made in His own image." The discussion is conducted with perfect courtesy, and Dr. Finlayson fully recognises the vigour, freshness, and eloquence of the writer. But it was simply impossible for him to acquiesce in a method which ignored those facts and teachings in which from the first he had found the only solution for the riddles of the world. " In considering the dealings of God with men, we may prefer to follow the analysis of parental affection and discipline rather than the analysis of mere natural selection. In contemplating the possible issues of God's dealings with our race, we decline to limit ourselves to the study of pollen and seeds, pigeons and vultures, tigers and apes. We think we can learn something from Gethsemane and Calvary." The Incarnation, as interpreted by St. John, would have been a puzzle to him if its only result had been the perfecting of a few chosen souls in the highest quality of life. His acute intellect could not fail to see the essential inconsistency between Prof. Drummond's teaching on spiritual growth and his teaching on spiritual degeneration. Nor would his sense of truthfulness allow the cardinal principle of Prof. Drummond's theory, that a life of moral goodness and virtue is to the life of worship towards God precisely as a non-living mineral is to a living plant. In fact, there is hardly a page in this most valuable little book which does not expose some dangerous fallacy of the brilliant essayist. The nature of the subject hardly lends itself to the poetic eloquence to which Dr. Finlayson elsewhere rises; but there is no better example of the lucidity of his thinking, the clear-cut precision of his style, and the classical self-restraint of his expression. His own creed even to the last had changed but little from that which he had formed in early manhood. The doctrines, which had then been regarded as so heretical, had come to be classified as moderately orthodox; and the width of his theological views had left ample room and verge enough to include within their compass all that the growing thought of men had added "in the process of the suns." What was changed was only the way in which such teaching was welcomed. It is perhaps worth adding that his published sermons found much acceptance far beyond the limits of his own body, and that the use which others made of them was not always quite legitimate.

Dr. Finlayson's love for poetry was very genuine; he was an excellent reader and reciter, and his memory was well stored with favourite passages; but perhaps the attraction lay more in the substance of the thought than in the literary form. Tennyson always seemed to be for him rather the interpretive thinker of the generation than the consummate artist in words; and Browning's rough-hewn massive thought had a charm for him never present in the purer poetry of Swinburne or Wm. Morris. Sometimes in lectures, and more than once in a sermon, he expounded with much force and clearness the results of his sympathetic study of a poem, not a little to the delight of his audience.

But after all it was not Dr. Finlayson's varied culture and intellectual gifts which gave him his essential power and his place in the hearts of his people. His sermons were so impressive because of the life out of which they so naturally sprung. He preached, as he had said when first he came that a minister must preach, more by his character than by his words. His life was one of rare disinterestedness and forgetfulness of self. How much this contributed to the peace and harmony of his church it is impossible to estimate; but many examples could be given of the way in which he habitually put his own interests absolutely out of the question. At one time an important change was made in the method of raising the necessary funds for the church. Dr. Finlayson was in hearty sympathy with the plan which the deacons adopted, that of free-will weekly offerings in the place of pew-rents; but he never expressed his own opinion so long as it could bias the judgment of others. It was a slight but characteristic illustration of this that he never would accept a fee for marriage or funeral duties; his services were always freely put at the command of any of his people who desired them. The same unselfishness lent a singular charm to his intercourse with others in society, and especially in his home-life. It was the source of the truest courtesy, one which was marked by the candour inseparable from his truthfulness, but which never forgot the considerateness of a genuine kindliness. Dr. Mackennal, in *The Independent*, spoke with perfect justice of the rare combination in him of a critical faculty of mingled directness and subtlety, and of a conscience of great scrupulousness, qualities which may easily lead to a harsh censoriousness, but in him were tempered by simplicity of affection and breadth of sympathy. To this rare combination was perhaps mainly due his remarkable influence over the younger ministers of the district, and the students of the neighbouring theological college. They were drawn to him by the feeling that they were sure to find a clear understanding of their difficulties, whether practical or speculative; and an absolutely candid, but at the same time most sympathetic, judgment as to their course of action. One of them wrote: "A person who went to him in any case for counsel or sympathy or assistance might sometimes be surprised, and—at first—not quite agreeably. He may have gone thinking him to be mere 'sweetness'; but he finds 'light' as well, and very searching light too. He receives real kindness—such probably as a more effusive friend would not take the trouble to give—but he also gets insight; he is made to view impartially and justly the matter he has come about, and his own relation to it." The same old friend, Dr. Mackennal, with delicate intuition, pointed to another very noteworthy feature in his life. He must have known that he had the intellectual gifts needed for rising to eminence, and that only the coming on of physical weakness hindered this. Yet he never repined or lost his cheerful brightness. "He lived so much with God that he could not but be content." And here in truth lay the secret of his great, though often unconscious, influence. "The stillness of the eternal was round about him; he made 'our noisy years seem moments in the being of the eternal silence.'" With such a man reverence was the only conceivable attitude of the soul; flippancy was as impossible as untruth or meanness. And so all who were privileged to know him felt that great as was the blessing of the teaching, so fresh and elevating and true, there was something more than the preacher in the man. He dwelt himself so constantly in the presence and the power of spiritual things that his life appeared the strongest proof of their reality. Of all the chapters of the New Testament there was none which he chose more frequently as a lesson than the beginning of the First Epistle of St. John; and no words recall so well, to those who knew him, the aim and the significance of his life:—

"That which was from the beginning, that which we have heard, that which we have seen with our eyes, that which we beheld, and our hands handled, concerning the Word of life (and the life was manifested, and we have seen, and bear witness, and declare unto you the life, the eternal life, which was with the Father, and was manifested unto us); that which we have seen and heard declare we unto you also, that ye also may have fellowship with us; yea, and our fellowship is with the Father, and with His Son Jesus Christ."

TENNYSON'S "IN MEMORIAM."

[Delivered in Rusholme Public Hall, Manchester, March 24th, 1871, and on various subsequent occasions.]

IN a volume of criticism recently published, Tennyson comes in for a large share of the critic's scorn. Even his physiognomy is described with an affectation of supercilious contempt. As a poet, he is called " sugar sweet" and "pretty, pretty"; and then (by way of compliment, I suppose, to the ladies) it is added that he is " full of womanly talk and feminine stuff!" This volume is entitled "Modern men of letters honestly criticised." Verily, honesty and wisdom do not always go together. "Dogberry" was doubtless an honest enough man in his way; at least, the word 'honest' was very often in his mouth: but, for all that, Dogberry was very nearly "written down an ass!" A similar fate may possibly lie in store for the 'honest' critic who speaks of the author of the " Idylls of the King" as a mere "drawing-room poet," a "half-hearted and polished rhymester," "full of womanly talk and feminine stuff." But indeed—to say the truth—it is difficult to believe that there is not more spite than honesty in this kind of "talk," which is certainly *not* "womanly." Whether it be even "gentlemanly" is a question which ("appealing from Philip drunk to Philip sober") we might perhaps leave to be decided by the author of "The *Gentle Life.*"

Let Tennyson be 'tried by his peers,' and a very different verdict is recorded. Thus, Robert Browning, in a preface to some selections from his own poems, published by Moxon—who had just previously issued some selections from the works of Tennyson—says regarding his own little volume: "This contentedly looks pale beside the wonderful flower-show of my illustrious predecessor—dare I say? my dear friend; who will take it, all except the love in the gift, at a mere nosegay's worth." Now, *there* you have words both manly and womanly—a compliment at once dignified and graceful. Browning *may* be, in some respects, a greater poet than Tennyson: he has certainly more at least of the dramatic faculty: but he is too much of a *man* to allow any petty jealousy to blind him to the manifold and real merits of the Laureate's productions. And, in likening his own selections to a "pale nosegay," as contrasted with the "wonderful flower-show" of his friend, he hits the most characteristic feature of Tennyson's poetry—its richly-coloured, variegated, and highly-cultured beauty. The forest, with its strong oaks and its sweet wild-flowers, has a grandeur and beauty peculiarly its own: but we need not therefore refuse our admiration to the rich and noble garden, with its beautiful shrubberies, its skilfully-arranged borders, its rare and costly plants. To read the works of Tennyson is like walking through such a garden. Not but that there is strength as well as beauty in his writings. The garden is a very extensive one, and possesses many fine trees that strike their roots deeply into the soil; but still, a rich beauty is its prevailing characteristic. *The Idylls of the King* win our admiration with their grand terraces and noble vistas. *The Princess* charms us with its gay parterres and sparkling fountains. *Maud* is a bit of rockwork—intentionally bold and rugged in aspect, but festooned with delicate wild-plants and with here and there some richer flowers, a favourite nook, we are told, with the gardener himself. And from the *Miscellaneous Poems* you might cull many rich and beautiful blossoms. It is not as a thinker that Tennyson is pre-eminent. There is solid thought in his poetry; but he is essentially an Artist. It has been objected that he over-elaborates, that he spends too much time and skill over the details of his work. He *does* elaborate. Such effects in landscape-gardening are not to be produced without labour. Such flowers as these are not to be found growing in the hedge-rows. But flowers are not necessarily waxen, simply because pains have been taken to produce them. Tennyson is an Artist, but not an Artificer. He may not be so simply or grandly natural as Wordsworth; for, even in such a simple poem as *Dora*, the Artist's hand is clearly manifest. His poetry is certainly not like that "careless-ordered garden" in the "Isle of Wight," to which he invites his friend Maurice. But neither is it a Dutch-cut garden, laden with sickly odours. There is unvarying art; but there is also artistic variety. The walks are always well-kept; but they are often winding. The odour of the flowers is rich; but through the whole garden there blows a healthful breeze,—the living breath of a true interest in human affairs, and a true sympathy with all that is noble in humanity.

And in *this* "garden" also "there is a sepulchre," or, say rather a monumental enclosure—a piece of ground, marked off from the rest, shadowed by the dark yew-trees, and yet with the light of heaven glinting in upon it—and in its midst a monument chiselled with almost classic severity, although here and there, in detail, richly and exquisitely carved. And around this monument, sacred to the memory of a departed friend, the poet has planted with loving hand such flowers as love the shade. This monumental enclosure is the poem now before us—perhaps, on the whole, the finest elegy which has ever been written in any language.

"IN MEMORIAM," then, is a series of odes *in memory of* Arthur Henry Hallam, the eldest son of Hallam the historian. This young man was born in Bedford Place, London, on the 1st of February, 1811. As a boy, he was characterized by great sweetness and conscientiousness of disposition, and by precocious talents and thoughtfulness. When he was nine years of age he could read both French and Latin "with tolerable facility," and "felt a keen relish for dramatic poetry." At the close of his course at Eton, he accompanied his parents to the Continent, and passed eight months in Italy. Here he learned to speak the Italian language with perfect fluency, and became intimately acquainted with the works of Dante and Petrarch. In 1828—when nearly eighteen years of age—he became a student of Trinity College, Cambridge. Here he made the acquaintance of Alfred Tennyson, who was of the same College, and who was only a few months older than himself. The acquaintance seems to have speedily ripened into friendship; and Hallam became by-and-bye betrothed to one of Tennyson's sisters. During his residence at the University, Arthur Hallam evinced not only poetical tastes and genius, but also great partiality for metaphysical and philosophical studies. His College prizes testify to his ability; and the literary remains which his father has given to the world indicate remarkable powers both of thought and expression. These "remains" consist of several sonnets and other pieces of poetry, and also of several prose essays on miscellaneous subjects—including one on the old problem of Moral Evil, which betokens much earnestness of religious thought and feeling. Yet his College associates tell us that these compositions—remarkable as they are—give but "an inadequate conception of his actual power," and that "of him—above all his contemporaries—they agreed in forming the loftiest expectations." After taking his degree at Cambridge in 1832, Hallam was entered on the boards of the Inner Temple, and began the study of law. In the autumn of the following year, he was travelling with his father on the Continent. He was taken ill at Vienna with "an intermittent fever." The "symptoms were slight": but a "sudden rush of blood to the head" put an instantaneous end to his life on the 15th of September, 1833. His body was brought from Vienna to England, and buried, on the 3rd of January, 1834, in the manor aisle of Clevedon Church, on the estate of his grandfather, Sir Abraham Elton, and situated on a lone hill overhanging the Bristol Channel. Thus, at the early age of twenty-two, passed away one to whom the genius and affection of his friend have now given an extensive and enduring fame.

I.—This, then, is the first aspect in which we may view "In Memoriam," *as a monument erected before the eyes of men, in memory and in honour of Arthur Hallam.*

There can be no doubt that Tennyson regarded his friend, whilst living, as one who was destined to "make his own mark" in the world. It was only natural, therefore, that he should wish to celebrate the name of one who, if he had lived, would have made *himself* celebrated. The poet would fain give the world *some* sense of what it had lost, and, at least, he would link his own name indissolubly with that of one to whose influence he had been so deeply indebted. Thus, whatever fame he himself might acquire—whether it were much or little—would be reflected upon the name of his friend. And, accordingly, you will observe that Tennyson kept these odes in his desk until he had himself acquired an established reputation. We may gather from the poem itself that it was written, in substance, within a few years after Hallam's death, but not until seventeen years had expired was it given to the world. Tennyson was a young man of twenty-four when he lost his friend; but when *In Memoriam* was first published, he was a man of forty. He thus endorsed, in the maturity of his prime, that estimate which he had formed of Hallam in the enthusiasm of his youth. Doubtless too, in the interval, he had been touching and retouching the poem with the loving hand of the artist, seeking to make it worthier at once of Hallam and of himself. And it was only a few months before he was made Poet-laureate that he at length unveiled to the public gaze this monument which he had erected to the memory of his friend.

Now, "there are monuments and monuments." Thus, for example, over the tomb of Sir Walter Scott in Dryburgh Abbey there is a plain massive slab of granite, with a simple inscription carved upon it. Compare this with the monument erected to the memory of Scott in Glasgow, which consists of a lofty column of stone, crowned with a statue of the great novelist. Compare both of these, again, with the monument erected to Sir Walter in Edinburgh. This is not only richer and more elaborate; but also, in addition to a beautiful marble statue of the novelist, contains a large number of niches filled with miniature sculptures of characters and scenes from his novels and poems. This is emphatically *the* Scott monument: the idea of Scott dominates and pervades the whole design. Now there are different kinds of elegy, corresponding to these different kinds of monument in stone. Look at Burns's "Elegy in memory of Matthew Henderson." There you have the simple expression of mourning—with the name of the departed, as it were, inscribed upon it. There are numberless elegies of this type. Remove the inscribed name, and the monument might stand just as well for almost anybody else. Then, look again at Milton's *Lycidas* in memory of Edward King, or Shelley's *Adonaïs* in memory of John Keats. There you have an elegy of a fuller type. You have not only the building up of "the lofty rhyme"; you have also, as it were, in addition, the sculptured statue; you have several allusions which serve so far to specify the departed. But *In Memoriam* is an elegy of the most specific type. Before *this* monument could be made to stand for any one else, it would be necessary not only to alter the name and remove the statue, but also to strike off, as it were, many little sculptured niches which all point to the one departed friend. The idea of Arthur Hallam dominates and pervades the whole poem. The particulars which I have already mentioned concerning his brief career might almost all be gathered by a careful reader from the odes themselves; and certainly, these particulars ought to be kept in view, if we would fully understand many of the minuter allusions and references of the poem. Thus, I have said that Hallam and Tennyson were fellow-students of the same College : and one of the odes has special allusion to Cambridge, with its College halls and chapels—the river Cam, with its boats and bridges—the "gray flats" outside the town—and the long and beautiful avenue of Trinity College itself :—

> " I past beside the reverend walls
>   In which of old I wore the gown,
>   I roved at random thro' the town,
> And saw the tumult of the halls ;
>
> " And heard once more in college fanes
>   The storm their high-built organs make,
>   And thunder-music, rolling, shake
> The prophets blazon'd on the panes ;
>
> " And caught once more the distant shout,
>   The measured pulse of racing oars
>   Among the willows ; paced the shores
> And many a bridge, and all about

"The same gray flats again, and felt
 The same, but not the same ; and last
 Up that long walk of limes I past
 To see the rooms in which he dwelt."

I have mentioned the fact that, after leaving Cambridge, Hallam began to study law in London; and I have also referred to his intimate acquaintance with the Italian language, and his admiration of Dante and Petrarch. I have said too that he was betrothed to a sister of Tennyson's, and it appears that he used often to run down from London to see his friends at Somersby Rectory in Lincolnshire. In one of the odes we have allusions to these various circumstances :—

"How often, hither wandering down,
 My Arthur found your shadows fair,
 And shook to all the liberal air
 The dust and din and steam of town:

"He brought an eye for all he saw;
 He mixt in all our simple sports;
 They pleased him, fresh from brawling courts
 And dusty purlieus of the law.

. . . . . .

"O bliss, when all in circle drawn
 About him, heart and ear were fed
 To hear him, as he lay and read
 The Tuscan poets on the lawn:

"Or in the all-golden afternoon
 A guest, or happy sister, sung,
 Or here she brought the harp and flung
 A ballad to the brightening moon."

And this mention of "happy sister" is not the

only allusion to the tender relationship at which it hints. In the marriage-ode appended to the poem there is a retrospective glance at the happiness experienced when

> " first *he* told me that he loved
> A daughter of our house";

and, in another ode, when picturing to himself what *might* have been the course of Arthur's life if Death had not snatched him prematurely away, the poet describes what seemed at one time the probable future:—

> " I see thee sitting crown'd with good,
>   A central warmth diffusing bliss
>   In glance and smile, and clasp and kiss,
> On all the branches of thy blood;
>
> " Thy blood, my friend, and partly mine;
>   For now the day was drawing on,
>   When thou should'st link thy life with one
> Of mine own house, and boys of thine
>
> " Had babbled 'Uncle' on my knee;
>   But that remorseless iron hour
>   Made cypress of her orange flower,
> Despair of Hope, and earth of thee."

Thus, again, there are one or two allusions to the place and also to the suddenness of his death:—

> " My blood an even tenor kept,
>   Till on mine ear this message falls,
>   That in Vienna's fatal walls
> God's finger touch'd him, and he slept."

There are several references to the place of his

burial—the Church of Clevedon, on the Bristol Channel :—

> "The Danube to the Severn gave
> The darken'd heart that beat no more;
> They laid him by the pleasant shore,
> And in the hearing of the wave."

More specially the Chancel is referred to where the villagers partake of the Sacramental Cup,

> "where the kneeling hamlet drains
> The chalice of the grapes of God."

And, in one of the odes, the poet pictures to himself the appearance of the "marble" tablet inside the church as the "silver" moonlight "steals" over it,—or, again, as it "glimmers" in the early morning "dawn." One of the most beautiful portions of the poem has reference to the ship that brought Hallam's remains from Vienna to England. More than three months elapsed between the death and the funeral; and the poet represents himself as during this interval often going out in thought to meet the coming ship, as she moves on "thro' circles of the bounding sky," laden with her "dark freight, a vanish'd life." He seems to quit, for "an hour" at a time, his own body, whilst his fancy plays in reverie about the "prow" and "sails" of the approaching vessel. When the storm rises on the Autumn evening, he is restless, and fears that the winds may perhaps be tossing and endangering the ship. On the other hand, the stillness of the calm Autumn morning harmonizes with the "calm despair" of his own heart, and with his desire that the ship may have a calm passage home:—

> "Calm is the morn without a sound,
>   Calm as to suit a calmer grief,
>   And only thro' the faded leaf
> The chestnut pattering to the ground:
>
> "Calm and deep peace on this high wold,
>   And on these dews that drench the furze,
>   And all the silvery gossamers
> That twinkle into green and gold:
>
> "Calm and still light on yon great plain
>   That sweeps with all its autumn bowers,
>   And crowded farms and lessening towers,
> To mingle with the bounding main:
>
> "Calm and deep peace in this wide air,
>   These leaves that redden to the fall;
>   And in my heart, if calm at all,
> If any calm, a calm despair:
>
> "Calm on the seas, and silver sleep,
>   And waves that sway themselves in rest,
>   And dead calm in that noble breast
> Which heaves but with the heaving deep."

Now, these and similar minute allusions to the circumstances of Hallam's career impart to this monumental elegy a very specific character. But the poet has also endeavoured to give us some idea of the genius and goodness of the departed. He would have us see his friend as reflected in his own admiration of that friend's worth. This is the man he "held as half-divine,"—who always "outstript" him "in the race,"—for "whose applause he strove,"—for whose "blame" he had "such reverence,"—who was "strong as he was true,"—who grew "by year and hour" "not only in power and knowledge," but also in "reverence and charity." He would have us "guess" his friend's "greatness" by "the measure of his own grief." To himself that greatness is all the more apparent now that his friend is gone.

> " As sometimes in a dead man's face,
>   To those that watch it more and more,
>   A likeness, hardly seen before,
> Comes out—to some one of his race:
>
> " So, dearest, now thy brows are cold,
>   I see thee what thou art, and know
>   Thy likeness to the wise below,
> Thy kindred with the great of old."

The poet goes back, too, in thought to the days of youthful debate at College, and describes how Hallam —his "form" dilating with enthusiasm, and his eyes shining brightly under brows like "Michael Angelo's" —used to speak with "powerful" and "graceful" eloquence and with an accuracy of "aim" that hit "the mark." He tells us, moreover, that Hallam was not the man to take his religious "faiths" on mere tradition:—

> " He fought his doubts and gathered strength,
>   He would not make his judgment blind,
>   He faced the spectres of the mind
> And laid them."

We are told, too, of his powers of conversation—his "affluence in discursive talk"—his "critical clearness"—his "impassioned logic." And then the poet will have us know that all this ability was associated with real goodness. His "manners" were "gentle" and "noble," yet entirely natural. There was no need of pretence or affectation. He "best seemed the thing he was." "He bore without abuse the grand old name of gentleman." His manners encouraged "the weak"—softened "the stern"—silenced "the flippant." His soul was lofty, yet not "ascetic"; his affections were warm, yet "pure"; and his strength was so blended with sweetness as to evoke the confidence even of little children :—

> "High nature amorous of the good,
>   But touch'd with no ascetic gloom;
>   And passion pure in snowy bloom
> Thro' all the years of April blood;
>
> .   .   .   .
>
> "And manhood fused with female grace
>   In such a sort, the child would twine
>   A trustful hand, unask'd, in thine,
> And find his comfort in thy face."

Such, then, is the likeness that Tennyson has here carved for us; and the sculptor has done his work so well that the world cannot soon overlook the name of Arthur Hallam. My own conviction is, that as long as the English language lives Tennyson will be read: and, as long as Tennyson is read, the friend of his youth cannot well be forgotten. Death had seemed to rob young Hallam of all earthly renown; but the poet, by rearing this monument, has robbed Death of at least a portion of his triumph.

II.—A second aspect in which we may view *In Memoriam* is *as an expression of private grief and personal affection.*

It is a significant circumstance that this poem was published anonymously, and that only the initials of Hallam's name were inscribed upon it. Now, this could not be because Tennyson had any desire to conceal either the authorship of the odes or the name of his friend. He was well aware that both would very soon be known to the world. Indeed, there was no attempt at secrecy. The initials "A. H. H." were sure to provoke inquiry. The poem, moreover, issued from the house of Tennyson's usual publishers; and, in point of fact, the authorship was, from the first, no secret. But, by withholding his own name from the title-page, and also by giving simply the initials of his friend's name, the poet meant to indicate the private and personal character of many of these odes.

This was not an elegy in memory of any well-known man, whose talents or virtues the poet had admired from a distance: this was an elegy in memory of the dearest friend of his youth—of one, moreover, who was unknown to Fame. There is here, therefore, no mere echo of public laudation,—no mere expression of a general sentiment. The praise—the love—the grief—here uttered are all intensely personal. The poet *does* wish to give the world some adequate idea of his friend; but, in order to do this, he must admit the world so far into the privacy of his own heart. To publish some of these odes was like publishing extracts from a diary that had been kept under lock and key. Yet he will venture to reveal even his own secret emotion rather than allow his friend's worth to remain unrevealed. At the same time, in the very act of unveiling the monument, the poet marks his own sense of the delicacy and sacredness of the personal affection that has reared it. And accordingly, to this day—although the poem has now passed through so many editions—it still bears on it, as at the first, the simple initials "A. H. H.," and is still published without the author's name. The monument *is* for the public to look at; but the public are not to forget that it stands on private ground.

Now, this ought surely to have been enough to prevent everything like rude comment on the tender emotion which breathes through so many of these odes. Tennyson himself seems to have felt that, in publishing them, he was laying himself open to the rough criticism of unappreciative natures who would fail to treat with delicacy either his affection or his grief. One critic might accuse him of being weak, womanish, and sentimental. Another might insinuate that the expression both of his love and of his sorrow was exaggerated, or that he was making an unnecessary and unbecoming display of his emotions. Another might accuse him of morbidly brooding over his private griefs, when he ought to be taking an active and healthy interest in the affairs of the world. The poet anticipates all this criticism in one of his odes:—

> " I sing to him that rests below,
>   And since the grasses round me wave,
>   I take the grasses of the grave,
> And make them pipes whereon to blow.

> " The traveller hears me now and then,
>   And sometimes harshly will he speak;
>   'This fellow would make weakness weak,
> And melt the waxen hearts of men.'

"Another answers, 'Let him be,
   He loves to make parade of pain,
   That with his piping he may gain
The praise that comes to constancy.'

"A third is wroth: 'Is this an hour
   For private sorrow's barren song,
   When more and more the people throng
The chairs and thrones of civil power?

"A time to sicken and to swoon,
   When Science reaches forth her arms
   To feel from world to world, and charms
Her secret from the latest moon?'

"Behold, ye speak an idle thing:
   Ye never knew the sacred dust:
   I do but sing because I must,
And pipe but as the linnets sing:

"And one is glad; her note is gay,
   For now her little ones have ranged;
   And one is sad; her note is changed,
Because her brood is stol'n away."

I think, then, we are bound to believe in the genuineness both of the grief and the affection expressed in this poem. As to the charge of "sentimentalism" and "effeminate weakness," that, surely, can be brought only by those who confound manliness with stoicism, or who have never experienced the awful blank which death can make in a human life. No doubt there *are* tears which are unmanly; but there is also a tearlessness which is inhuman. There was One who "wept" at the grave of Lazarus, and was not ashamed of His weeping. It is pride that dries up the fountains of tenderness; and pride is the Devil's "virtue." There are some young men, it is true, who would not for worlds be seen shedding a tear; but perhaps they may live to see a day when they will long for the relief which tears might bring. They would be ashamed now to be seen taking an infant into their "manly" arms; but perhaps, when their arms are a trifle manlier, they will understand better what manhood means. Hector of Troy was none the less a hero because he could lay aside his gleaming helmet when his infant-boy cowered back at sight of its nodding crest. The bravest are often the tenderest. To be manly does not mean to be inhuman.

> "I dare do all that may become a man;
> Who dares do more, is none."

It is true, again, that the affection which breathes through *In Memoriam* is, in its exquisite tenderness, more like that which may subsist between a man and a woman, than that which usually characterizes the friendship of two men. But surely this need not lead us to suspect any affectation. You must remember that *this* friendship was formed in early life, when the hearts of these two young men were warm and fresh: and such friendships are sometimes characterized not only by unreserved confidence and even playful tenderness, but also, on one side at least, by an almost reverent admiration. And then you ought further to remember that this "fair companionship" was "broken" early—before it was subjected to the strain of time—whilst yet the bloom of youthful enthusiasm was upon it,—and that the dear friend, heretofore admired, was now, as it were, transfigured by death. Certainly this friendship is beautiful to look upon: its comparative rareness only makes it the more refreshing.

This was no mere dining at the same club—no mere smoking of cigars together—no mere joining in the same jollity. Here was a real union of heart and mind, mutual esteem, unselfish sympathy.

> "Ah yet, ev'n yet, if this might be,
> I, falling on his faithful heart,
> Would breathing thro' his lips impart
> The life that almost dies in me;
>
> . . . . . .
>
> "My Arthur, whom I shall not see
> Till all my widow'd race be run;
> Dear as the mother to the son,
> More than my brothers are to me."

Such tenderness as this reminds us of another elegy, also intensely personal, written by another poet: "I am distressed for thee, my brother Jonathan; very pleasant hast thou been unto me; thy love to me was wonderful, passing the love of women." The poet who was "sentimental" enough to write *that* was the man who went out, singly, to meet Goliath of Gath!

Some, however, may be disposed to think that the elaboration of such a poem as *In Memoriam* is incompatible with such intensity of grief as it professes to embody. They cannot understand how a sorrow so deep should be able to utter itself, deliberately, in a long series of carefully-finished odes. But here we must not forget that the writing of this poem extended over a period of some years after Hallam's death,—and that, as the poet himself tells us, it was only "by fits" and starts that his sorrow "broke into song": there were often times when his grief was too deep for utterance.

Then we ought also to remember that these two friends were both lovers of poetry. We know that at one time, whilst they were at College together, they had contemplated publishing a joint volume of their poems; and young Hallam has himself left on record his admiration of Tennyson's poetical faculty. It was surely natural that, under these circumstances, the survivor should employ the faculty which his friend had appreciated, in order to express his own sorrow and affection. His friend had "cared for" his "poor flower of poesy":—

> "But since it pleased a vanish'd eye,
> I go to plant it on his tomb,
> That if it can it there may bloom,
> Or dying, there at least may die."

And we can well believe that the very exercise of writing these odes would often be a positive help to him in his sorrow,—as being a work which both occupied his mind and relieved his heart.

> "I sometimes hold it half a sin
> To put in words the grief I feel;
> For words, like Nature, half reveal
> And half conceal the soul within.
>
> "But, for the unquiet heart and brain,
> A use in measured language lies;
> The sad mechanic exercise,
> Like dull narcotics, numbing pain."

And this benefit of "measured language" has been experienced by many a reader, as well as by the writer, of these odes. We all know how song can relieve by expressing emotion. To have our griefs set to music is often an alleviation. Thus it is that many a mourner has been helped by the reading of this poem. Each "heart knoweth its own bitterness": and so, the very privacy of *In Memoriam* has made it dearer to thousands. Many a bereaved one has his own "Arthur," and, in the intensely personal affection and sorrow which pervade this poem, he sees the reflection, and finds the expression, of his own emotion. He can appropriate many of its "words," and "wrap" his own grief in them, as in mourning "weeds" "against the cold."

III. A third aspect in which we may view *In Memoriam* is as containing what we may call *a natural history of the Sorrow of Bereavement*.

Every attentive reader of this poem must have noticed that there is in it a certain chronological progress. Certain anniversaries recur at intervals—such as Christmas-day and the day of Hallam's death—and it is easy to perceive that the poet is describing *successive* moods of feeling, and that he sets forth the change which gradually steals over his spirit as time rolls on. But what, perhaps, is not so commonly noticed, is that this chronological progress is *continuous*. I have already likened these odes to extracts from a diary; and I believe the resemblance is much closer than is generally recognized. I do not think it difficult to show that this poem covers an almost definite period of time. The prefatory ode of Invocation is dated 1849; but this was evidently written long after the others, and indeed speaks of them as "Confusions of a wasted *youth*." The marriage-ode, at the close, was written nine years after Hallam's death; but even this stands apart by itself, as being of the nature of an afterpiece. The poem itself seems to me to cover a period of about *three years and a half*. Not that all the odes were necessarily written within that period—far less that they were all written in the order in which they now appear; but that they are designed to embody a continuous history of feeling extending over that period. Christmas-day occurs three times in the course of the poem; and that there is just one year between each Christmas and the next mentioned is indicated by the progress of the year through Spring and Autumn. After the third Christmas, we have once more the mention of Spring; and then, shortly afterwards, the poem closes. Now, it is only natural to infer that we are to look for chronological continuity before, as well as after, the first Christmas of the poem. If so, then this first Christmas, coming, as it does, after the mention of Hallam's funeral, cannot be the Christmas immediately succeeding his death. For, as I have already said, although Hallam died in September, 1833, yet he was not buried until January, 1834. Thus the Christmas of 1833 came *between* the death and the funeral, and so is not specially mentioned. Even a forced festivity would scarcely be possible, just when the ship was arriving with its "precious relics." I regard, therefore, the first Christmas mentioned as being the first after the funeral—the Christmas of 1834. And this agrees with the fact that the third Christmas of the poem is represented as occurring shortly after the poet came to reside in a new parish, where the sound of the bells was unfamiliar. For it appears that it was in 1836 that the Tennyson family left Somersby Rectory. I am thus confirmed in the view which I have taken of the chronological continuity of this poem, as extending from the later Autumn of 1833 to the Spring or Summer of 1837.[1]

Under this aspect, then, *In Memoriam* contains a natural history of the Sorrow of Bereavement. The poet depicts the successive moods that sweep over his spirit, the various questionings that naturally arise within his mind, and the gradual change which passes over his grief, as the seasons come and go. One of the most beautiful features of the poem arises out of the skill with which Tennyson indicates this gradual change, and contrasts his experience in the earlier stages of his sorrow with his experience later on, when time has done its healing work. Thus the odes that open the poem stand in marked contrast with the odes that close it. The former breathe a passionate fear lest, through any philosophical attempt to moderate

---

[1] The editor has left the argument and dates untouched; the author seemed, indeed, to have good authority for his statements, as appears from the following letter he received from the late Rector of Somersby :—

SOMERSBY, *Jany.* 13*th*, 1871.

Dear Sir,—Mrs. Tennyson continued to reside at Somersby Rectory some time after the Dr.'s death. To the best of my recollection she would leave about June or July 1836, when I had to come into residence. The date I sent you is quite correct.—I am, Dear sir, Yours truly,

L. B. BURTON.

Further inquiry, however, shows that the Tennysons left Somersby in the early part of 1837. In a letter to R. Monckton Milnes, dated Jany. 10th, 1837, the poet speaks of all his people being about to quit Somersby, never to return (see *Life of R. Monckton Milnes*, vol. i. p. 180); and it seems that the sale of the furniture of the Rectory was advertised in the *Lincolnshire Mercury* to take place on May 22nd and 23rd, 1837.—J.F.

grief, love should lose its intensity; they express a morbid desire that love should prove its constant fidelity by cherishing a constant gloom; and they indicate how this gloomy Sorrow within tends to darken all Nature without, and to rob the heart of its faith in a wise and universal Order. The closing odes, on the other hand, breathe the spirit of joy in Nature, and the calm assurance that "all is well"; and they indicate that, although love is not less, but is even more than ever, yet it now exists, not as a dark and darkening Regret, but as a bright and brightening Hope. The first ode dreads the "victor Hours": the last ode triumphs over the "conquered years."

These contrasts of experience, due to the lapse of time, are, moreover, pursued into detail; and the transitional stages through which the mourner gradually passes are marked with delicacy and skill. At first the dark yew-tree in the churchyard is so congenial to his spirit, that he is filled with a "sick" longing to be as faithful, in his own melancholy, to the departed, as the yew is "stubbornly" faithful in its unchanging gloom. He cannot bear the thought that the coming of Spring will ever make him cheerful again. He sinks into a state of sullen torpor; and yet he doubts whether he ought to "embrace" or to "crush" such sorrow. When he sleeps, he never dreams of his friend, but is burdened "all night" by a "nameless trouble." When he goes, in the "early morning," to look at the house where his friend used to live, that house appears all "dark" and "unlovely," and he shrinks within himself as he thinks of the "hand that can be clasp'd no more." To tell him that there are thousands besides himself who are mourning the loss of friends, only increases the bitterness of his sorrow. Sometimes the whole thing looks like a dream, and he finds it difficult to realize his loss. The "Shadow" of Death darkens for him both the Present and the Future: it is only the Past that is bright; and the memory of its departed joy makes the pathway of life very "dreary." Thus a whole year passes away. Then comes the first Christmas after the funeral. He had almost wished never to hear "the merry, merry bells of Yule" again. But when they do ring, they bring him "sorrow *touch'd with joy.*" He cannot altogether escape the power of early associations. He tries to keep Christmas-eve after the old fashion, just for custom's sake; but the gaiety is a "vain pretence of gladness," and the forced mirth is followed by silence and tears. By-and-bye the Spring comes, but it brings him no joy yet; only he can see now that even the yew-tree, which in his earliest grief he had called unchanging, *does* respond to the quickening influences of the season. His sorrow is not quite so gloomy. His feeling is that this sorrow must ever remain with him, but that it may have its "lovelier" aspects, as well as its "harsher moods." He has his comforting thoughts as to the abiding love of the departed. He begins to take a kindly interest in others, and when he sleeps at night now, he has visions of his friend's face—the happy days of the past are reproduced in his dreams. But still, when the anniversary of Arthur's death comes round, it renews the old gloom. It is the 15th of September, and it comes a wild, showery day; but he feels that, if it had come calm and fair, it would have been quite as chill and cheerless to *him*. Thus, a second year has passed away; and presently Christmas-eve has to be kept again. And now the mirth is no longer forced—it almost appears, in the midst of the festivity, as if sorrow had grown less; but he comforts himself with the thought that his Regret can never die, and that it is only made less poignant by long familiarity. It is clear, however, that his grief is by this time altered in its character. When the new year comes he finds himself even longing for the flowers of Spring. A quiet "content" takes possession of his mind. He begins "to count it crime" to "mourn for any over-much." He finds solace in a second friendship, although he feels that it can never be quite like "the first." The "sweet air" of the Summer evening imparts to him a sense of "new life." The warble of the nightingale, that seems to blend joy with grief, typifies his own feeling; almost in spite of himself, he is glad. There *was* a time when he "would not have felt it to be strange," if the ship that was bringing Arthur's remains had landed him at the quay, a living passenger; but now, if Arthur were to appear to him, he would regard it simply as an illusion of the brain. And now, again, the 15th of September comes round; and this time it comes with "balmy breath": and he can now take a kind of comfort from the thought that there are multitudes besides himself to whom the day brings "memories of death." Thus a third year has passed away. The next Christmas, indeed, is spent without festivity, but that is simply because they have recently left the old family-home; and when the bells begin to "ring in the new year," the poet finds himself in *full* sympathy with their cheerful, hopeful chimes—

> "Ring out the grief that saps the mind,
> For those that here we see no more;
>
> . . . . . .
>
> "Ring out, ring out my mournful rhymes,
> But ring the fuller minstrel in."

And when the 1st of February comes—the anniversary of Arthur's birthday—he keeps it with festal cheer and books and music. Rather than cherish sorrow, he would reap the "wisdom" that sorrow brings. And now, with the advent of the new Spring, his "Regret becomes an April violet, and buds and blossoms." *Now*, when he goes to look at the "house" where his friend used to live, the street seems even bright and gladsome, and he feels as if "in thought" he were clasping his friend's hand again. He is looking forward to re-union, rather than backward to separation. There is

> "Less yearning for the friendship fled,
> Than some strong bond which is to be."

Thus, then, time has done its healing work. The mourner who at first dreaded its influence, has lived to be thankful for it. It has "touched into leaf" the "crown of thorns." And yet, although there is so great a change in the tone of his feeling, he is conscious that *he himself* has not changed. His love abides unaltered. Formerly, it was like "Hesper," the evening star, brooding over the departed Sun; now, it is like "Phosphor," the morning star, anticipating the coming Dawn. Yet "Hesper" and "Phosphor" are, after all, just the same star in different positions at different periods of the year; and, in like manner, it is only the attitude of his spirit that is altered—his love is the same as ever :—

"Sad Hesper o'er the buried sun
  And ready, thou to die with him,
  Thou watchest all things ever dim
And dimmer, and a glory done:

"The team is loosen'd from the wain,
  The boat is drawn upon the shore;
  Thou listenest to the closing door,
And life is darken'd in the brain.

"Bright Phosphor, fresher for the night,
  By thee the world's great work is heard
  Beginning, and the wakeful bird;
Behind thee comes the greater light:

"The market boat is on the stream,
  And voices hail it from the brink;
  Thou hear'st the village hammer clink,
And see'st the moving of the team.

"Sweet Hesper-Phosphor, double name
  For what is one, the first, the last,
  Thou, like my present and my past,
Thy place is changed; thou art the same."

It is as *illustrative* of this altered attitude of spirit that we find appended to *In Memoriam* a nuptial ode. This ode was written on the marriage of one of the poet's sisters to one of the poet's friends, probably the "true in word and tried in deed," to whom he had already offered the "imperfect gift" of a second friendship. I hardly see why I should hesitate to name him—Professor Lushington, of Glasgow University—for, as an old student of his, I have pleasure in echoing the poet's praise of him:—

"And thou art worthy; full of power;
  As gentle; liberal-minded, great,
  Consistent; wearing all that weight
Of learning lightly like a flower."

The bride was not the sister who had been betrothed to Hallam, but she had been known to Hallam; "he too foretold the perfect rose." And now, this marriage-day—nine years after Hallam's death—is the brightest day the poet has yet experienced since his sad bereavement. He finds that he can enter with thorough heartiness into all the festivity and gladness of the wedding. It is not that he has forgotten his first friend; he thinks of him as perchance present, though unseen,

"And, tho' in silence, wishing joy."

His old Regret has gone, but not his old love—

"Regret is dead, but love is more
Than in the summers that are flown."

And so, whilst true as ever to the memory of the departed, he can enter with living healthful sympathy into all the joy of the bridal. There *was* a day when the churchyard was to him only a place of congenial gloom; but now, when he follows bride and bridegroom out of the church porch, he feels that even the grave "has its sunny side." Thus the marriage-ode is no mere literary excrescence: its addition to the poem is justified by the laws of art; for it gives a crowning illustration of that progressive history of feeling, of which the poem itself contains the record.

IV.—The fourth and last aspect in which I shall view *In Memoriam* is *as embodying the protest of the Heart in favour of spiritual Faith.*

The soul that has just been stricken by a sore bereavement is often confronted with the great questions of human destiny. Brought face to face with the fact of death, the soul is no longer satisfied with a mere traditional creed. Even "scepticisms," which were formerly mere objects of curiosity, may perhaps now demand to be made subjects of inquiry. The soul longs for spiritual assurance.

That friend whom I so dearly loved, does he still exist, or has he ceased to be? Is there, after all, a soul that survives the dissolution of the body? And, if there *is* a soul, is it at death re-absorbed into the universal spirit, or does it still exist as a separate individual? And, if so, is it meanwhile in a state of sleep, waiting until it receives the resurrection-body, or is it even now in a state of conscious activity? Does my friend see me? Does he remember me? Does he love me still, or has he forgotten the circumstances of his earthly existence, now that he has been born into the higher life? or does he regard the old friendship as unworthy of him, now that he is holding converse with the "circle of the wise" above? If he sees me, and knows all my faults, will he not love me less? Shall we recognize each other again when we meet in another world? Now that he has got so far beyond me, can I ever be his companion there as here? And is there really a Christ, who, when He was on earth, raised the dead,—a Divine Redeemer in whom we can trust as "The Resurrection and the Life"?

Such are the questions that naturally present themselves to the bereaved heart, and that are touched by Tennyson in the course of this poem. *Touched:* that is all. The poet does not profess to discuss them. He attempts no philosophical investigation. He enters into no theological argument. He simply brings the questions, as a poet may well do, into the light of imagination and affection. He looks at the analogies of nature and of human experience. He considers the various questions in relation to his own deepest feeling. He lays weight on spiritual intuition—on that which is "likest God within the soul." When analogy and intuition seem to point in different directions, he leans to intuition. He trusts nature less than human nature on the great questions of human destiny. And, as a man who has "loved and lost," without professing to solve these questions, he meets them with an answer born of the cravings and instincts of his own heart.

He believes that his friend still lives. His heart refuses to accept the doctrine that what he loved was merely a piece of organized matter, now mouldering in the churchyard. Nor can he believe that his friend has lost individuality and been re-absorbed into the "general soul." *That* is a "faith as vague as all unsweet." Perhaps the soul may be sleeping: if so, it is a comfort to think that, when it wakes again, all the old love will wake with it, the same as ever. But, for his own part, he clings to the belief that the soul is not sleeping—that, as "*here*, the man is more and more," so *there* the soul is, even now, making constant and conscious progress. He loves also to think that his friend has carried his memory with him, and that the eternal landscape of the past lies all "clear" before him. He hopes that his friend still loves him : surely love is "too precious" a thing to "be lost": and even the superior nature may surely "spare some sympathy" for the inferior. He wishes the departed to "be near him"—to "look him through and through"; for surely our friends who are with God can look upon our faults with a godlike charity. He clings to the faith, born of love, that they "shall know each other when they meet again," and "each enjoy the other's good." He clings even to the hope that all God's creatures may "at last," when God's purposes are "complete," exist in the conscious enjoyment of life. It may be but a "dream"; God knows best; and there are analogies of "Nature" that seem to contradict the expectation; but still his heart bids him "trust," however "faintly," "the larger hope." Nor does he conceal his faith in Christ. To him Christ is no mere imperfect moralist. The Gospels are the record of

> "the *sinless* years
> That breathed beneath the Syrian blue."

To him the miracles are no myths: Christ is "the Life indeed," who brought back Lazarus from "his charnel-cave." Yea, Christ is to him the "Word made flesh," who

> "wrought
> With human hands the creed of creeds
> In loveliness of perfect deeds,
> More strong than all poetic thought."

Some have ventured to call Tennyson a "Pantheist." Well, as Carlyle has it, "call him Pantheist or Pottheist," he has certainly here uttered himself in favour of faith—faith in God and Christ and a personal immortality. Doubtless the poem has its echoes of the scepticisms peculiar to our own age; but this only makes it the more valuable, as embodying the protest of the heart against them:—

"If e'er when faith had fall'n asleep,
　I heard a voice 'believe no more'
　And heard an ever-breaking shore
That tumbled in the Godless deep;

"A warmth within the breast would melt
　The freezing reason's colder part,
　And like a man in wrath the heart
Stood up and answered 'I have felt.'"

The scepticisms of our time are born chiefly of the ultra-scientific spirit. Fascinated by the discoveries which have so greatly widened for them the region of the natural, men are losing their faith in the supernatural. They begin to regard humanity as lying entirely within the sweep of the same laws that rule in nature. Now, possibly it may be of but little consequence whether we believe that the first man was made by God out of "the dust of the ground" or developed by God out of an ape; but, if men go on to infer from this "doctrine of development" that human thought and love and aspiration and conscience are all mere affections of nerve and brain, and that when nerve and brain cease to act the man ceases to be, then this *inference* may have its serious issues. Certainly the great battle which Christianity has now to fight is the battle with a scientific materialism, and in this conflict the *In Memoriam* of Tennyson, appealing as it does to cultured minds, and the outcome, as it evidently is, of a personal experience, is fitted to render valuable service to the cause of spiritual faith :—

"I think we are not wholly brain,
　Magnetic mockeries. . . . .

> "Not only cunning casts in clay:
> Let Science prove we are, and then
> What matters Science unto men?"

The poet would remind the *savant* that the human *heart* has an "eye" as well as the human *intellect*, and that, in the formation of our beliefs on the profoundest of all themes, we are *bound* to take into consideration the yearnings and intuitions of the soul. Another poet of our time, whom perhaps we may justly call "Pantheistic," has said, in the melancholy of his unbelief—

> "Nor does our being weary prove that there is rest."

No, not "prove" it perhaps *logically*; for, as Tennyson says, the highest truths "never can be proved" after that fashion. But if there be a God of justice and mercy, then surely the elements of human nature must be in correspondence with the facts of the universe. Human *hunger* does point to a provision of *food*. Human *fatigue* does point to a provision of *sleep*. The Almighty Father has a "rest" for the "weary." We may well therefore "trust the truths that never can be proved." We may well believe that our spiritual cravings point to spiritual realities—that there *is* a "Bread of Life" for the hunger of the soul:—

> "Strong Son of God, immortal Love,
>   Whom we, that have not seen thy face,
>   By faith, and faith alone, embrace,
> Believing where we cannot prove;

> "Thine are these orbs of light and shade;
>   Thou madest Life in man and brute;
>   Thou madest Death; and lo, thy foot
> Is on the skull which thou hast made.

"Thou wilt not leave us in the dust:
   Thou madest man, he knows not why;
   He thinks he was not made to die;
And thou hast made him: thou art just.

"Thou seemest human and divine,
   The highest, holiest manhood, thou:
   Our wills are ours, we know not how;
Our wills are ours, to make them thine.

"Our little systems have their day;
   They have their day and cease to be:
   They are but broken lights of thee,
And thou, O Lord, art more than they."

The man who wrote *that* you may call "Pantheist" if you please; I am content to close my lecture with the music of these words ringing in our ears.

CHRISTIANITY AND "THE RELIGION OF THE FUTURE."

[Originally written in 1878: subsequently revised and slightly altered.]

I. THE CHRISTIAN ESTIMATE OF THIS LIFE.

"*THE Religion of the Future,*" says Mr. George Henry Lewes, "*must no longer present a conception of the world and physical laws, or of man and moral laws, which has any other basis than that of scientific induction. It must no longer put forward principles which are unintelligible and incredible, nor make their very unintelligibility a source of glory, and a belief in them a higher virtue than belief in demonstration. In a word, this transformed religion must cease to accept for its tests and sanctions such tests as would be foolishness in science, and such sanctions as would be selfishness in life. Instead of proclaiming the nothingness of this life, the worthlessness of human love, and the imbecility of the human mind, it will proclaim the supreme importance of this life, the supreme value of human love, and the grandeur of the human intellect.*"

I quote this passage because it is one of the characteristic utterances of modern scepticism. It may be taken as fairly representing the attitude of a school of thought which seems to be at present on the increase in England, and which, through various channels, is captivating some of the minds of the younger generation. The school to which I refer is distinguished by intellectual ability, and by a fearlessness which occasionally passes into audacity. Its adherents agree in rejecting all "supernatural religion"; and they trace their rejection largely to the teachings of science and to the atmosphere which is generated by the scientific spirit. They also agree in regarding what has been called the "religion of humanity" as being practically the "religion of the future." If there be a God, He is "The Unknown and The Unknowable." He has never, they say, revealed Himself to men in such a way as that we are warranted in feeling assured that He is our Loving Father. The world beyond death is, they say, probably a mere dream, born of the natural instinct which clings to life. The highest, and indeed the only, religion which is possible on truly rational grounds is, they tell us, the practical religion of spending our life for the benefit of our brethren, and thus losing our individual selfishness in devotion to the general good. And the only immortality on which we can safely reckon is an immortality of the influence which we can exert on others, and which may live long after we ourselves have passed into nothingness, or rather into "nature." Such is the creed which some are now preaching with even passionate enthusiasm, an enthusiasm which may well seem strange to some of us, but which is, perhaps, to be explained partly by their conviction that they are fighting against superstition and proclaiming the most unselfish ideal of conduct, and partly by the inspiring power which is wielded by the true and noble idea of Human Brotherhood.

But surely we may recognize all that is honest and earnest in such men, and yet deplore the conclusions at which they have arrived, and which they are seeking to propagate. We may believe that what is loftiest and best in their attitude and utterances is due to that very revelation of God in Christ which they regard as incredible. We may well shudder to think what our race might become, if its only hope of progress lay in a doctrine of human brotherhood, divorced altogether from any faith in God or immortality, and accompanied, perhaps, by the doctrine that man is a conscious automaton! And, whilst we believe that these men may even be doing good by some of their protests, we may also feel bound to protest, in our turn, against what we believe to be their dangerous errors; and we may well feel anxious to guard the minds of the young against a one-sided philosophy which would rob them of all practical faith in the gospel of Jesus Christ.

The passage which I have quoted from the writings of Mr. Lewes is one which might well be studied, clause for clause; for, short as it is, it bristles with points which challenge our Christian position. I propose, however, to confine our attention to the closing sentence, which contains a kind of epigrammatic summary of the contrast between the religion which is supposed to be passing away, and "the religion of the future" which is expected to replace it. "The kingdom of *Man* is at hand," says one of the writers of this school. "The religion of the future," says Mr. Lewes, in the sentence which I propose to examine, "the religion of the future, instead of proclaiming the nothingness of this life, the worthlessness of human love, and the imbecility of the human mind, will proclaim the supreme importance of this life, the supreme value of human love, and the grandeur of the human intellect." Now, here we have a threefold indictment, and a threefold ideal, the one corresponding to the other. An indictment is brought against the religion of the past and present, including, I presume, the Christian religion, that it has "proclaimed the nothingness of this life, the worthlessness of human love, and the imbecility of the human mind." And an ideal is presented of "the religion of the future," that it "will proclaim the supreme importance of this life, the supreme value of human love, and the grandeur of the human intellect." Let us look at *the first point* in this threefold contrast. "The religion of the future," we are told, "instead of proclaiming the nothingness, will proclaim the supreme importance of this life." Here, I say, we have both an indictment and an ideal.

Let us look, first, at *the indictment*. Is it fair, or philosophical, to affirm that the Christian religion "proclaims the nothingness of this life"? It is, indeed, quite true that, in the history of the Christian church, there has often been manifest a tendency to under-estimate the significance and value of the present life. The glorious rays of the "Sun of Righteousness" so dazzled the eyes of many that they were almost blinded for a time to the things of this world, just as, indeed, the marvellous revelations of modern science have so fascinated and absorbed the thoughts of some, as almost to shut out from *their* view the whole kingdom of the spiritual. Then, too, many of the early Christians seem to have been living in expectation of the immediate return of Christ, and the winding-up of all terrestrial things; and it was only natural that the expectation of such a transcendent crisis should colour their whole feeling and conduct. The furniture of a house may be of great value; but surely no one would blame a man severely, if, in the hour of earthquake, he thought but little of his furniture. Then, again, the glorious revelation of the heavenly world, with its high and pure felicities, so captivated the minds of many who were only too familiar with the struggles and sorrows of life, that they even longed for death, and sometimes rushed on martyrdom. Then, further, a false philosophy, which regarded matter as the seat and source of evil, led to those monstrosities of an inhuman asceticism, which did so much to misrepresent the true spirit of Christianity. The church, in its revulsion from the sensualities and earthliness of the world, has too often cut itself off from the great common life of man, and indulged in a sickly and unnatural pietism. It must be confessed that, even in some hymns which are still sung in Christian assemblies, there is a certain unreal and exaggerated presentation of the Christian attitude towards the things of this world. And I think we ought all to be careful how we lend our countenance to any such unreality in the expression of our religious life. I do not mean that we should never sing hymns which are beyond our own present spiritual experience; for these I think we may sometimes sing, as indicative of our aspiration rather than of our attainment. But we ought not to sing hymns expressing a contempt of the present world, which we not only *do* not feel, but which we *ought not* to feel. Surely we may magnify the grace of God for the higher blessings of redemption, without despising, or affecting to despise, the minor blessings and comforts of life. The exaggerations of the Secularist or Positivist School of thought may be partly a reaction from this sentimental pietism, and may have exercised, so far, a healthful influence on the Christian church. The teachings of science, also, regarding the intimate connection between the mind and body, have their own value in checking the tendency which is often manifested by an earnest religious life in the direction of a morbid asceticism.

But now, whilst we thus make all these confessions and admissions, we may well repeat the question whether it is either fair or philosophical to charge the Christian religion with " proclaiming the nothingness of this life "? Is it fair to fix the attention on the excesses of fanaticism or even the exaggerations of pietism, and to speak of Christianity as if it had never been represented by other forms of the religious life, or as if it had never exercised any beneficial influence in modifying and moulding the institutions, laws, and customs of society ? Would it not be more philosophical—before bringing such an indictment against the religion of the past—to examine the conduct and teachings of Christ Himself, the general spirit and tendency of the New Testament, and the practical influence of Christianity on this very life which it is said to ignore and to despise ?

Look at the recorded history of Jesus Christ.

Where do we ever find Him "proclaiming the nothingness of this life"? It is true, we hear Him saying that "a man's life consisteth not in the abundance of the things which he possesseth"; but even the secularist, I presume, would assent to that. We find Christ protesting against an exaggerated and unspiritual estimate of the things of this world; but, even whilst He dissuades His disciples from over-anxiety as to "what they shall eat and what they shall drink," etc., it is not on the ground that these things are valueless, but that "the Heavenly Father knoweth that they have need of all these things." Yea, some of His arguments against this feverish anxiety are drawn from the very value of human life in the sight of God. "Is not the life more than meat, and the body than raiment?" Will He who has given the greater blessing withhold the less? Did not Christ also distinctly warn His disciples against courting martyrdom? "When they persecute you in one city, flee ye to another." Did He not Himself deliberately avoid the ascetic life, accepting the invitation to the wedding-feast, and to the supper which His friends made in His honour at Bethany? And what is the meaning of all Christ's miracles of healing and beneficence? Did He go amongst the diseased, and tell them that all their pain was not of the slightest consequence? Did He not show His intense sympathy with them in their afflictions? and did not His works of healing reveal His appreciation of all healthy conditions of human life? Was it not, moreover, part of the very plan and purpose of Christ to set up "a kingdom of God" *on this very earth*—a "kingdom" which would extend itself throughout the wide world—which, "like the leaven," would gradually "leaven the whole lump"—and which, linking men to the one Father, would bind them to one another as brethren? Was all this a proclamation of "the nothingness of the present life"?

Or, look at the writings of the New Testament generally, and consider whether they are fairly open to this charge. Consider the emphasis with which the loftiest principles are brought to bear on the ordinary tasks and commonest relationships of life. Consider how Paul worked at his trade of tent-making, and supported himself with his own hands, whilst preaching the gospel. Consider how he availed himself of the privileges of his Roman citizenship, in order to protect his life from his persecutors. Consider how he protests against the perversions of a morbid asceticism and a fanatical abstinence, and speaks of the body as "a temple of the Holy Ghost." Think, too, how he warns the Thessalonians against that condition of mind which was begotten of their idea that the "day of the Lord" was immediately "at hand," and how he exhorts them "with quietness to work, and eat their own bread." Remember the counsels which are given in almost every epistle to practical godliness in daily life; counsels to husbands and wives, to parents and children, to masters and servants, exhortations to honesty, and purity of speech, and truthfulness, and hospitality, and care for the poor, and respect for magistracy. Look, too, at Paul's words addressed to Timothy: "Godliness is profitable unto all things, *having promise of the life that now is,* and of that which is to come."

Could such an utterance as this have been born in the atmosphere of a religion which "proclaimed the nothingness of the present life"? I think, then, we may claim that, whatever may have been the errors of some Christians, this indictment against Christianity is answered by an appeal to the spirit and teachings of Christ and His apostles.

And now let us turn to the *ideal* which is presented to our minds of the expected "religion of the future," when it is said that it will "proclaim the supreme importance of this life." There is certainly a "long interval" between "nothingness" and "supreme importance." There are many things which we may regard as *very* valuable, and yet which we may not think to be the *most* valuable things in the universe. The question, of course, here is: What is meant by speaking of the "supreme importance" of this life? Surely it cannot be meant that there are absolutely no higher considerations than those which have regard to the duration and happiness of our earthly existence. In his own *History of Philosophy*, Mr. Lewes has shown us how he can admire the martyrdom of Socrates and the noble self-denial of Spinoza. It cannot be meant that every individual should be taught that his own earthly life is to be regarded by himself as of supreme importance, to be preserved even at the cost of violating duty. I suppose, therefore, that what is really meant is to institute a contrast between "the life that now is" and the life which, according to the Christian doctrine, "is to come." The new religion is to tell us that such a life beyond death is a mere dream of the imagination, or is at best a peradventure—that it ought, therefore, to be left out of calculation and regarded as of minor importance, and that we ought to fix our whole thought on the duties, circumstances, and conditions of our present existence. Now, if this were simply equivalent to a protest against the selfish idea that our whole business in this life is to save our own souls in the next, or against the idea that a man, through the hope of heaven or the fear of hell, is to spend his earthly life in neglect of the plainest earthly duties to which God is calling him, then we might gladly welcome such a protest. But if it be meant, as I suppose it is meant, that we ought to give up all thought of a future life as being of no practical moment, and that we ought to live in this world as if the present life were all, then, I say, may God save us from any such new religion! To proclaim in this sense the "supreme importance" of the present is really to make it of less importance than it is. If you turn means into ends you do not necessarily increase their value. A road may be of far more "importance" to me, when I regard it as leading to a certain city, than it can be when you tell me that there is "no thoroughfare," but that it is a good road as far as it goes, and that I had better make the best of it! You do not surely diminish the importance of school-life when you tell a boy that his present diligence may help to fit him for the duties of manhood. And, even so, although you may appear to be magnifying the present existence when you suggest that it is all, and that there is nothing beyond it, you are practically diminishing its importance. For the value and grandeur of human life depend on the value and grandeur of the nature that lives it. Hence the gospel, which has "brought immortality to light," has also everywhere deepened the sense of the sacredness of human life. It abolishes infanticide: it condemns suicide: it builds hospitals: it cares for the aged, the sickly, the deformed, and the weak: it ministers tenderly even to the dying in their last moments, for it looks at human beings as the children of God and the heirs of immortality. It tells us that our dear ones who have gone before us have not gone beyond the Father's care: it comforts us with the blessed hope of meeting them hereafter in the Father's house. But it does not tell us that the present life is nothing. Threescore years and ten are indeed but a span as compared with the life that never ends; but even the fraction of an immortal life is a grander thing than the sum total of a life that perishes for ever in death. Regard the present as the vestibule of a future existence: look at it as the school in which God is training His children—the arena in which character is being drilled and disciplined for eternity; and then even the "trivial round" and "common task" acquire a new sacredness and significance. Certainly Christianity does *not* "proclaim the nothingness of this life," and as certainly it does not proclaim that this life is all or is to be lived as if it were all. It tells us that we are "pilgrims on the earth," and every one must acknowledge it. This at least is a fact beyond all doubt. "Here we have no continuing city": we are simply travellers. But travellers *whither?* "That is the question." Some say to the grave: the gospel says to the world beyond, and, in saying this, really magnifies the importance of the journey. And the life of "godliness" and goodness—the "eternal life"— the life of God in the soul of man—THIS is the one thing of *absolutely* "supreme importance" both "in the life that now is" and in that which "is to come."

II. THE CHRISTIAN ESTIMATE OF HUMAN LOVE.

LET us now examine the second point in Mr. Lewes's threefold contrast. The "religion of the future," he says, "instead of proclaiming the worthlessness of human love," will proclaim its "supreme value." Here again we have both an indictment and an ideal. And with reference, first, to the *indictment*, I would ask the question, Is it true that the Christian religion "proclaims the worthlessness of human love"? It must, indeed, be admitted, as before, that in the history of the Christian church, it is possible to point both to doctrines and to practices which have been fairly open to such a charge. Those who are not familiar with the history of asceticism would be astonished by finding to what an unnatural and inhuman extent Christian men and women have sometimes carried the doctrine and practice of self-denial. But it is well enough known that from an early period in the history of the church, it was the custom to look down upon marriage, and to hold up the unmarried state as being the highest type of the religious life, and as being certain to meet with the highest reward in the heavenly world. One can easily understand how the life of the monastery, with its false ideals of piety, would lead to a contempt of those affections which lie at the root of our ordinary relationships. And, when celibacy came to be the law of the church for the whole of its clergy, we cannot wonder that, when the teachers and leaders of the Christian community were men thus cut off from family ties, human love should have been less valued. Add to this that the doctrine of original sin and of the inherent depravity of human nature was sometimes taught in a form so exaggerated as to cast a dark shadow on all the natural instincts and affections of humanity.

Mr. Lecky, in his interesting book on *The History of European Morals*, has collected some strange and striking illustrations of the excesses of austerity engendered by these perverted ideals of the Christian life. He tells us, for instance, of one "holy" man who, being earnestly besought by his own sister—who had not seen him for many years—to come and visit her on her death-bed, refused at first to go, on the ground that it would be a departure from the saintliness of his life, and who, being afterwards moved to visit her, did so in disguise, so that she did not know at the time that he was the brother whom she had longed to see. He tells us also of another "holy" man, who, having occasion to carry his own mother over the ford of a river, covered his hands carefully with cloths before he did so, lest he should be defiled by touching a woman!

But now, surely, it is the part of a philosopher to distinguish between fruit and fungus, between the healthy religious life quickened by the spirit of Christianity, and these morbid outgrowths of an ascetic "sainthood." Is it not the case that the spirit of the gospel has already in large measure shaken off these perverted ideals? Yea, is it not the case that, in the very infancy of the church, the spirit of the gospel frequently uttered its protest against the tendency to these inhuman extravagances? And I appeal to the whole spirit and tone of the New Testament, and ask whether any simple, impartial reader of its pages would ever come to the conclusion that the Christian religion "proclaims the worthlessness of human love"?

Look at the spirit and teachings of Christ Himself. Can any one fail to see that Christ loved human beings with a deep and true affection? Is it not clear that one of His great purposes was to link men to one another in the bonds of brotherhood? Does He not often inculcate compassion and kindliness? Think of the parable of the "Good Samaritan." Does He not lay emphasis on the duty of forgiveness? Think of the parable of the "Unmerciful Servant." Does He not exhort us even to "do good to our enemies," and to pray for them, and that, too, because we are to "love" them still in spite of their enmity? Does He not tell us that "the second great commandment" of the law is, "Thou shalt love thy neighbour as thyself"?

But it might, perhaps, be replied:—All this relates to a general love—a kind of spiritual affection—which Christ wished men to cherish towards each other as members of the same race, and as children of the same Father in heaven: it does not touch His attitude towards the closer loves, and the ordinary relationships of human life. Now this objection would surely come with rather bad grace from those who speak so enthusiastically of the "religion of humanity," and of the duty of merging private interests and considerations in devotion to the general good! And we might well ask whether "human love" ceases to be "human love" when it goes forth in kindliness and sympathy towards all men, or when it recognizes spiritual kinship, or when it looks on others in the light of the Divine Fatherhood?

But, indeed, we need not hesitate to accept the challenge, even with regard to Christ's estimate of the ordinary relationships and the closer affections of humanity. Where, then, I ask, is the evidence that Jesus either despised or overlooked the natural ties and claims of family, or friendship, or country? It is true, indeed, that when His mother sought to dictate to Him, and His brethren sought to interfere with Him, in His great work, He calmly asserted His independence. But do we not read that, as a boy, He was "subject" to Joseph and Mary in Nazareth, and have we not every reason to believe that He loved His mother with a special affection? Do we not read that, amid the awful agony of the Cross, He thought of that mother's welfare, and commended her to the care of "the disciple whom He loved"? And this very phrase—"the disciple whom He loved"—what does *this* imply but that the human heart of Jesus had its special friendships? We read that Jesus loved Martha and Mary and Lazarus: we know how He "wept" at the grave of His friend. Does all this look like denying the value of human affection? When Jesus took three of His most intimate disciples into the recesses of the garden, that they might be near Him in the hour of His great sorrow, was this intense craving for human sympathy an evidence that He set no value on human love? Are there not indications also that the treachery of Judas was one of the bitterest elements in His cup of anguish? And can *He* be charged with being dead to the love of country who shed those tears of grief over doomed Jerusalem?

Or, look again at Christ's teaching, and think how He recognized the sacredness of human relationships, and the value and beauty of natural affections. When the mothers brought their little ones to Him that He might "bless" them, think how tenderly He took them into His arms, and how lovingly He spoke of their claims. Remember how He increased the sanctity of the marriage-bond by limiting the right of divorce. Think how He condemned some of the Pharisees, who, under pretext of serving God more devotedly, neglected their own parents and imagined that by their "Corban" they could rid themselves of their duty to father and mother. Remember also how, in the parable of the "Prodigal Son," He pictures the forgiving love of a true father as an emblem of the divine love itself, and how, in the same parable, He holds up the conduct of the unbrotherly brother as a mirror in which the Pharisees might see the reflection of their own harsh and unloving self-righteousness. Was all this the teaching of one who proclaimed "the worthlessness of human affection"?

Or, again, look at the general spirit and tendency of the apostolic writings. It is true that, in one of his epistles, St. Paul advises celibacy as a matter of Christian prudence, in consideration of the then troubled condition of the times; but even this advice he gives conditionally, with a due regard to special temperaments and circumstances. In other epistles he protests against a false asceticism, and condemns those who "forbid to marry." It does not occur to him that a "bishop" is less fitted for his post by being a husband and a father. He exhorts husbands to "love their wives, even as Christ loved the church." He lays special emphasis, too, on the claims of blood-relationship: "If any provide not for his own, and specially for those of his own house, he hath denied the faith, and is worse than an infidel." And his touching allusions to the friendship of Onesiphorus and others, his craving for Timothy's presence, his beautiful salutation to "Rufus and *to his mother and mine*," all show the value which he attached to human sympathy and affection. If, then, Mr. Lewes, in saying that the "religion of the future" will *not* "proclaim the worthlessness of human love," means to suggest that Christianity has done so, I think we may venture to claim that—whatever some Christians may have done—the whole tenor of the New Testament proves that the Christian religion, as such, is not fairly open to any such charge.

But now, let us pass on to look at the *ideal* which is presented to our minds when it is said of the "religion of the future," that it will "proclaim the supreme value of human love." Here, I ask first of all, What is meant by this phrase "supreme value"? Is it simply meant that pure, true, unselfish love is the highest manifestation of goodness in humanity? But surely the religion of the Cross—if it means anything at all—means that the highest life is the life of loving and lawful self-sacrifice. A Christian apostle has celebrated the praises of this love in a manner which the most eloquent of modern Positivists will find it hard to match. "Love suffereth long, and is kind; love envieth not; love vaunteth not itself, is not puffed up, doth not behave itself unseemly, seeketh not its own, is not provoked, taketh not account of evil; rejoiceth not in unrighteousness, but rejoiceth with the truth; beareth all things, believeth all things, hopeth all things, endureth all things. . . . But now abideth faith, hope, love, these three; and the greatest of these is love." THE GREATEST OF THESE IS LOVE, for there needs no "religion of the future" to tell us *this*.

Or again, is it meant that the natural affections which bind us to one another are of "supreme value," in the sense that their claims are necessarily above all other claims, and that we ought not to endanger these affections for any consideration? Surely this cannot be meant; to assert this would be to strike at the root of all morality. "He that loveth father or mother more than Me," said Christ, "is not worthy of Me." And whatever any Positivist may think of this remarkable and lofty claim, he would surely never dream of denying that considerations of private affection ought to yield to the claims of conscience and duty. He would not defend a father who should commit a fraud in order to promote the welfare of his children. And I cannot doubt that he would admire the character of the man or woman who should cleave to truth and honour, at the cost of endangering—or even of losing—the love of the dearest relative or friend. Mr. Lewes, therefore, cannot mean to proclaim that human love is of such "supreme value" that it is entitled to demand from us the sacrifice of morality.

What, then, does he mean? Probably this: that the love which human beings cherish towards each other and towards their race is man's chief treasure; that we know of no higher love in the universe; and that a love for humanity ought to prompt us to the noblest life, without any thought of a personal God or of a personal immortality. The Positivist would substitute the religion of humanity, the worship and love of the human race, for the worship and love of the living, personal God. It is here that we differ from him. We deny the "supreme value of human love," if it be meant by this that there is nothing higher in the universe. Noble and precious indeed is the pure, unselfish affection which human creatures can cherish for one another: it is certainly one of our dearest possessions. But there *is* one thing which is higher and more precious still, and that is the love which the Father in heaven bears towards every human soul. "God is love": and His love towards us is the one thing which is of absolutely "supreme value." It is His love which is the fountain of all other love; it is His love which has given us the friends who care for us; it is His love which bestows upon our own hearts the faculty of loving. And any religion which shuts out from view God and immortality, whilst it may appear to be increasing the worth of human love by speaking of it as "supreme," does in reality lessen its significance and preciousness, and tends to dry up some of the sources of its inspiration.

Thus, suppose we regard the love of a mother for her child, or the love of youth and maiden, however pure and noble, as being merely a subtle form of animal instinct; suppose we regard the love of friends and country and humanity, and all the unselfish devotion which flows from these affections, as due simply to certain movements in the brain, which men cannot control; and suppose, further, that we regard all these affections as not only having their origin in dust, but as also going back into dust in the grave, is it possible that we can still attach the same sacredness, significance, and value to human love? Or, if this planet of ours is destined in the course of ages to become uninhabitable, and if science compels the Positivist to believe that humanity, as such, is thus destined to be blotted out of the universe, what becomes of the "immortality of his influence," and how does the worship and love of "humanity" appear in the light of this final consummation? Surely the value of human love must depend on the value of the nature that loves and is loved. Surely human affection becomes a much grander thing when we believe that, however it may be associated with the bodily frame, it is the affection of a spiritual and immortal creature, "made in the image of the Creator." The love of a mother for a child, does it not become far more significant and precious when we regard it as implanted by the God whose very nature is love? Our own dear ones who have passed away through death, what of their love for us? Will it become more holy and precious in our thought if we think of it as converted into ashes, dust, and gas? Is it not far more valuable when we think of it as abiding still, when we feel that we can *still* love, not a mere memory, but a living friend, whom we hope yet to meet again in "the Father's house"? Yes: when it is immortals that love immortals, the love itself becomes a grander and more precious thing. Then it is seen that love is too sacred a thing to be tampered with, and to be made the mere sport and plaything of an hour; that no man, even though he be a human colossus, like the German Goethe, has any right to trifle with human affections. Then, too, when all men are seen to be the children of God, spiritual creatures destined for immortality, we feel that there is a far higher basis for the love and the service of humanity. The "brotherhood of man" has its true foundation in the "Fatherhood" of God. And so, any "religion of the future," which ignores God and immortality, may preach, as it will, "the supreme value of human love," but this "supreme value" will not be so valuable as the human love which is seen to have its spring in the higher love of God, and which even death itself cannot destroy.

III. THE CHRISTIAN ESTIMATE OF THE HUMAN INTELLECT.

WE come now to the third point in Mr. Lewes's threefold contrast. "The religion of the future," he says, "instead of proclaiming the imbecility of the human mind, will proclaim its grandeur." Here, once more, we have both an indictment and an ideal.

Look, first, at the *indictment*. Supposing it to be here suggested that Christianity "proclaims the imbecility of the human mind," I ask whether this charge can be substantiated by adequate evidence. The question is not whether many foolish things have not been uttered in the name of Christianity, for this, of course, must be admitted. It must be acknowledged that Christian men, in dwelling on the necessity for faith, have sometimes under-estimated the powers of the human intellect, and undervalued the kind and amount of knowledge which comes from the exercise of these powers. It may be that they have sometimes even represented the call to faith as a demand to believe incredibilities. And it is quite true that narrow and ignorant Christians have often spoken with contempt of human learning, and have gloried in clinging to beliefs which science has demonstrated to be no longer tenable. But even this falls a long way short of "proclaiming the imbecility of the human mind"; and, moreover, the essential question is not as to what mistaken or narrow Christians may have said on this subject, but as to what is the attitude of the Christian religion, *as such*, towards the human intellect.

Look, then, at the teaching of Christ and His apostles—look at the general tone and spirit of the New Testament—and consider whether it is fairly open to the charge of "proclaiming the imbecility of the human mind." Jesus Christ does not, indeed, come before us in the Gospels either as a man of science or as a philosopher—technically so called. He was educated in no human school of learning or philosophy. "According to the flesh," He was a man of the people, and, until He was thirty years of age, lived the life of a Galilean peasant. It was no part of His mission to engage in scientific research, or to examine how far the exercise of reason could carry men in the pursuit of knowledge. It was not even any part of His specific mission to urge men *directly* to the due cultivation of their intellectual powers. His was other and far higher work. He came as a Prophet—a Seer—a religious Teacher and Reformer—yea, as the Revealer of the Eternal God. He came to reconcile men to their Father in heaven—to make them true and loyal citizens of the kingdom of righteousness and love.

His appeal was made specifically to the heart, the conscience, the will—the deeper spiritual nature of man. But where is the proof that Christ, in the prosecution of this great work, "proclaimed the imbecility of the human mind"? Do we ever find Him speaking scornfully of human learning? Do we ever find Him proclaiming the worthlessness of the knowledge which comes from the use of the perceptive and reflective faculties of the mind? Do we ever find Him warning His disciples against the cultivation of their intellectual powers, or telling them that it was not of the slightest consequence whether they were enlightened or ignorant. On the contrary, much of Christ's teaching presupposed the exercise of common sense in his hearers. His parables and aphorisms took it for granted that men would use their reason, and would distinguish between the letter and the spirit of His words. It is indeed true that Christ chose as His first apostles men who were "unlearned," perhaps because they were the first who proved susceptible to His spiritual influence, perhaps because it was desirable to show that the progress of His kingdom was dependent on spiritual rather than on intellectual forces. But, on the other hand, there are indications that some of these apostles—Peter and John, for example—were men of considerable mental vigour; and it is certain that the apostle of the Gentiles, who appeared later on the scene, was a man of well-disciplined and cultured mind, and of great intellectual force. We are, therefore, I think, justified in affirming that the fanaticism which despises mental training and secular knowledge was foreign to the spirit of Jesus; and, although Paul speaks slightingly of the Greek "philosophy" of his own time—which was largely a thing of rhetorical word-mongering and subtle disputation, casting no real light on the universe of matter or of mind—yet there are indications in his writings that he was ready to appreciate any true "wisdom" or any real "knowledge" *rightly* "so called." It would even appear as if he saw in the gospel of Christ an element which brought a certain satisfaction to the intellectual nature. "We speak wisdom," he says, "among them that are perfect." His own epistles, too, make their appeal to the reasoning faculties. He calls upon his readers to exercise their minds on the questions which he discusses. "I speak as to wise men; judge ye what I say." "Brethren, be not children in mind; howbeit in malice be ye babes, but in mind be men." And throughout the whole history of the church, down from St. Paul's day until our own, there have been men of strong and cultured minds who have consecrated their intellectual powers to the service of Christ, and employed them in the defence and propagation of His gospel.

It is doubtless true that Christ and His apostles did not set supreme value on intellectual culture; did not suppose that "a man's life consisteth in the abundance" of the knowledge "which he possesseth." It is also true that Christ distinctly recognized the limitations of the intellect, in relation to the perception of spiritual realities. "I thank Thee, O Father, Lord of heaven and earth, that Thou hast hid these things from the wise and prudent, and hast revealed them unto babes." Here, doubtless, it is implied that to the childlike heart, and not to the mere disciplined intellect, does God reveal "the things" of His "kingdom." We are not, indeed, to infer that the possession of human "wisdom" and "prudence" necessarily hides from a man the things of God; although, in point of fact, intellectual attainments bring with them their own temptations, and sometimes puff a man up into a self-conceit which robs him of the childlike spirit. But, if the "wise" and "prudent" are also "babes," if they remain true to the instincts of their spiritual nature, if they do not allow their knowledge to blind them to their deepest needs, if they remain simple and sincere, trustful and receptive, then to them also, as thus childlike, will come the revelations of the eternal world. This same fact is brought before us by the Apostle Paul, when he speaks of "the wisdom of this world as being foolishness with God," and implies that mere human philosophy, mere intellectual research, is inadequate to discover spiritual realities. "The world by its wisdom knew not God." The "things of the Spirit of God" are "spiritually discerned." The gospel which seemed "foolishness" to the philosophical Greek was an appeal to the spiritual nature of man, and brought a "wisdom" higher and more precious than any which could be attained by the mere exercise of the intellectual faculties.

But now, was all this equivalent to "proclaiming the imbecility of the human mind"? Is it proclaiming the imbecility of the human eye to assert that it cannot hear the thunder? Is it proclaiming the imbecility of the human ear to say that it cannot see the sun? Is it proclaiming the imbecility of the reasoning faculties to say that no one can logically demonstrate that his own mother loves him? Would a politician be accused of disparaging art if he were to say that a man's eminence as a landscape-painter did not necessarily qualify him to judge of a political question, and that many a man who had never handled a pencil might have a clearer apprehension of the bearings of a political crisis? Would a musician be accused of disparaging the scientific faculty if he were to say that the inventor of the phonograph is not necessarily the more qualified to appreciate a sonata or an oratorio? Do we pour contempt on mathematical ability when we say that a man may be able to calculate an eclipse, and yet may possibly have less knowledge of what is meant by "being in love," than some other man who perhaps does not know how an eclipse is produced, but whose whole being is thrilled in presence of the maiden of his choice? Why, then, should a prophet or apostle be accused of disparaging the human mind when he affirms that the mere exercise of the intellectual powers does not necessarily give insight into "the things of God"? Every faculty has its own limitations. It may be mighty in its own sphere, but beyond *that* sphere it may be helpless. Marvellous are the powers of the human intellect, and great are the results which it has achieved; but there are other faculties in our nature besides the purely intellectual, and these may be powerful in regions where the intellect, as such, is weak. Scientific research is mighty; but who can "by searching find out God," or heaven? You cannot put God under a microscope! You cannot see heaven through a telescope! You cannot hear "the still, small voice" of the Spirit with a microphone! And philosophy, too, may be mighty and useful in its own domain; but it cannot logically demonstrate the existence or the character of God, or the fact of a future life. Yea, is not this precisely what many of our modern philosophers who reject Christianity are constantly telling us? They call themselves "Agnostics." They affirm that if there be a God He is "the Unknown and the Unknowable." They tell us that their philosophy can find no evidence of a future life on which they can rely. And yet, when we so far echo their words and say, " Yes, the mere intellect, as such, *is* 'agnostic' "; it cannot know "the things of the Spirit of God," for they are "spiritually discerned," must we be charged with "proclaiming the imbecility of the human mind"? No, we do not deny the marvellous powers of the perceptive and reasoning faculties of man. But we say that the revelation of God in Christ appeals, specifically, to other capacities of our nature; that the Father in heaven can and does make Himself known to His children; that, in His manifestations of Himself, He appeals to the spiritual instincts, yearnings, and aspirations which He has implanted within us. And therefore we say that, in this special region, the tender conscience, the loving heart, and the childlike spirit which recognizes its own needs, and trustfully looks out of itself for their satisfaction, can see further and acquire a fuller knowledge than any intellect, however disciplined in faculty, or stored with learning, which insists on believing nothing that is incapable of logical proof or absolute "demonstration." Well does Tennyson, in one of his recent poems, make the "Ancient Sage" appeal thus to the young man:—

> "Thou canst not prove the Nameless, O my son,
> Nor canst thou prove the world thou movest in,
> Thou canst not prove that thou art body alone,
> Nor canst thou prove that thou art spirit alone,
> Nor canst thou prove that thou art both in one :
> Thou canst not prove thou art immortal, no
> Nor yet that thou art mortal—nay my son,
> Thou canst not prove that I, who speak with thee,
> Am not thyself in converse with thyself,
> For nothing worthy proving can be proven,
> Nor yet disproven : Wherefore thou be wise,
> Cleave to the sunnier side of doubt,
> And cling to Faith beyond the forms of Faith!"

Look now at the *ideal* which is here presented of the "religion of the future," viz., that it "will proclaim the grandeur of the human intellect." And here I remark on the threshold, that this would hardly seem to be any part of the specific function of "religion." Religion, as such, has hitherto been supposed to stand in direct relation to the moral and spiritual rather than the intellectual nature. It springs out of man's "sense of the Infinite": it expresses those feelings of reverence and awe which lead to worship: it supplies the impulses and motives which shape moral character and conduct. Now, a "religion" which should ignore God, and at the same time place in the foreground "the grandeur of the human intellect," might tend rather to foster self-conceit and self-worship, than to deepen a healthy humility and awe. Moreover, even Mr. Lewes, whilst he speaks of the "supreme value of human love," does not speak of the "supreme value" of intellectual culture. I suppose he would say that any "religion" is defective which does not take direct and special cognizance of moral character; and he would affirm that the "religion of humanity" aims at the production of healthy moral action. Surely then, instead of harping on " the grandeur of the human intellect," it ought rather to proclaim the surpassing grandeur and importance of virtuous character and virtuous conduct, and to supply the inspiration which may lead to a life of well-doing. It is indeed true that—other things being equal—a man is all the better for having a well-disciplined and well-stored mind; his virtues will then become more intelligent, and his very knowledge may be helpful to him on the path of moral and spiritual progress. But, on the other hand, it is not always so: "other things" are not always "equal." We cannot shut our eyes to the fact that intellectual vigour and learning do not always go hand in hand with virtuous character. A philosopher may be utterly selfish. A poet may be a sensualist. A man may have studied the effects of alcohol on the physical constitution, and yet be himself a drunkard. Or a man may even make his knowledge an instrument in the hands of vice. Whereas a man of but little mental vigour and less learning may be living a beautiful life of simple honesty, purity, temperance, and unselfishness. Is this any reason for keeping men in ignorance, or undervaluing the importance of secular education? Certainly not. But it is a reason for not over-estimating the value of mere intellectual culture. And surely, in the light of such facts, it would seem to be one of the chief functions of any "religion" to lay special emphasis on the transcendent importance of moral and spiritual character, and to warn men against the worship of intellectual power, and especially against the idea that any amount of genius or learning can compensate for the lack of simple virtue. This is what Christianity does. It places "graces" above "gifts," love above knowledge, godliness above learning, and spiritual insight above philosophy.

But, although Christianity thus places intellectual culture in a subordinate position, the mind of man appears, nevertheless, a really "grander" thing in the light of the gospel, than in the light of that "religion of humanity" which ignores God and immortality, and "proclaims the grandeur of the human intellect." If we give up the idea that there is a "soul" in man—if we believe that memory, judgment, and imagination are simply the product of brain-impressions and brain-agitation—if we believe that the intellectual powers of man have been gradually evolved out of the most rudimentary forms of matter, apart from any creative or presiding intelligence—if we believe that when the body dies the individual ceases to be—shall we be likely thus to have loftier conceptions of the human mind? Does it heighten our conception of the intellect that created "Hamlet" and "Lear," to believe that it was once "potentially present" in some material atoms, and that it has all, long ago, gone back again into atoms—no longer to live or to think? Do we not obtain a far "grander" conception of the "human intellect" from a religion which tells us that, whatever may have been the mode of creation, man was "made in the image of God"; that, whatever may be the close and subtle relations between mind and brain, it is " the inspiration of the Almighty that giveth understanding," and that the powers of thought and reason survive the dissolution of the body? Surely the intellect of an immortal being, who is a child of the Eternal Creator, is, in itself, a "grander" thing, than the intellect of a being who has emerged, by some blind fatality, out of the "primeval slime," and who perishes utterly and for ever in death!

The fact is that the gospel—with its doctrines of the Fatherhood of God, the Incarnation of the Eternal Word, the Indwelling of the Holy Spirit, and the Resurrection of the Dead—necessarily gives a loftier view of the whole nature of man than can be given by any mere "religion of humanity." And, whilst it is no part of the specific function of Christianity to be ever harping on "the grandeur of the human intellect," yet it does remind us of our duty to consecrate our *whole* nature to God, and it tells us that all our faculties are "talents" committed to our trust by the Divine Master. Whilst it places character above learning, and godliness above intellectual vigour, and the pure and childlike heart above the wisdom of the philosopher, its whole spirit nevertheless exhorts us to keep "a healthy mind in a healthy body," to despise no knowledge of that universe which God has made, and to discipline and store our minds so that we may become the more useful in His service. "In malice be ye babes; but in mind, be men!"

IV. CRUCIAL TESTS OF A "RELIGION."

WE come now to the actual contrast which exists between the religion of the gospel and this proposed "religion of the future" in their respective relations to the fundamental needs of human nature and to the critical circumstances of human experience. The relative value of different kinds of food and drink is measured by their adaptation to the healthy natural cravings of the body, and by their fitness to maintain the health and strength of the physical frame. The worth of any friendship also is tested by the crises of life—"a friend in need is a friend indeed." And a "religion," to be truly worthy of the name, ought to supply proper food for the healthy cravings of our deepest nature, ought also to stand our friend and helper in the hour of our sorest necessity. Let us, then, apply these tests to the old religion of the gospel and to this new "religion of the future." I will take three cases of human nature in its need.

And, first, I will take the case of a poor man toiling hard to obtain the bare necessaries of life for himself and his family. Say that, for generations, his fathers before him have also been poor working men, and have had the same struggle to "keep the wolf from the door." This man has had no chance of getting a good education: his intellect is comparatively uncultivated, and he has no reasonable prospect of bettering his circumstances in life. Now, what has the new religion to say to this man? Here it may no doubt be alleged that, were the principles of "the religion of humanity" to become more prevalent, and to be widely acted upon, cases of extreme poverty would become more rare, and the whole *status* of the working-classes would be elevated. Well, be it so; I do not stay to discuss this point; I do not care to dispute it, for I daresay it will not be denied, on the other hand, that were the principles of Christianity more thoroughly acted out, this also would create great changes in society, and especially in the condition of the labouring poor. Christ Himself was a working-man; His first apostles were fishermen; the earliest believers were almost all drawn from the ranks of the poor—some of them were Roman slaves. The whole spirit of the gospel too is friendly towards the struggling; it is also opposed to drunkenness, dishonesty, oppression, and many of the other causes of poverty; and it inculcates justice and generosity—thoughtfulness for the claims and need of others. But here the man is, in this position, and he sees no reasonable prospect of bettering it. What, then, has the new religion to say to this man? Will it do him much good to "proclaim the grandeur of the human intellect"? This may only make him more discontented with his own poor education and lack of intellectual culture. Or, will it do him much good to proclaim "the supreme importance of this life," to tell him that he had better make the most of his present lot, for that he never knows how soon he may die, and be changed altogether into ashes and dust? The man looks round about him and sees multitudes in circumstances of luxury, or at any rate of comfort; and when his heart is almost eaten up with envy, you come to him with this gospel of "the supreme importance of the present life!" Is this the way to make the man's spirit brave and strong and patient?

But, then, this new religion also proclaims "the supreme value of human love." Well, this is something: this is much; for human love does naturally sweeten the lowliest lot, and brighten the poorest home. And yet, if the poor man comes to believe that these children whom he loves are under no divine care, that they are simply dependent on himself and on society, and that they are growing up to a lot as hard as his own, and perhaps harder, I am not sure whether his very love for them might not even increase the bitterness of his poverty, and lead him to wish that he and they were all at rest for ever in the grave! But now, see what the gospel of Christ has to say to this poor man in his poverty. It tells him that, whoever may be to blame or not to blame for the circumstances in which he now finds himself, one thing is certain, that he and those whom he loves are under the eye and the care of the Father in heaven. It tells him that not a sparrow falls to the ground without this Father. It tells him that God cares for the poor and the ignorant as really and truly as for the rich and the learned; "there is no respect of persons with God." It tells him that God's curse rests on all injustice, tyranny, and oppression; and that, in proportion as the spirit of Christ extends and prevails, the conditions of social life will improve. But it tells him, also, that how a man behaves himself in his circumstances is of more importance than the circumstances themselves. It tells him that character is more important than comfort; that faith in God is a better treasure than this world's gold. It tells him that if he will only live as a "child of God" he is "an heir of the kingdom which God hath promised to them that love Him," and that this present life is a school in which God is educating and drilling us for the world beyond. It assures him that the Christ who died for all men sympathises with him in his struggles, and that although God in His wisdom may see fit to permit these hardships, He can make them all "work together for good." Suppose a man really believes this gospel, and feeds his nature on this spiritual "bread," and prays every day to an Almighty and All-loving Father, and looks forward to a heavenly home, is he not more likely to carry himself with a quiet dignity, to seek the redress of his grievances in a right spirit, and to bear his troubles—as many of the Christian poor do bear them—with heroic courage and patience? Surely *that* religion must be the best friend of man which can thus stand by him and strengthen him in the midst of hardship and poverty?

Take, again, as a second test, a case of temptation and sin. Here, we shall suppose, is a man of education—of genius, if you will—who is strongly tempted to some act of wrong-doing. A terrible struggle is going on within the man's soul. Perhaps the inclination which he is tempted to gratify is of a refined rather than a coarse nature; but he cannot reconcile its gratification with his sense of duty and honour. Now, here the man needs a religion which can do the very utmost to enforce the demands of conscience and to hold him back from transgression. What, then, has the new religion to say to this man? Will it "proclaim the grandeur of the human intellect"? Why, this may only tempt him to think that genius ought not to be bound by the moral laws that are adapted for ordinary mortals. Or, will it remind him of the "supreme importance of the present life"? But this is precisely what he does not need to be reminded of: it is the present that is pressing in upon him with its strong desires, offering him present pleasure, or wealth, or fame, or power. Or again, will you tell him of "the supreme value of human love"? But what if it be this very love that is tempting him? What if he wishes to shield his wife and children from coming hardship? Or, what if there be some passionate affection which he longs to indulge, and the value of which appears to be so "supreme" as to override all other considerations?

Look, now, what Christianity has to say to this man at this critical moment. It tells him that he is responsible to the living God, his Maker, for every action of his life. It tells him that neither "life" nor "love" is of such value as to be worth buying or gratifying at the cost of sin. It tells him that the laws of morality are as binding on the learned as the unlearned. It warns him that he must yet "appear before the judgment seat of Christ," and that a terrible retribution may follow the evil-doer, even in the world to come. It reminds him that he is a child of the Eternal God, and that Christ died to "redeem him from all iniquity." It assures him that no one and nothing can really "harm him," if he will only be "a follower of that which is good," and that he may well dare to do the right, and leave results with the God of righteousness. Need I ask which of these two religions supplies the motives that are *most likely* to hold a man back from wrong-doing in the great crisis of temptation?

But alas! even the highest motives do not always succeed in keeping a man from iniquity, and so I will now suppose that this man has yielded to temptation, and has sinned his sin. Remorse seizes him; he fears, it may be, the wrath of God; he fears, perhaps, the punishment of hell; or, it may be that his sin has been brought to light, and he has to suffer its punishment at the hands of human society or human law. And now, what has "the religion of humanity" to say to this poor, wretched soul? Will it tell him that he need not fear God or hell, for that, *probably*, there is no God and no future life? But can it *prove* this? Can it make him *absolutely certain* that these forebodings of conscience point to no reality? Or, will it speak to him of the "supreme importance of the present life," when perhaps all his prospects for this life have been ruined by his crime? Or, will it tell him that his remorse is a mere agitation of his brain? Or, will it perchance even suggest to him that he is simply a machine, and that he could no more help sinning his sin than the sun can help being eclipsed, that his deed was simply the unavoidable result of his tendencies and his circumstances? Is this to be the miserable and debasing comfort of "the religion of the future," this drugging of the conscience with an insidious narcotic labelled "scientific philosophy"? Consider now what the gospel has to say to this wretched, guilty man. It tells him that there is mercy even "for the chief of sinners." It tells him that the Son of God came "to seek and to save that which is lost." It tells him that "the Lamb of God" died to "take away the sin of the world." It calls upon him to repent, and not to despair. It offers him pardon and cleansing. It tells him that God does "not despise the broken and contrite heart." It tells him that he may be a new man yet, that he may begin to live a new and higher life. It tells him that, although he may have to suffer some of the consequences of sin even till his dying day, yet he may endure these as the discipline of a Father who has forgiven him, and who is seeking to prepare him for a place among the redeemed in heaven. Here is, indeed, "bread" for the hungry—this "good news" of "grace" to the sinful, guilty, wretched soul. Well might the apostle exclaim, in the presence of Roman power and Greek philosophy, and well may we exclaim, in presence of "the religion of humanity"—"I am not ashamed of the gospel of Christ; for it is the power of God *unto salvation.*"

Take as our last test a case in which "the shadow of death" is creeping over a happy home. Here we shall suppose is a young man of brilliant powers and brilliant promise—"the only son of his mother, and she is a widow." He was standing on the threshold of his chosen life-work: he was looking forward to the time when he should be able to help his mother and sisters in the struggle of life, and to found a new home with her whom he loves. But now, without any blame whatever on his part, he is stricken down by disease, and both he and his friends know how it must terminate. What has the "new religion" to say to him and to them at this terrible crisis? Will it speak of "the grandeur of the human intellect"? Alas! this young man feels that his mental power, in which he formerly rejoiced, is already lessened by his illness; and is it any comfort to know that the brain, which has won him college honours and prizes, will soon have gone into atoms in the churchyard? Or will you speak of "the supreme value of human love"? Is it not a kind of mockery to remind him now of the preciousness of that which he is about to lose for ever? Or will you speak of "the supreme importance of the present life"? What! speak thus to this young man who is about to be torn away from it all? Or will you tell him of the duty of serving "humanity," and try to comfort him with the thought that, though he himself is to perish, his influence will live? Ah! but this is one of his sorest trials: he has done so little for the world: he has all along been preparing for his life-work, and now he is dragged away from it for ever! Or will you tell him to brace himself up and face the inevitable "like a man"? Ah! "like a man": yes; but what if he is too thoroughly human to play the stoic thus—too much of a man to be untrue to the deepest instincts and feelings of his nature? What shall we think of a "religion" which thus fails so utterly in the hour of sorest need? But the gospel of Christ does not thus fail. It does not indeed deny either the awfulness or the mystery of the crisis. It does not profess to remove the natural sorrow which the separation of death brings to loving hearts. But, at least, it darts some rays of light into the darkness—it speaks some words of comfort and hope. It tells this young man that he is in the hands of a "Father" who does many things that are mysterious, but not one thing that is cruel. It speaks to him of "the Father's house of many mansions"; it tells him that his powers of thinking and loving cannot be destroyed by death. It tells him that his work is not done—that God can be served in other worlds than this. It holds up before his eye the Cross of Christ as the revelation and pledge of infinite mercy, and as the example of faith and resignation. It may indeed be still a hard thing to die; but, at any rate, there is here an offer of " bread " and not of a " stone " to the hungry soul. And when the eyes are closed at last, and the sorrowing friends are weeping at the grave, the gospel comes to them, and speaks of Him who is " the Resurrection and the Life "—who, in His own person, has conquered death, and who can yet re-unite them to the loved one who is gone.

This is the religion which we are told is destined to pass away before the new "religion of humanity!" —a religion without God and heaven! No; never. Never, so long as throbbing human hearts remain true to their deepest instincts, their noblest yearnings, and their purest love!

TRANSLATIONS FROM HEINE.

Auf Flügeln des Gesanges.

My darling, I will bear thee
   Away on the wings of song,
To the lovely plains of the Ganges,
   To the spot I have known so long.

There lies a blossoming garden
   In the moonlight quiet and clear;
The lotos-flowers are awaiting
   Their little sister dear.

The violets twitter and titter,
   And look up to the stars above;
And the roses whisper each other
   Their fragrant tales of love.

The shy gazelles are leaping,
   Or in shady coverts lie;
And the waves of the sacred river
   In the distance are rushing by.

There we'll lie down together,
   Beneath the palm-tree's crest,
And dream our dream of gladness,
   And drink of love and rest.

Die Lotosblume ängstigt.

The lotos-flower retireth
  Before the Sun's fierce light,
And with drooping head awaiteth
  In dreams the coming night.

The Moon, who is her lover,
  Awakes her with his rays,
And sweetly she unveileth
  Her modest, lovely face.

She blooms, and glows, and brightens,
  And shyly stands up again;
In her fragrance she weeps and trembles
  With love and love's sweet pain.

Es stehen unbeweglich.

The stars above, all motionless
  For centuries in the skies,
Stand gazing on each other
  With loving, yearning eyes.

They utter all a language
  So beautiful and grand!
Yet none of the philologists
  Can this language understand.

But 'tis long since I have learnt it,
  And it ne'er forgot can be;
The face of my best belovèd
  Was a Grammar unto me!

Herz, mein Herz.

My heart, be not with sorrow shaken,
   But thy lot bear, as of yore;
   For the spring will yet restore
What the winter's blast hath taken.

Think how much life still retaineth!
   The world is beautiful as wide!
   And, O my heart, whate'er betide,
Thy power of loving still remaineth!

Leise zieht.

Echoing softly through my heart,
   Sweetly sound the bells;
Ring far and wide your tinkling song
   That of the springtime tells.

Ring out to where flowers sweet and rare
   At yonder house are meeting;
And when you see a little rose,
   Say that I send her greeting.

Im wunderschönen Monat Mai.

When all the buds were blowing
   In the wondrous month of May,
Then also in my bosom
   Love blossomed in a day.

When all the birds were singing
   In the wondrous month of May,
Then I confessed my passion.
   As at her feet I lay.

Aus meinen Thränen.

OUT of my tears spring forth such flowers
   As grow in blossoming dales,
And all my very sighs become
   A choir of nightingales.

And when once thou lovest me, my child,
   These flowers shall to thee belong,
And at thy window shall be heard
   The nightingale's sweet song.

Wenn Zwei von einander scheiden.

WHEN two dear friends are parting,
   They cling in fond embrace,
And each the "Farewell" sigheth
   With sad and tearful face.

Our Farewell had no weeping—
   No sigh—our grief to tell;
Only—when all was over—
   The tears in silence fell!

Hör' ich das Liedchen klingen.

I HEAR the song a-singing,
   Which my love sang long ago;
And my heart is wildly throbbing,
   As if 'twould break with woe;

A dim, vague longing drives me
   To the forest where no one hears,
And there my sobbing sorrow
   Dissolves itself in tears.

Lorelei.

I KNOW not how it happens
   My mind is filled with gloom;
It may be the haunting presence
   Of an ancient tale of doom.

The air is cool, and quietly
   The Rhine's deep waters run;
The mountain-top is gleaming
   In the rays of the setting sun.

On a rocky height is sitting
   A maiden wondrous fair;
Her golden jewels glitter,
   And she combs her golden hair.

With a golden comb she combs it,
   And she sings a thrilling strain—
So piercing sweet and musical
   The echoes ring again.

Alone in his skiff, the boatman,
   Entranced by the sound and the sight,
Sees not the rocky ledges—
   Sees only the form on the height.

At last, both the boat and the boatman
   Sink under the whirling wave;
Thus the siren witch of the Lurlei
   Sings her victims to their grave!

In mein gar zu dunkles Leben.

ONCE into my life all gloomy,
   Shone an image sweet and bright;
That sweet image now hath faded,
   Leaving me in deepest night.

Little children, when in darkness,
   Are attacked by terrors strong;
And, to drive away those terrors,
   Sing aloud some nursery song.

I too sing—a child distracted,
   And with grief and gloom oppress'd;
And my song, though not delightsome,
   Hath relieved my burdened breast.

Allnächtlich im Traume.

IN dreams, every night, whilst sleeping,
   I see thee so gracious and sweet,
That with wild and passionate weeping
   I cast myself down at thy feet.

Sadly thou look'st on me calling,
   And shakest thy fair head of curls;
From thy dear, sweet eyes are falling
   The tear-drops like beautiful pearls.

Thou giv'st me a wreath of cypress,
   And dost whisper with gentle tone:
I wake—and thy words are forgotten,
   And the cypress wreath is gone!

Ich hab' im Traum geweinet.

In sleep I wept, whilst dreaming
    That thou wert lying dead;
I woke, and still were dropping
    The tears upon my bed.

In sleep I wept, whilst dreaming
    That thou hadst forsaken me;
I woke, and still for sorrow
    Wept long and bitterly.

In sleep I wept, whilst dreaming
    That thou wert faithful and good;
I woke, and still are streaming
    My tears of gratitude.

Du schönes Fischermädchen.

My pretty fisher-maiden,
    Come, draw thy boat to land;
And, sitting down beside me,
    Talk with me, hand in hand.

Thy head on my heart reclining,
    Fear thou no harm from me;
Thou trustest thyself daily
    To the wild and stormy sea!

My heart the sea resembles;
    It heaves, and ebbs, and flows:
And precious pearls and beautiful
    Within its depths repose.

Der Brief.

THE letter you have written
  Has done my heart no wrong;
You say you'll no more love me,
  But then—your letter's long!

'Tis quite a little manuscript,
  Close-written to the marge!
One does not pen twelve pages,
  In giving a discharge!

Du bist wie eine Blume.

As sweet and pure and lovely
  As any flower thou art;
I look on thee, and sadness
  Doth creep into my heart.

On thy dear head it seemeth,
  As if my hands must meet,
Beseeching God to keep thee
  Thus lovely, pure, and sweet.

Ein Fichtenbaum.

FAR north a lonely pine-tree
  Stands on a barren height,
And the snow and ice enwrap it
  With a coverlet of white.

It sleeps, and dreams of a palm-tree
  Far off in the Eastern land,
That, all alone in silence,
  Mourns on the burning sand.

Sie haben mich gequälet.

How many folks have vexed me
   With worries small and great;
Some vex me with their loving,
   And others with their hate.

My glass they've sometimes poisoned,
   And the very bread I ate;
The one set with their loving,
   The other with their hate.

But she who most hath vexed me
   With a grief all griefs above,
Hath never shown me hatred,
   And hath never shown me love!

Am fernen Horizonte.

FAR off on the horizon,
   Enwrapt in a misty shroud,
The city with its turrets
   Appears as if built of cloud.

A moist breeze, faintly blowing,
   Ruffles the water gray;
With dull, slow stroke the boatman
   Rows me sadly on my way.

Once more the sun, forth-breaking,
   Shines brightly from above,
And shows me again distinctly
   The spot where I lost my love.

Schöne Wiege.

Lovely cradle of my sorrows,
   Lovely graveyard of my peace,
Fare thee well! thou lovely city;
   Now our intercourse must cease.

Fare thee well! thou sacred dwelling
   Where the dear one sheds her grace;
Fare thee well! thou spot so sacred,
   Where I first beheld her face.

Had I never looked upon thee,
   O thou lovely Queen of hearts!
Never then had sorrow pierced me
   With such keen and deadly darts!

I never wished to stir thy feeling,
   Never have I asked thy love;
I only wished in thy sweet presence
   Peacefully to live and move.

But with bitter words and cruel
   Thou hast driv'n me from thy door;
And now madness stirs within me,
   And my heart is sick and sore;

And my limbs—a heavy burden—
   On my staff I drag away,
Till my head, with sorrow weary,
   In some far-off grave I lay!

Mein Kind, wir waren Kinder.

My child, we once were children,
   Two children blithe and gay;
We crept into the hen-house,
   And hid ourselves in the hay.

We cackled like the poultry,
   And the people, passing by,
Thought that our "Cock-a-doodle!"
   Was really the cock's shrill cry.

The old chests in our courtyard
   We carpeted inside,
And dwelt therein together
   In our house so grand and wide!

The elderly cat of our neighbour
   Oft paid us a morning call;
We received her with bows and curtseys,
   And compliments great and small.

We asked after her health politely,
   With all the airs of a prince;
We have made the same inquiries
   Of many an old puss since!

We often sat like old people,
   And talked of the olden time,
And grumbled that all was better
   When we were in our prime;

How Love, and Faith, and Justice
   Were like to disappear;
How gold had grown much scarcer,
   And coffee was so dear!

Ah! past are those games of childhood,
   And all things are passing away—
The gold, and the world, and the old times—
   Even Love and Faith decay!

Wenn ich an deinem Hause.

At morn, as I pass thy dwelling,
   Thou child of sweetest grace,
It gives me a gleam of pleasure
   At the window to see thy face.

With thy dark brown eyes inquiringly
   Thou dost the stranger scan:
"Who art thou, and what aileth thee,
   Thou strange and sickly man?"

I am a German poet,
   Well known in the German land;
When men speak the names most famous,
   Amongst them mine will stand.

And what ails me, little maiden,
   Ails many a one in my land;
When men tell of woes the saddest,
   Amongst them mine will stand.

Wie des Mondes Abbild zittert.

As the image of the moon
    Quivers in the ocean wild,
Whilst the moon herself in heaven
    Wanders on serene and mild;

So thou wand'rest on, my love,
    Heart serene and full of rest,
Whilst thine image, mirror'd bright,
    Quivers in my trembling breast.

Das gelbe Laub erzittert.

THE yellow leaves are trembling
    And falling at autumn's breath;
And all things sweet and lovely
    Are fading to their death.

The sunshine is flickering sadly
    On the forest above the dell;
It might be the last fond kisses
    Of the summer's sad farewell.

I feel as if for sorrow
    I could weep my soul away;
That image again reminds me
    Of our sad parting-day.

I could not help but leave thee,
    And I saw death on thy brow!
I was the summer departing,
    The dying forest thou.

Ein Jüngling liebt ein Mädchen.

A YOUTH is in love with a maiden
   Who long for another has sighed,
And that other loves another
   And takes her for his bride.

Then the maiden, vexed and weary—
   To bring her heart relief—
Marries the first that asks her,
   And the youth is whelmed with grief.

It is an old, old story,
   But alas! 'tis ever new;
And to whomsoe'er it happens,
   It breaks his heart in two!

Der Herbstwind rüttelt die Bäume.

THE night is damp and chilly,
   The autumn wind doth moan,
As, wrapt in my dark grey mantle,
   I ride through the wood alone;

And as I ride, my fancies
   Are riding on before,
And gaily and lightly bear me
   To my beloved's door.

I see the servants' tapers,
   I hear the barking curs;
And up the winding staircase
   I dash with clanking spurs.

The bright, warm, carpeted chamber
    Is fragrant with all its charms;
And there my darling waits me—
    I rush into her arms.

The leaves in the wind are rustling,
    And the oak-trees near the stream
Are saying—"Thou foolish rider,
    What means this foolish dream?"

Und wüssten's die Blumen, die kleinen.

If the little flowers only knew
    That I am so pained at heart,
They would all in sympathy weep,
    To heal my bitter smart.

If the nightingales only knew
    That I am so sick and sad,
They would warble their cheerful notes,
    To make me well and glad.

If the bright stars only knew
    That I am so full of grief,
They would all come down from their height,
    To bring my soul relief.

But alas! none of these can know;
    One only knoweth my smart:
And 'tis she herself that hath torn—
    Hath torn my bleeding heart!

TO MY MOTHER.

(Two Sonnets.)

I.

It is my wont to carry my head high,
  And somewhat proud and stubborn are my ways;
  Ev'n if the king should look me in the face,
I would return his look with steady eye.
Yet, mother dear, whenever thou art nigh,
  In presence of thy sweet and blessèd grace,
  My haughty temper from its loftiest place
Descends, and meekly at thy feet doth lie.
  Is it that thy brave spirit conquers mine,—
  Thy spirit which doth all things well divine,
  And soareth upward into heaven's sunshine?
Ah! to mine eyes the tears of sorrow start,
When I remember with how many a dart
I must have pierced thy loving, faithful heart!

II.

Once I forsook thee, on a wild, mad quest;
  It was my wish to roam the wide world through,
  To see if I could find love deep and true,
And, finding love, to clasp her to my breast.
In every street I sought for love's sweet rest;
  At every door, with hands outstretched anew,
  I begged some crumbs of love, however few,
But only met with hatred, scorn, and jest.
    Thus seeking love, I wandered on strange ground—
    Still seeking love—but love I never found;
      Then home I turned, with hopes all dead and past:
Thou cam'st to meet me; and, with glad surprise,
Lo! there I saw—all swimming in thine eyes—
    The sweet and long-sought love, now found at last.

Das Meer erglänzte weit hinaus.

FAR off in the glow of the setting sun
    Out yonder gleamed the sea;
We sat by the fisherman's lonely house,
    Still and alone sat we.

The billows heaved, the mist arose,
    The gulls flew to and fro;
From thy sad eyes, so full of love,
    The tears began to flow.

I saw them falling on thy hand,
    Down on my knee I sank;
And from thy white and lovely hand
    Those tears away I drank.

Since then my yearning spirit droops,
    My frame a shadow appears:—
'Twas surely poison that I took,
    When I drank that woman's tears.

PROPRIETY AND POLITENESS.

[Delivered in Rusholme Public Hall, Manchester, April 24th, 1872: based on a paper published in *The Christian Spectator*, July, 1864.]

THE word "propriety" is etymologically akin to the word "property." "Property" is that which is a man's *own*—which belongs peculiarly to a given individual; "propriety" designates that course of conduct which is proper to a certain occasion—*which belongs peculiarly* to a given set of conditions. "Politeness," according to some, means, originally, the manners acquired in *city-life*, just as "courtesy" originally meant the manners acquired at the "courts" of kings; and just as "boorishness," "clownishness," "rusticity," are words pointing originally to the manners of those born and bred in the rural districts. It appears, however, that the word "politeness" is akin rather to the word "*polish*," and thus referred originally to smoothness and refinement of speech and behaviour.

But, of course, all such words are now used with considerable latitude of meanings. They have come, moreover, to have at once a superficial and a deeper significance. Thus, we speak of a *true* propriety and a *true* politeness. An action may be condemned by many as "improper," which, under the circumstances, is really the most proper—*i.e.*, the most fit and becoming thing to do. And even a metropolitan lady, of most *polished* manners, may fancy that she is not violating any of the rules of *politeness*, and yet all the while be committing what, in the deeper sense of the word, is nothing but vulgarity!

There is a great deal of so-called "propriety" that is purely conventional, and we are all more or less bound by such conventional usages and. rules. Many of these are so harmless, and in themselves so utterly indifferent, that it is not worth while deviating from them; and such deviation, without any reason whatever, would only indicate a foolish pride. Nevertheless, whilst every modest man will be glad for his own sake to acquiesce in all the purely indifferent proprieties of social life, there is, on the other hand, abundant reason why we should refuse to be chained down by the formal rules of society, and why, under certain circumstances, we should deliberately set at naught some of these conventional usages.

For, to begin with, it must be confessed that a merely artificial propriety tends greatly to stiffen the whole man, and to take away from our life that freshness, elasticity, and naturalness which constitute one of its most delightful charms. Between the real human being and the mere slave of propriety, there is about the same difference as exists between the living flower on which the dewdrops glisten and the same flower dried in the botanist's portfolio; or, to use Mrs. Barrett Browning's figure, between the bird that lives and sings in the thicket and the bird that "leaps from perch to perch" in the cage. Blackbirds or "lions," 'tis all the same, "society" would keep us in the "cage"; and, so long as we sing within the wires, or roar within the bars, according to *her* pleasure, she will gladly give us her approval on which to feed. The actor's meed of applause will be ours so long as we violate no dramatic propriety, and break through none of the traditions of the stage. And there are not a few who are as accommodating in this matter as Bottom the weaver in *Midsummer-Night's Dream;* they will play Pyramus or they will play Thisbe, or they will play the lion; and if the lion's voice should be considered improperly loud, they "will roar you as gently as any sucking-dove" or "an 'twere any nightingale!" But, whether we think of these artificial demands of society as cage-wires or as stage-traditions, we feel that to be *enslaved* by them is altogether uncongenial to our nature. Many of us show our appreciation of a freer and more natural life by the value we set on that characteristic of our homes which we best name their "homeliness." Now, we might surely infuse a little more of this happy liberty into the social circle without breaking down the barrier which makes home such a pleasant retreat. I am not saying that we ought to go out into society in slippers and dressing-gown, but I do say that there ought to be more frankness and naturalness in our general social intercourse. We are not to act towards "each new-hatched, unfledged comrade," as if he were a long and well-tried friend; but we need not therefore treat him as if he were an inhabitant of some other planet. Some men are so wonderfully afraid of "wearing their heart upon their sleeve," that they lay themselves open to the suspicion of having no heart at all.

There is too much of the well-dressed mummy

about our social gatherings. In the case of some of our fashionable evening parties, propriety is a kind of "death's-head at the feast." Recreation "dies of dignity." Host, hostess, and guests are too polite to be human. One almost wishes that the solemn waiter would trip for once on the carpet, so that a hearty human laugh might relax the stiffness of the company! A great deal of the talk is forced and unnatural. Spontaneous converse would be much more profitable. But a conventional propriety too often acts as a social *non-conductor*. I know I am uttering heresies; but I believe that even the *dressiness* of evening parties plays no unimportant part in this work of social *insulation*. It is not so easy to get at the real humanity through all those elaborate preparations of the *toilette*. Nor does this difficulty always vanish in proportion to the frequency with which such parties are attended. On the contrary, there is something in their very atmosphere which tends to check all freshness and spontaneity of intercourse. Who does not feel that the *truly* "proper" and becoming thing would be for men and women to meet each other—even for the first time—with a certain measure of genial frankness and mutual kindliness and sympathy?

But not only do the demands of an artificial propriety tend thus to stiffen our nature, and rob our social intercourse of the charm of freshness and simplicity, they also tend to destroy individuality of character. It is quite refreshing now-a-days to meet with a man who has the moral courage to be simply —*himself*. Society has a "pattern on her nail"; and after that pattern she would carve her devotees. Almost every one of us has been more or less dwarfed by current maxims and standards: very few have the fortitude to develop fully what is distinctive in their nature. And there are many who allow themselves to be "Dutch-cut," so that a proper and dull uniformity takes the place of a marked and varied individuality. Thus men lose enthusiasm: to be enthusiastic is to be "vulgar." A gentleman comes to be *tacitly* defined as a man who always maintains an outward serenity. "A gentleman," said Beau Brummell, "never perspires!" Equanimity comes to be regarded as the highest of virtues. Indignation against iniquity is unbecoming. I fear St. Paul was very ungentlemanly when he "withstood Peter to the face!" I am afraid Martin Luther did a highly "improper thing" that day he nailed his theses to the door of the church in Wittenberg! I begin to suspect that all the loftiest deeds in the history of the world—born as they have been of individuality and enthusiasm—have been only a series of "improprieties!" The truth is that what is admired by many as equanimity, is frequently the mere pride or selfishness of a mean and little soul. Equanimity is admirable only when it is based on *magnanimity*. And no man need live at second-hand. Every man may have a character as distinctively his own as his face is. And we may well overlook all merely formal proprieties which threaten to interfere with the true and "proper" growth of our *individual* life.

Our very opinions and beliefs are not safe from the dictation of society. The man who dares to differ on any important political question from the coterie in which he moves is likely to be met with a half-contemptuous astonishment. There are works of art which we are expected to admire, as a matter of course, whether we like them or not; and if we venture to hint our want of appreciation, those who echo the prevailing cry will inwardly despise our lack of taste. Many a man who gives himself out as a *connoisseur* is such simply in the sense of being *knowing enough* to have found out what it is considered "the proper thing" to admire! Then, again, it is well for a man to be religious, if only he is not pious. To attend worship once on the Sunday is sound "etiquette." Irreligion and religious earnestness are alike unfashionable. *Somewhere* between Atheism and Methodism there is a "happy medium" of moderate orthodoxy and decent religiousness, which society delights to recognize as *the* respectable and proper thing.

Now, I say, fight against all this *hum-drum-ism*, to the very death. Recognize and assert your individuality. Not that I would have you cultivate a mere eccentricity. To be peculiar for the sake of peculiarity is a token, not of strength, but of weakness. A *passion* for heresy of any kind indicates a very immature and unripe individuality. And mere "crotchetiness" is individuality "run to seed." But THINK for yourself. In religion, in politics, in every region, ask not for what beliefs are fashionable and proper, nor, on the other hand, for what opinions are peculiar and novel, but ask for what is *true*. ACT, too, for yourself. Even when you act with others, or in deference to the wishes of others, let your action be the result of individual resolve, and not of mere gregarious instinct. And—BE yourself. Develop that which is distinctive in your own natural temperament and faculty, so long as it is not morally unhealthful. You are not meant to be the mere echo, or "double," of any other man. You are not merely so much human nature, to be cast into the common mould of society, and turned out after a common type. You need not *exaggerate* the importance of that which is distinctive in your own personality; but still, you ought to remember that it may be on that very side of your nature that you are fitted to be *most* serviceable. First, and above all, see to it that you are upright and good; next,

> "to thine own self be true;
> And it must follow, as the night the day,
> Thou canst not then be false to any man."

Still further, there is danger lest the conventional demands of society should sometimes be permitted *to override the claims of duty and affection*. There was a time when to run the risk of committing murder in a duel was, under certain circumstances, the only "proper" thing for a "gentleman" to do, and when it required no ordinary degree of moral courage to take the highly improper step of refusing a challenge. The days of duelling in this country are gone; but there are still sins committed in the name of society against truth, and light, and conscience. What is all that "keeping up of appearances" which lands so many people in extravagance, debt, and dishonour, but just a sacrifice made to this fetich of "society"? I verily believe there are men who would go to the scaffold if necessary for their political or religious convictions, who yet have not the moral courage to reduce their expenditure at the bidding of simple honesty. They would be a great deal happier in a smaller house where they could live within their means; they would sleep more soundly on their pillow; they would gain in self-respect, as well as in comfort; very often—if they only knew it—they would ultimately gain in the real respect of the very people whom they dread; but meanwhile they shrink from social ostracism, the Medusa-head of Mrs. Grundy at once fascinates and terrifies them, "gorgonizes them with a stony British stare," so that their very will is paralyzed. And, accordingly, they go on dressing in the proper fashion, as if it were a sufficient remuneration for any tradesman to have the honour of supplying *them* with goods! And they go on feasting their neighbours at other people's expense, and call it "hospitality!" And then, by and by, comes the crash—and the whole thing has an ugly aspect of swindling—and Mrs. Grundy, with the politest of bows, "passes by on the other side."

Even Christian men are sometimes led to overlook or shirk their duty through false notions of propriety. The clergyman and the dissenting minister might agree in many things to co-operate for the good of the parish, were it not that the clergyman has been taught to regard the dissenting minister as his social inferior. What right has the pastor of *Salem Chapel* to occupy a position of social equality with the rector of Carlingford? I presume, too, that even if Lady Western were a devout woman, and were to become attached to Nonconformity and its modes of worship, the most improper thing she could do would be to become a member of the church at *Salem Chapel*. And, as for the Nonconformist minister—the Rev. Arthur Vincent himself—see how he is scared from his duty through being constantly haunted by this same ghost of "propriety!" Did his Divine Master then send him to Carlingford to be a model of artificial politeness, or did He send him to be "an example to the believers in godliness and charity"? Was it his grand mission to raise *the social status* of Nonconformity, to make it a proper and respectable thing for ladies of rank to come to chapel? or, was it not rather his mission to save the souls of human beings—whether gig-possessors or not—and to fit these souls for a heaven where even Lazarus "the beggar" finds a place in "Abraham's bosom"? Our poor Mr. Vincent—was it at Homerton he learnt that a lady, riding about in her carriage and shopping, is necessarily a finer specimen of humanity than an honest and industrious tradesman standing behind his counter, "diligent in business"? But—selling butter!—ah! here was the "head and front" of poor Tozer's "offending"! Had it only been any other article! But—*butter!!*—here was the awful degradation! One hopes that, for his own comfort, our squeamish Nonconformist pastor ate his toast dry! And then—those suppers in the butterman's back parlour—they were really more, were they not, than flesh and blood could bear? True, the people were kind, and their hearts were warm, but their grammar was sadly defective, and their manners somewhat unpolished. And has not an apostle somewhere said that the "three" things which "abide" are grammar, politeness, and charity, and that *the least* of these is charity? Has not another apostle said that "the ornament of a meek and quiet spirit" is as nothing compared with the crest on a fine equipage or the glitter of a diamond ring? Our young minister used to preach some very eloquent sermons: I wonder whether he ever took for his text, "I will glory of the things which concern mine infirmities ... through a window, in a basket, was I let down by the wall." The Rev. Arthur Vincent of Carlingford *in a basket!* What an excellent frontispiece for the next edition of *Salem Chapel!* And, by the way, has not Mrs. Oliphant told us a great deal about one Edward Irving, about his true nobleness and dignity? But how he is outshone, after all, by this Arthur Vincent! There is more heroism in the world than we had dreamed! Here, in obscure Carlingford, we find a man *noble and heroic enough* to give up the work of the Christian ministry, rather than endure the unpolished manners of some wretched Dissenters, whom he had undertaken to enlighten and elevate! Whereas, will it be believed that Edward Irving—with all his nobleness—so far forgot himself on one occasion as actually to carry, on his own shoulders, the pack of a fatigued Irish pedlar? Will it be believed that, on another occasion, he actually went into the house of a poor infidel shoemaker, and discoursed with him on the qualities of leather? Is it not dreadful to think that, had the infidel been a "butterman," this minister of the gospel might have so far committed himself, as even to talk about—*butter!* And the worst remains to be told. This same Edward Irving was actually seen in the streets of London—in broad daylight—carrying his own baby in his arms, with Mrs. Irving walking by his side! How any *heroic* man could be guilty of such glaring "improprieties," I must really leave Mrs. Oliphant to explain!

Thanks, then, to *Salem Chapel* for the illustration which it gives us of the manner in which men will occasionally shirk some of the loftiest *duties*, through a fastidious and altogether undue regard for the conventionalities of society. And *affection* sometimes fares no better than duty at the hands of propriety. Our love and our friendship are, it seems, to be "cabin'd, cribb'd, confin'd," at the bidding of society. We are not to be too intimate with any who are beneath us in the social scale; and yet we wonder how poor benighted Hindoos can keep up their wretched system of *Caste!* "Sir Aylmer Aylmer, that almighty man, the county god"—coming of a family who have been "partridge-breeders for a thousand years"—will see his daughter pine and droop and die, rather than let her wed the man she loves, even although he is her equal in refinement, intelligence, and virtue. It would be a most "improper" pollution of the noble Aylmer blood! Nay, it is exceedingly doubtful whether it is a proper thing to cherish a warm or deep affection at all; and, as for manifesting it, that is quite out of the question. The dog "Crab," in the *Two Gentlemen of Verona*, seems to be, in this respect, a model of decorum; although, according to Launce himself, he is "the sourest-natured dog that lives." "My mother weeping; my father wailing; my sister crying; our maid howling; our cat wringing her hands; and all our house in a great perplexity; yet did not this cruel-hearted cur shed one tear: he is a stone, a very pebble-stone, and has no more pity in him than a dog; a Jew would have wept to have seen our parting; why, my grandam, having no eyes, look you, wept herself blind at my parting!" We can have no doubt that this cur was regarded, in fashionable dog-life, as a perfect model of propriety. Not that Crab altogether lacked affection; but, evidently, he "hated a scene!"

On the other hand, it must be confessed that many of the ordinary rules of propriety and politeness are not so arbitrary and conventional as at first sight they may appear. Some of them have the soundest basis in that practical wisdom which is the fruit of experience. Young men and women are sometimes apt, in their inexperienced enthusiasm, to be too radical and revolutionary in their social ideas. They chafe and fret under restraints which appear to *them* to be a most unnecessary thwarting of natural inclination. But the truth must be told, that some of those restrictions which thus seem *artificial*, are really dictated by a wider and deeper knowledge of that which is *natural*. Many a young woman has made shipwreck of life, because she has resented, as the croaking of superannuated timidity, what was really the wise counsel and warning of ripened experience. Some of those little "proprieties," to which she paid not the slightest heed, were really—if she had only known it—as floating buoys, that might have protected her from the dangerous sandbank.

I have already protested against allowing mere arbitrary regulations to override the claims of duty and affection. But equally, I must *now* protest against violating the ordinary rules of decorum, in a mere spirit of caprice and self-will. Many of these rules commend themselves to your own sense of what is truly fit, becoming, and appropriate. Other rules which are in themselves purely arbitrary, it may nevertheless be foolish, and even dangerous, to disregard, unless you have some sound and adequate reason for doing so. To court singularity is not to be truly singular. To court singularity is to be vain or proud, and surely there is nothing very singular or uncommon about vanity and pride.

But it is not only the young who are in danger of violating a real propriety, in their revolt against that which is merely conventional. Some of our modern ladies of culture and experience seem to me to err in the same direction. When the women of the Corinthian Church began to assert their "independence" by laying aside, in the public assemblies, the head-dress which it was customary for the Greek women to wear, you remember how St. Paul—with that marvellous philosophic insight of his, which saw great principles in little things—fell back on what we might call the "rubric of nature." I cannot help thinking that were the apostle back again amongst *us*, to hear some of our English ladies speaking from public platforms, to mixed audiences, on questions which are scarcely fit for public discussion at all, he would not unlikely have remonstrated with them in the old words—"Doth not Nature itself teach you?" I admire the courage of these ladies, I honour their zeal, I sympathize with their object; but I venture to think that, in doing violence to their own natural delicacy of feeling, they are offending against a true propriety. It may, perhaps, be mere squeamishness on my part: but I confess that, when "Augean stables" are to be cleansed, I would rather see it done by *Hercules* than by *Minerva!* There *is* a reasonable as well as a conventional propriety. There is also a deeper as well as a superficial *politeness.* Many of the rules of *etiquette* are of the most arbitrary character, as may be seen in the fact that what are considered "good manners" in one generation may even be considered bad manners in the next. And, as almost all knowledge is valuable, so a certain acquaintance with the current maxims of conventional politeness is not to be despised. Such knowledge may save us from unintentionally annoying our neighbours, and may save ourselves from a host of petty irritations. The danger lies, not in knowing these things, but in attaching too much importance to them. Let us remember that it requires no great intellect or virtue to graduate in the school of etiquette. A man may know how to conduct a lady into a dining-room, and yet have very little reverence for womanhood. He may know how to manage his knife and fork to perfection, and yet he may sometimes eat and drink rather more than is good for him. He may be able to carve with dexterity, and yet if he had to earn his own living with his own brains, he might not have very much to carve! Let us look facts in the face. We need not despise the laws of etiquette; but still they are not the Decalogue! To put a knife into one's mouth at dinner is, no doubt, very bad; but still, after all, there *are* worse vices in the world! We have need to cultivate our aesthetic faculty *more on the spiritual side.* It would be well if our fastidiousness had more of the moral element in it, so that we might be quicker to recognize the beauty of goodness and the ugliness of evil. Dean Ramsay tells a story of a Scotch elder who, when a certain

Lady Glenorchy in a fit of spleen had got into the way of passing the collection-plate without a contribution, and sailing majestically up the aisle of the church with the politest of curtseys, ventured rather bluntly to remonstrate with her. '"My lady," said he, "gi'e us less o' your mainers, and mair o' your siller!" I am afraid I cannot quite praise this elder for his politeness; but certainly he was not far wrong in thinking that a bad temper is more unseemly than an awkward gait, and that generosity is more beautiful than gentility. A woman may be, in her manners, as polished as a marble statue—*and* as cold! "Rosamond" in *Middlemarch* was elegant and graceful enough; she was always extremely polite; she never flew into a passion; she never violated the serenities; she never contradicted her husband: she only—*only*—wrecked his life!

There *is*, however, a politeness which has its seat in the character, and which springs from true kindliness and charity of soul. The secret of this deeper politeness lies in putting ourselves by imaginative sympathy into the position of others, so that we may act towards them as we would wish them to act towards us. True politeness is as the polished wood: conventional politeness—when it stands alone—is simply veneer. There are those, however, who make the mistake of despising the polish even of the substantial wood. They are upright, sincere, and truthful, but they are deficient in courtesy. Their "independence" has a tinge of surliness. Even their benevolence may be more like a blow than a kiss. In their revulsion from insincerity they assume a roughness foreign to their nature; they pride themselves on their straightforwardness and even bluntness. *They* " never mince matters "; *they* always " speak out what they think ! " That is, they are so vain of their strong boots, that they don't mind treading on their neighbour's corns ! Some of our young gentlemen are so terribly afraid of being thought " ladies' men " that they affect rudeness. They prefer the gymnasium to the dancing-school, and no one blames them for *that;* but why should they not cultivate manners as well as muscles ? It is good to have a robust body, a robust mind, and a robust character; but why should not the rock of strength be clothed with the beautiful flowers of refinement and courtesy ? It is written of the charity which "seeketh not its own," that it "doth not behave itself unseemly." This charity is the grand thing to cultivate. This charity is the wellspring of the deepest politeness,—a politeness which is all the more beautiful, because it is free from fussiness and parade. You may remember how Tennyson—in describing the friend of his youth—draws a distinction between the merely genteel man and the true gentleman :—

> " The churl in spirit, howe'er he veil
>   His want in forms for fashion's sake,
>   Will let his coltish nature break
> At seasons thro' the gilded pale :
>
> " For who can always act ? But he,
>   To whom a thousand memories call,
>   Not being less but more than all
> The gentleness he seem'd to be,
>
> " Best seem'd the thing he was, and join'd
>   Each office of the social hour

> To noble manners, as the flower
> And native growth of noble mind;
>
> .   .   .   .   .
>
> "And thus he bore without abuse
> The grand old name of gentleman,
> Defamed by every charlatan,
> And soil'd with all ignoble use."

"Wisdom is justified of all her children." The childish men, who are living as if life were a game to be played at after a stereotyped fashion, may peevishly complain of those who will not "dance to their piping" nor "mourn to their lamenting." But the manly children of Heavenly Wisdom, wherever they be, who are refusing to bow down before the idol of "society," who are disdaining to set their whole life to the key-note of mere custom, and who are thinking earnestly for themselves,—these men are abundantly "justified." It becomes ultimately manifest that a true propriety regulates their conduct. An inward purity of heart and singleness of motive are the best guarantee for a demeanour that will be marked by the most becoming modesty, and yet be free from all that prudery which is simply an inverted impurity. There is a limit in wit which a deep reverence refuses to pass. There is a point in self-revelation at which a true modesty instinctively pauses. There is a silence which self-respect teaches. There is a delicate considerateness which kindliness inspires. And therefore, whilst we ought to be on our guard against mere conventionalities whenever they would rob us of our naturalness, or destroy our individuality, or pervert our judgment, or crush our affections, or lead us astray from the path of duty, we ought also, on the other hand, to recognize everything which commends itself to a true discretion or a cultivated taste, as being really beautiful, becoming, or appropriate. Christianity brings in "nobler modes of life," and with these come "sweeter manners," as well as "purer laws." The grand thing—here as everywhere else—is, not that we "cleanse the outside of the cup and platter," but that the heart be thoroughly purified, and that we constantly remember how we are responsible for our beliefs, our affections, our conduct,—not to public opinion, with its shifting, transitory regulations,—but to Him whose laws are unchanging and eternal.

THE REAL AND THE IDEAL.

[Reprinted from *The Christian Spectator*, 1858.]

WHEN Cervantes sent forth into the world that redoubtable hero, Don Quixote, "Knight of the Woeful Figure," and, mounting him on his gallant steed, Rozinante, dismissed him in quest of noble adventures, he did not forget to give him, in the person of Sancho Panza, one who was in every respect fitted to be the squire of such a chivalrous knight. By this we mean, not that the squire and his donkey were the best companions for Don Quixote de la Mancha and his gallant steed, in so far as the purposes of the noble knight were concerned, but that the squire and donkey aforesaid do most effectually serve the purpose of Cervantes himself. For, although the whole work is an exquisitely keen satire on the sentimental romances which were so much in vogue when the author lived, yet nothing could be further from his intention than to cast ridicule upon all fictitious composition. This is manifest from several considerations. From this, chiefly, that in order to secure his purpose, Cervantes did not write a dry, moral disquisition on the absurdities of the tales of chivalry, but a work of fiction, the different parts of which are bound together by a marked relationship, and the whole of which is pervaded by an artistic unity. And herein he showed his wisdom. He did not discard the weapon of his opponents, but turned it against themselves. His work of ridicule was at the same time one of example. He endeavoured to redeem fiction to its proper sphere —to strip it of the unmeaning follies which had gathered around it. And rarely, in the history of literature, has the success of satire been so marked and so abiding. For though, as has been remarked, his attempt to stem the torrent of prejudice which then existed in favour of the tales of chivalry was apparently as "Quixotic" as the adventure of his own hero against the windmills, yet it is a fact (and a very important fact too, as illustrating the power of the pen) that, from the publication of *Don Quixote* is dated the downfall, in Spain, of the taste for these absurd and chimerical romances.

We repeat, then, that it was not the purpose of Cervantes to cast ridicule upon all fictitious composition. And we think, therefore, that whilst he has painted in his hero a man who lives wholly in an ideal world, which has no connection whatever with the world around us, his teaching would have been incomplete, and his influence less powerful, had he not contrasted this extreme with its opposite, and shown us in Sancho Panza, a man who is "of the earth, earthy," who is destitute of a single particle of fancy or imagination, and who is led to follow his master, through all his wanderings, only by the hope that he may possibly be a gainer in the end, and perchance become king over that imaginary "island," which the Don is constantly promising to him as the reward of his fidelity. Here, then, we have before our view a contrast of the Real and the Ideal, in their ultimate extremes. The noble spirit of chivalry, misdirected to the achievement of impossible adventures, in circumstances purely ideal,—this is portrayed on the one hand; and here, whilst we laugh, we pity. The coarse, utilitarian spirit, grovelling in the dust,—clever in its own way,—quoting bundles of shrewd proverbs,—greedy of gain,—without one spark of nobleness or fancy,—this is portrayed on the other hand; and here we laugh also, but, whilst we laugh, we despise. We feel at once that we would rather be the knight, mistaking windmills for giants,—supposing every inn to be a magnificent castle, and every woman to be a lady of exalted rank and virtue,—than shrink within the narrow dimensions of the soul of the squire, who has no lofty idea of any woman whatsoever, to whose degraded spirit everything on earth seems common.

The contrast between the Real and the Ideal,—the spirit of chivalry and that of mere utility,—could hardly be better exemplified than by that famous episode of the history, where, when Don Quixote is all impatient to investigate the cause of those terrible noises which are astonishing both himself and Sancho, the latter, trembling like a coward, says to his master, "Pray, sir, why will you thus run yourself into mischief? What need you go about this rueful misadventure? 'Tis main dark, and there's ne'er a living soul sees us; we have nothing to do but to sheer off, and get out of harm's way! *Who is there to take notice of our flinching?*" The squire's views of chivalry and honour seem to have been much akin to those of our own illustrious Jack Falstaff, who, by the way, appeared upon the world's stage only a few years earlier than Sancho. Some of our readers will remember his famous soliloquy :—

"Well, 'tis no matter; Honour pricks me on. Yea, but how if Honour prick me off, when I come on? how then? Can Honour set to a leg? No.—Or an arm? No.—Or take away the grief of a wound? No.—Honour hath no skill in surgery, then? No.—What is honour? A word.—What is that word? Honour.—What is that Honour? Air.—A trim reckoning!—Who hath it? He that died o' Wednesday. Doth he feel it? No.—Doth he hear it?—No. Is it insensible, then? Yea, to the dead.—But will it not live with the living? No.—Why? Detraction will not suffer it. Therefore, I'll none of it! Honour's a mere 'scutcheon, and so ends my catechism!"

It is manifest that although this soliloquy gives evidence of a mind somewhat more philosophic than Sancho's, yet Sir John comes to the very same conclusion. He is your shrewd, utilitarian philosopher, who thinks he sees things as they *really* are, and sneers at those who look at the world around them through the medium of the imagination. And we fear that this philosophy of Jack Falstaff has leavened in no small degree the spirit of our age, and is working at this moment with dangerous influence in spheres from which it ought to be most rigidly excluded.

It has now become quite a common-place to remark that ours is eminently a "practical" age, and that the "spirit of the age" has reached its highest development in the Anglo-Saxon character and life. If a submarine telegraph is to connect the old and the new worlds, the Anglo-Saxon declares himself ready for the task; if the greatest steamship which the world has ever seen is to be built, an English dockyard is the place, and English engineers are the men for the work; if the African continent is to be trod, an Anglo-Saxon Livingstone is the man to do it, and if the suppression of a mighty mutiny is not altogether an impossible thing, depend upon it that it can and will be effected by such men as Havelock and Campbell.

Now we do not mean here to make light of that industrious character of the English people which has done so much for our country and the world. Especially would we guard ourselves against the charge of depreciating those mighty results which have been achieved by the practical researches of scientific men. We honour the man of business whose commercial sagacity teaches him how he may best turn honest industry to profitable account. We respect the sound common-sense and inventive genius which have done aught to increase the happiness and comfort of our race. But we say most emphatically, that these great blessings do not come to us unalloyed, but are attended with numerous and mighty dangers. When the genius of man is almost exclusively occupied with the world of matter, he is in danger of forgetting the far more important world of mind and heart. When our attention is so much occupied with that which is popularly called *the Real*, because it is visible, tangible, palpable to the senses, we are apt to depreciate that which we call *the Ideal*, because it is inward, and lies further from the senses. The man who gives his whole soul to the prosecution of commercial pursuits is very apt, if not absolutely certain, to carry the principles of his ledger into every sphere of his life; to divide his fellow-beings into debtors, creditors, and partners (his wife being one of the latter!), and to look upon all human action and endeavour in the light of "profit and loss." And thus it is, that an eminently scientific age is in danger of falling into materialism, and an eminently commercial age of falling into utilitarianism. We do not say that these are necessary results; we only say that, taking human nature as it is, they are results which are natural. We rejoice to believe, with Christopher North, that "the philosopher who knows what a rainbow is, does not therefore cease to regard with delight the glory as it spans the storm"; and that "a drop of dew on a flower, or a tear on the cheek, will be felt to be beautiful, after all mankind have been familiarly acquainted with the philosophy of secretions." Yet, on the other hand, it remains true that no one is in greater *danger* of falling into a merely prosaic existence than your keen man of science, who has so accustomed himself to observe the details of nature, that, when a flower which he has never seen before is presented to his view, his uppermost thought may have little reference to its rare beauty, but rather to "genus" and "species," and his own "herbarium" at home! And it must also be acknowledged that there is a tendency in the keen pursuit of commerce and money-making to degrade the aspirations of the human soul.

Now it cannot be denied that the age in which we live is at once eminently scientific and eminently commercial. Science and commerce are acting and re-acting upon each other—the exigencies of commerce demanding fresh scientific discoveries, and the results of science facilitating and extending commercial pursuits. And the consequence is just what we have stated, that the men of our time are in great danger of exaggerating the importance of what they call the real and practical, and, in pursuing the utilitarian, of losing sight altogether of the chivalrous and the noble. Do we not constantly meet with men who seem to be sinking into mere calculating machines, who carry the principles of arithmetical computation into almost everything they do? Our "utilitarian" young man of the world is a very wise individual. *He* is not to be "caught by sentimentalism," —not he! "He knows what's what." Money is with him the great power in this world. He has an eye to profit, somehow or other, in all that he says and does. He may not exactly go the length of Sancho Panza, when he says, that "the man who fills his belly wins his heart"; but he is just as fond as Sancho of quoting shrewd proverbs. His favourite maxim is, "A bird in the hand is worth two in the bush." He never thinks of asking himself the question—"What shall it *profit* a man if he gain the whole world and lose his own soul?"—or if he do ask the question, he forthwith opens a new account, in his private ledger, with the next world, and sets down to his "credit" a certain amount of church attendance, which he calls "worship," and of creed repetition, which he calls "faith." It is true the "worship" and "faith" are a "kind of bore" to him; but then, this young gentleman wishes to "make the best of both worlds!" Speak to him of scrupulous truthfulness; he does not see the *use* of being so very exact, but he does see the use of an occasional "white lie," which does no harm, and is rather respectable than otherwise. Speak to him of the chivalrous endeavour of some noble man; he will perhaps sneeringly tell you that "no man is a hero to his own flunkey," forgetting, as Carlyle so pithily remarks, that the fault may very possibly lie with the flunkey! He is always advising us "to take the world as it is," or "to wait until we know the world as *he* does." He sneers at "love in a cottage." "Everybody, of course, knows *that* to be the merest moonshine"; so, "when once he has a respectable establishment, he will take unto himself a wife," which, being interpreted, means that he will enter into marriage as he would into a Joint Stock Railway Company. Speak to him of the pleasures of the beautiful, and the joy of the imagination; he will tell you that "he leaves the *ideal* to dreaming poets; as for his part, he likes to stick to *real* life!"

But is it true that those things only are *real* which are palpable to the senses? Is the *ideal* necessarily unreal? Does not the imagination oftentimes create for a man what is just as *real* to him as those things which he sees or handles? There is an axiom which is worthy of attention here, and which may help us towards a solution of these questions. It is this, that the "eye only sees that which it brings with it the power of seeing." As Carlyle somewhere remarks, "The same landscape may paint itself, in exactly the same way, on the retina of Newton's eye and on the retina of the eye of Newton's dog; but still, to Newton the landscape is a very different thing from what it is to his dog!" And how absurd would it be for the dog to insist that he sees the landscape as it *really* exists, whilst his master is looking at it through a *false* medium. The principle is of universal application. Everything depends on the state of the soul. Take a clodpole like Peter Bell;

> "A primrose by the river's brim
> A yellow primrose was to him,
> And it was nothing more."

But to a soul like that of Robert Burns, the mountain-daisy, turned over by the plough, is suggestive of the sweetest thoughts; and he who has felt the beauty of nature can sympathize with Wordsworth when he says, in language which it would puzzle Peter Bell to comprehend:—

> "Thanks to the human heart by which we live,
> Thanks to its tenderness, its joys, and fears,
> To me the meanest flower that blows can give
> Thoughts that do often lie too deep for tears."

Nay, further, the aspect of external nature will appear different to the same man in different states of mind and feeling. To the hero of *Locksley Hall*, the sky overhead and the beach at his feet seem bright and beautiful, so long as the love of Amy remains to him; but when she proves faithless, then the shore is only "barren," and the moorland very "dreary." Again, to the old miller, the wheel and the dam and the meal-sacks are the merest common-places of his trade; but if we would learn how they appear to the imagination, we must listen to him who is in love with the "Miller's daughter":—

> "I loved the brimming wave that swam
> Thro' quiet meadows round the mill,
> The sleepy pool above the dam,
> The pool beneath it never still,

> The meal-sacks on the whiten'd floor,
>   The dark round of the dripping wheel,
> The very air about the door
>   Made misty with the floating meal."

Thus it is that, to use the words of Emerson, "the passion rebuilds the world for the youth." His imagination actually creates. On no true principle can it be said that he is only looking at the things which are round about him through an unreal medium. As well might the dog insist that his master sees beauties which are not *really* in the landscape; as well might a blind man insist that there is no "primrose by the river's brim" because he cannot see it. And, indeed, the same philosophy which asserts that there is no beauty really existing in the landscape or primrose, will, if followed out, lead us to deny the real existence of either primrose or landscape.

The "ideal," then, is not necessarily unreal. The man whose mind is devoid of the poetic element, does not, as he supposes, see things as they really are, but only sees them partially. He sees none of those realities which are visible only to the man of imagination. It is *he*, therefore, who looks at things through a false medium, or at least, through a cloudy atmosphere. For the universe of God is open only to the eye of the *seer*; and a man becomes a true seer just in proportion as he cultivates all the faculties of his being. And, therefore, the true culture of the imagination does, so far as that can go, help a man to see things as they really are. In the *Noctes Ambrosianæ* the "shepherd" waxes most eloquent on this subject :—" Nae man o' a high order o' mind either thinks or feels through 'an unreal medium.' But I'll tell you, sir, what he does—

he thinks and feels through a fine medium. He breathes the pure air o' the mountain-tap, and he sees through the *clear* air a' the dwallins o' man, and richt through their roofs intil their hearths and their hearts. Did Burns think and feel through an unreal medium, when,

'In glory and in joy,
Following his plough upon the mountain-side,'

his soul saw the Cottar's Saturday Night, and in words gave the vision imperishable life ? Na, na, for as sure as God is in heaven, and He has given us His word on earth, that picture is a picture of the truth; and Burns, in drawing it, saw, felt, and thocht through that *real* medium, in which alone all that is fairest, loveliest, brichtest, best in creation, is made apparent to the eyes of genius, or permanent in its immortal works!"

The "shepherd" is right. Imagination purifies the vision. The ideal does not unfrequently pass into the real. To a stranger, for example, the countenance of my friend may seem only ordinary and common-place, whilst to me it seems noble and beautiful, because I look at it through the medium of the imagination, and every varying expression is to me a manifestation of the soul within. My friend is *really* beautiful to me, though he may not appear so to a stranger or an enemy. They look at him through a different medium; but they do not see all that can be seen.

Take one other and familiar illustration. Here is a soldier fighting on the field of battle. The colours of his regiment are in danger; he rushes to the defence of that old flag; he will shed the last drop of his blood ere he permit that flag to be taken. Will you step in, and tell him that it is *really* a piece of old cotton, a mere rag, which could easily be replaced? But here, again, the ideal has passed into the real. Imagination has created for that soldier a reality which is invisible to you. That flag is to him the symbol of his regiment's honour; its capture would be to him a token of his regiment's disgrace. It is thus that the actual is often transfigured by the spirit of poetry. It is "the real" we see; but we see it in the light of "the ideal." And the sight of such a transfiguration is most refreshing to the heart of man. For it remains in his memory, after he has come down from the mount; and, as he again pursues his journey along the common, dusty highway, the remembrance abides within him, as a well-spring of strength and joy.

"It is strange," says Emerson, "how painful is the actual world—the painful kingdom of time and place. There dwells care and canker and fear. With thought, with the ideal, is immortal hilarity, the rose of joy. Round it all the muses sing." This is true; but it is not all the truth. For, as Emerson elsewhere admits, the two kingdoms are not necessarily dissociated. The actual world may be seen in the light of the ideal. The care and canker and fear may be wondrously diminished. They may even give place to joy, as the story of many a noble martyr abundantly proves. And the words of St. Paul tell us of this same possibility—"Our light affliction, which is but for a moment, worketh for us a far more exceeding and eternal weight of glory; whilst we look not at the things which are seen, but at the things which are not seen; for the things which are seen are temporal, but the things which are not seen are eternal."

These words sound like poetry—they *are* poetry.

They are the words of a man who was often on the mount of transfiguration. He came into contact, as few men have ever done, with the "painful kingdom" of the actual. Yet his whole life seems to have been leavened with a poetic spirit. His letters, though dealing with the most practical questions, are full of imagination. His speeches are pervaded by a lofty tone. To Festus, the time-server, "willing to do the Jews a pleasure," the hero seems Quixotic—"Paul, thou art beside thyself; much learning doth make thee mad." The whole spirit of his career was that of nobleness and chivalry. And wherever we see him; whether on Mars' Hill, confronting the sneering philosophers of Athens, or in the dungeon of Philippi singing his midnight song, we have before us a man for whom the most common events of life have been irradiated by a light from heaven. Such a man has learned the secret of converting into poetry the dull prose of existence. And this is the great secret which we have all to learn. We are not meant to live a dreary, matter-of-fact life. For, just as a man may write a poetic or prosaic narrative of the same events, so, out of exactly the same materials, he may weave for himself either a poetic or prosaic life. And, just in proportion as a man cultivates aright all the faculties of his being,—and especially that kingly power of imagination which Wordsworth calls "the vision and the faculty *divine*,"—will the duties and events of ordinary life fall into their proper position, and be seen by him in that true light which a higher life can alone shed around them.

And now we are free to point out the connection which subsists between our subject and the Christian life. The mission of Christianity in our world is just to develop and ennoble all the faculties of our nature. Not until *all* the powers with which God has endowed us are redeemed from the service of evil, and elevated into the service of good; not until all these powers have been educated and developed according to the original design of the Creator, will the work of Christ be completed in the soul of man. The inference is obvious. As this, and nothing less than this, is the grand aim of Christianity, it follows that, in proportion as a man advances in the Christian life, does he possess that secret to which we have referred—the secret of viewing the actual in the light of the ideal, and so of converting into poetry the dullest prose of existence. For Christianity is full of poetry. In all ages, since its birth, it has appealed to the heart and imagination of man. Would that our theologians had always remembered this. Why will so many of them persist in thinking that their chief strength lies in arguments from miracles and prophecies?

And here we would make one other remark by the way. If what we have said be true, it is manifest that the technical, theological creed, even if perfectly sound in itself, can never be an *adequate* exponent of Christianity, for such a creed is, to a great extent, just the translation of poetry into prose. It may be well that we should have prose translations of the *Iliad*; but we do not suppose that our translation can ever be a substitute for the lofty grandeur of the Homeric verse. A sound logical creed may be very useful, if we remember that it is only as the "argument" of a poem. It becomes worse than useless when we begin to regard it as more important than the poem itself, or to suppose that it can ever fully represent the power and beauty which it but feebly indicates.

"There is a way," says the author of a little book[1] which we love for its wisdom and poetry, "there is a way of making truth plain and comprehensible, by unsouling it of all that is deepest and most precious in it. In the logical creed you lose the *livingness* of truth. Instead of butterflies glancing in the sun, you get them arranged by the hand of science, dead in their dusty case. Instead of odorous flowers, sucked by the honey-bees, kissed by the winds, and bathed in the dews, you get them dried in the botanist's portfolio." And, when once our theologians are content, in their teaching, to come back to the poetry of Scripture, they will find many an ear and heart open, which have been closed, justly or unjustly, against their formal creeds.

Christianity, then, we repeat, is full of poetry. Nor is the Christian life, therefore, unreal and visionary. Have we not seen that the poet has often an insight into realities, which are altogether invisible to the man who is destitute of imagination? Have we not seen that the life of Paul, the Christian, was not the less real, because it was irradiated and ennobled by a poetic spirit? And will the man of commerce become a visionary dreamer by looking at his daily business in the light of Christian life? Will his workmen become less real to him because he remembers that they are brothers, travelling with himself to the great hereafter, under the eye of the one Brother of all? Will his wife and children become the less real to him in pro-

[1] *Lazarus Revived;* James Culross, A.M. London: J. Heaton & Son. 1858.

portion as he loves them with a more unselfish love, and as he sees that halo of glory which the life of Christ sheds around the sanctities of home? Nay, verily; for we can never believe that the realities, either of this life or of the life to come, are seen as they should be by the man who has degraded himself into a money-making machine—who leads a dull, prosaic life, which he calls "practical"—who is honest only because "honesty is the best policy"—and who thinks of God's heaven as a "decided bargain" for a little troublesome painstaking on earth.

We would close these suggestions with one qualifying remark. We have been pleading for the culture of the imagination, as especially necessary in this age of commercial and scientific pursuit. But we must never forget that imagination is not the only faculty of our nature. In this world of the actual, our mission is not to dream, but to work. Give us Don Quixote *rather* than Sancho Panza. Heaven send us crusades *rather* than railway manias! But, why should we have either extreme? We are in the flesh, and have duties of the flesh to discharge; but this is no reason why we should become the slaves of sense. Our nobler part is that heaven-born spirit which binds us to the chivalrous and the beautiful, but neither is this a reason why we should neglect the most ordinary duties of our life on earth. And in proportion as we drink in the spirit of Christ shall we learn how we may live noble and self-sacrificing lives, without leaving the sphere of daily duty in which God has cast our lot. Every earnest and devout man has felt how the mount of prayer may become the mount of transfiguration.

The whole question which we have been discussing has been put in a very beautiful, and, as we think, true light, by the authoress of *Aurora Leigh*. After bitter experience, Aurora is compelled to confess that her "practical" cousin was so far right. But meanwhile, Romney also has found out his mistake, and comes to tell his "poet cousin" that it was *she* who had spoken the truth. It is the old story; each had been looking at a different side of the shield. The marriage of Romney and Aurora is a type of the truth. The actual must be wedded to the ideal. To use the words of Tennyson, which embody the same figure, we must not

"Divorce the feeling from her mate, the deed."

True human life is prose poetry. The seer is to be a *worker* in the world, not a mere dreamer or hermit; on the other hand, the worker is not to be a machine, but a *seer*.

THE PRACTICAL USES OF THE IMAGINATION.

[Reprinted from *The Congregationalist*, July, 1878.]

THE realistic spirit of our age and country is accompanied by its own peculiar dangers. One of these dangers lies in the tendency to adopt very contracted views of "the useful" and "the practical." Men ask the question "*Cui bono?*" with the narrowest notions of what *bonum* is—sometimes, indeed, as if it ought to be translated "bread and butter"! They ask the question, "Is this practicable?" in utter oblivion of the fact that results which are indirect and remote are often the most worthy of achievement. They talk about "substantial" advantages, precisely when they are speaking of the things that "perish in the using." And another of the dangers incident to the practical temperament lies in the tendency to disparage the imaginative faculty, and to neglect its culture. Many business men are scarcely conscious that they possess such a faculty at all; far less do they assign it a due place in the economy of human life. They know that they have powers of perception, memory, and judgment; these they are using every day; but "imagination" surely pertains only to poets and artists, who write and paint and—starve!

Now this, of course, is a great mistake. The Imagination—in its widest sense—may be popularly defined as *the image-making faculty of the human mind.* It may be described as that power which the mind has of making and holding up before itself pictures, either of what lies simply in the memory, or of what is suggested in accordance with the laws of association, or of what is evolved through the deliberate process of comparison. This is virtually the view of Sir William Hamilton, who affirms that "representation—the vivid exhibition of an object—forms the principal constituent of imagination," and who endorses the remark of a French philosopher that "there are as many different kinds of imagination as there are different kinds of intellectual activity." The images which the mind thus holds up before itself may be of the most varied character. They may be pictures of sensations, or of ideas, or of volitions, or of emotions. They may also be either simple or composite. They may be simple photographs, as it were, of what we ourselves have actually seen and felt; or they may be compositions of the most complex character, which in their entireness are altogether new, or possibly even without any counterpart in nature, although composed of elements the most simple and familiar. Think, for example, what pictorial novelties, what peculiar combinations of persons, of scenes, and of circumstances, our imagination produces in our sleep! And when, in your waking moments, you are trying to represent to yourself how your friend John Smith would think or feel or speak or act, if he were placed in certain circumstances, you are virtually using that same faculty which, working along with other endowments, enabled

Shakespeare to write his *Julius Cæsar* or his *Hamlet*. Of course, just as one man may be distinguished for his retentive memory, so another may be distinguished for his vivid and powerful imagination; but the pictorial, no less than the recording faculty, belongs naturally to every sound human mind, and is no less capable of development. The special purpose of the present paper is to commend the due cultivation of this faculty to men of practical temperament, by showing that its exercise enters as a factor into the production of the most important and practical results.

I. We may begin by considering the power of the Imagination *to increase personal comfort and happiness.*

Samuel Rogers used to tell how, at the time when plate-glass windows had just been introduced, he was dining in the house of a friend, and that, sitting at the table for an hour or two with his back to one of these windows, he was not only made very uncomfortable by imagining all the while that the window was wide open, but actually caught also a severe cold in consequence! And, if we remember rightly, it was Sydney Smith who, on hearing the story, exclaimed that this was surely a very foolish use to make of such a powerful instrument; for that the same vividness of imagination, if wisely directed, might enable a man to sit in a draught with impunity! It is at least an indubitable fact that the imagination does often influence to a great extent our personal comfort and happiness. Everyone knows what a power this faculty may wield, either for good or evil, in certain states of disease, and the skilful physician often takes advantage of this fact in order to promote a cure. So subtle and intimate is the connection between the mind and the body, that a right use of the imagination may have the most salutary effect even upon our physical condition. Perhaps it may be true that no one—

> " can hold fire in his hand
> By thinking on the frosty Caucasus,
> Or cloy the hungry edge of appetite
> By bare imagination of a feast " ;

but it is certainly true that martyrs at the stake have spoken of the flames as " a bed of roses," and that men have gone fasting for many an hour, when they have had " meat to eat " which others " knew not of." And it is also true that one man whose spirit is cheered by " visions of the brain " may get more real nourishment for his body from a homely meal, than some other man from a sumptuous banquet to which he sits down with no other thought than the " practical " one of gratifying his appetite. For there are many men who miss their mark, just because their eye is too intently fixed upon it!

How much personal discomfort, moreover, a man may often avoid, by imagining possible, or at least probable contingencies, instead of dashing forward recklessly to meet a future which he has never tried to image to his thought. How much enjoyment also is due to this same faculty, when we live over again in thought bright days that are gone, or picture in thought bright days that are to come. For " distance lends enchantment to the view " both of the past and of the future. It is quite proverbial how frequently the anticipation of happiness gives greater pleasure than even the reality. The past, too—

> "will always win
> A glory from its being far;
> And orb into the perfect star
> We saw not, when we moved therein."

Thus "the pleasures of memory" and the "pleasures of hope" are both, to a great extent, "pleasures of the imagination." We are all, further, familiar with the fact that the same external circumstances may assume very different aspects to different minds. To the two young souls under one umbrella, who are contemplating the same mental picture of a marriage-day not far distant, the storm of wind and rain through which they are walking is not at all the same thing that it is to the husband and wife whom they pass on the road, and who—on the principle, perhaps, that "two are better than one"—are each carrying their separate umbrella! Every lover is, more or less, a poet for the nonce. The real lies before him bathed in the light of the ideal. And can we say that the increase of happiness which is due to an imagination thus quickened by fresh affection is no practical advantage? Were such joy for sale in the world's markets, should we not see many a bank-note cheerfully paid down to buy it?

Nor will it be denied that a very substantial increase of happiness flows also from the appreciation of the beautiful in nature and art. It has been well said that "the eye only sees what it brings with it the power of seeing." Much depends on what sort of mind is behind the eye and on what sort of pictures are there. We remember a clever caricature representing a rising manufacturer "out" with his wife and daughters on his first visit to the Lake district. The manufacturer, sitting beside the coachman, asks, "And what water is this 'ere?" "That's Grasmere," replies the coachman; "ain't it beautiful!" "How strange!" says the practical man; "you ca' them all lakes and meres hereabouts; down with us they're called *reser-voyers!*" Worthy mate this of that other Englishman of whom we have heard, who, with his family, was—to use the characteristic Anglo-Saxon phrase—"*doing* Rome." Visiting one of the great picture-galleries, he comes to a celebrated painting in which the principal figure is John the Baptist. This figure catches his attention; he nods approvingly; and then comes the emphatic criticism, uttered in the hearing of everybody near him, "Quite *my* idea of 'the party!'" Now, who does not feel that there must be a very practical defect in the mind of a man to whom Grasmere is a "reservoir," or to whom the stern wilderness-preacher, seen through the vista even of eighteen centuries, has become simply —"a party"? Who does not feel that all men of whom these may be taken as caricature-types, are (whatever their profits may be) losers of substantial good? Surely it must practically increase the happiness even of a British manufacturer, when his imagination is sufficiently cultivated to enable him, now and again, after the toils of the day are over, to take down his Tennyson from his shelves, and forget for a little while his ledger and his factory, in following Sir Bedivere as he bears the wounded Arthur down to "the shining levels of the lake," or in listening to the Princess Ida as she holds converse with her maidens.

II. We pass on to notice the use which the Imagination subserves *in stimulating ambition and in sustaining perseverance.*

We were told in one of our earliest story-books how

a London apprentice, who had run away from his master's house because of the hardships of his lot, turned back to confront all these hardships again, when he heard the bells of Bow Church calling after him—

"Turn again, Whittington,
Lord Mayor of London!"

It is not at all unlikely that the story is substantially true. There was undoubtedly a Richard Whittington nearly five centuries ago, who fought his way through early difficulties, became one of the greatest merchants of his time, and was thrice elected to the mayoralty of London. And it would be strange if such a man—long before he was *Sir* Richard—had not been often upheld in his youthful struggles by bright imaginings of a possible future. Indeed, there have been few eminent men who have not heard, in their youth, the chimes of the prophetic bells. "The child is father of the man"; and the latent powers of the mind often carry within themselves the pictorial prediction of what they are fitted to achieve. The dawn of conscious ability flushes with its own light even the distant horizon of the future. Your unimaginative Esaus dream no dreams worth telling, and carve out for themselves no destinies worth recording. What is a "birthright" to them? A birthright cannot feed a hungry man; "pottage of lentiles" is a much more "substantial" thing! But your Jacobs, who have their visions of the ladder and the angels, and who hang up before the mind's eye pictures of coming good—these are the men who can sacrifice the present to the future, to whom "the seven years are but a few days" for the love they bear their Rachel, and who start enterprises, and found families, which leave their mark on the history of mankind. Such natures are often tempted to trickery in order that they may the more fully or swiftly realize their ideals; but take them on the whole, they are nobler in themselves, and they achieve more practical and permanent results, than those natures which are engrossed in chasing the fugitive pleasures of the passing day.

Nor is it merely the case that these visions of the imagination spring from latent power. There is also re-action here; the visions nurse the power to which they owe their birth. There is thus a double reason why our presentiments as to our own future tend to fulfil themselves. Our ideals, kept before the mind, quicken our powers, stimulate our perseverance, and maintain our patience. The young student of Christ's College, who has his visions of "adding somewhat to the permanent literature of his country," and whose lofty ideal of the poet is that "his own life ought to be a true poem," becomes by and by Oliver Cromwell's secretary, and the author of *Paradise Lost*. Yon Italian lad, who steals away from his desk in the notary's office to watch the artists at their work, will yet be known far and wide as Michael Angelo, the greatest of them all. That youth, who leaves his University with a profound contempt for Aristotle and the Aristotelian method, is Francis Bacon; and in that contempt lies the germ of the *Novum Organum*. In truth, most men who have achieved anything worthy of their powers, owe much to their own imaginings. None of us love disembodiment. We naturally wish to see our ideas incarnate and "clothed upon." The soul within us, like the sculptor of ancient fable, falls in love with the image of beauty which it has itself fashioned, and then appeals to us to make this image a living and breathing thing. And again, when men grow weary of their toils and of confronting the difficulties which obstruct their progress, what is it that revives their drooping energies? What but hope?—which, when it is at all definite, involves an exercise of the imagination. For hope simply holds up before our minds the picture of the possible future—the object we have in view—the position we desire to attain; and the sight of this picture rekindles our ambition and stimulates our flagging perseverance.

III. The exercise of the Imagination is also helpful *in the doing of justice and benevolence.*

Every honest, earnest mind will grant that whatever aids men in fulfilling their mutual duties, confers an advantage of the most practical and substantial character. Now, there are many cases in which a man cannot act righteously towards his neighbour, unless by imagination he places himself mentally, as near as may be, in that neighbour's position. Even the judge on the Bench, in using such discretion as the law allows him, is often enabled, by the exercise of this faculty, to elicit such evidence, or to allot such penalty, as tends to bring the human administration of justice into closer harmony with the divine. But every wise and good judge must feel that the very rigidity and apparent impartiality of our human law often make its operation exceedingly partial and unequal. The justice of such law can, for the most part, weigh in her scales only overt acts; and so it may be well that she should be blindfold; but the absolute and eternal justice must also weigh temptations, privileges, and circumstances; and so she has eyes "like unto a flame of fire," which behold the secret motive, as well as the outward deed. How grossly unjust many of our judgments are, simply for want of a little imagination! You set down a man as stingy and mean, when all the while he may perhaps be far more generous than yourself. Nor do we ever conduct controversy fairly, unless we represent to our own thought the views of those who differ from us. A man never holds his own convictions with a more honest and intelligent grasp, and never argues more convincingly on their behalf, than when he can fairly appreciate antagonistic opinions by having stood in imagination on the opposing platform. In our ordinary life, too, the simple endeavour to place ourselves imaginatively in the circumstances of others would often result in more equitable dealing. The man who is about to risk money that is not his own in some hazardous speculation, might be aroused, ere it is too late, to recognize the claims of honesty, if he would picture to his mind what, in the event of his being unsuccessful, would be the position and feelings of those who are now trusting in his honour. And there is many a clerk who would have his salary raised to-morrow morning, if only his rich employer, lying back to-day in his easy chair, would paint himself on the canvas of his own fancy as perched, throughout the long years, on that same counting-house stool!

Then, to pass from justice to benevolence: what a great deal of unkindness springs, not from any intention to inflict a wound, but from a thoughtless overlooking of the circumstances and feelings of others! A true politeness springs from imaginative sympathy. And herein it differs from a mere external courtesy, which, however polished, will often say and do really vulgar things, just because it cannot see with other eyes than its own. Vulgarity is constantly " treading on people's toes," just because it does not picture to itself the possibility of toes being in the way. Feelings are wounded, reputations injured, and motives misapprehended, simply for the want of a little imaginative thoughtfulness. There is a subtle tact and delicacy of conduct, which no mere artificial etiquette can give, and which flows only from our placing ourselves *en rapport* with others, so as to picture to our minds their attitude and wishes. Even a gift may be so bestowed as to make it more like a blow than a kiss. The very intentions of our benevolence may be frustrated by our failing to estimate aright the conditions and feelings of those whom we seek to benefit. We are to " remember those who are in bonds as bound with them "—as if we felt their chains upon our own wrists. And if those who have passed through sorrow themselves are often the best comforters of their brethren, is not this to be explained, partly, by the fact that their own experience enables them more easily and vividly to realize the trouble which they are seeking to alleviate ? But, surely, we need not wait for sorrow, disease, or death to come and open the fountains of our tenderness. The very anticipation of these in our thought would often be enough to disarm our harshness. It might often check the unjust or bitter word which is springing to the lip, were we simply to pause and imagine how the memory of such words will look to us when we are lowering the coffin into the grave! And what is the " golden rule " itself, which includes all justice and all benevolence, but simply an appeal to the imaginative faculty? We are to place ourselves, mentally, in the position of our neighbour, and picture to our thought his claims and his needs: "All things whatsoever ye would that men should do to you, do ye even so to them."

IV. We proceed to notice the province of the Imagination in *discovery and invention*.

It will be admitted that one of the greatest events of modern times—one of the most fruitful in practical issues—was the discovery of America. Now this event was due as much to the vivid imagination of Columbus, as to his dauntless courage or his nautical skill. It was the vision he cherished of the gorgeous East—of its wealth and beauty, and of the magnificent results which would flow from the discovery of a new path to it—that upheld the spirit of Columbus amid poverty and ridicule, and enabled him, through long years of obscurity, to cling with steadfastness to his projected enterprise, and to defend it with eloquence against the objections alike of science and theology. "The very children," we are told, "used to point to their foreheads as he passed, being taught to regard him as a kind of madman." The men of science considered that, after the studies and labours of so many generations, it was the grossest presumption in an ordinary man to conceive that there yet remained so great a discovery for *him* to make! Theologians set him down as a heretic, and quoted against him St. Chrysostom and St. Augustine and a whole host of "Fathers." But this man had "dreamed his dream," and was bent on finding "the interpretation thereof." His mind had gathered together various materials—ancient myths, floating rumours, scientific facts;—and out of all these his imagination had painted, in glowing colours, a picture of the new world which he would find by sailing towards the setting sun. With the monarchs to whom he unveiled his projects, and whose aid he asked, he would treat only on the loftiest terms, like a man whose prize was already within his grasp. The theologians he met on their own ground, quoting the poetical predictions of the inspired prophets as shadowing forth his contemplated discovery; for religion also lent its halo to the images of his thought. Of course, Columbus was no mere visionary; his ardent imagination was blended with the most practical energy and skill. But all that fund of practical energy, with even his skill as pilot at the helm, might have lain like a useless hulk upon the waters, unless his imagination had given it sails, and so borne it onward to the "desired haven." It was the vividness with which he pictured the undiscovered lands, which enabled him to consummate his grand enterprise in spite of obstacles and perils, not the least of which sprang from the occasional mutiny of his sailors—those "practical" men—who saw only death where he saw glory. And when at last he came to the reality, he was not disappointed; for what he then saw with his eyes was to him simply a mirror in which he beheld the reflection of his own imaginings. These conceptions of the New World which he entertained even after he had reached it, were of course full of error; we now know that many of them were but "airy visions of the brain." And yet, although Columbus was thus so greatly mistaken as to details, who would not acknowledge—looking at the America of to-day—

that the issues of his discovery have far surpassed even his brightest dreams?

Passing to the discoveries of science, we find that, in this region also, imagination lends the most valuable aid. One remarkable circumstance strikes us on the threshold: some of the sciences owe their very birth to the observations and researches of men whose patience was inspired by the most erroneous conceptions. Astrology, in search of some mystic relations between the starry firmament and human destiny, gives birth to Astronomy; and now the daughter-science enables men to "consult the stars" in far other fashion than that of which the mother dreamed. Grey-bearded Alchemy, bending over his crucible in quest of "the philosopher's stone," dies at last of utter weariness; but he leaves a son behind him to fulfil his dreams; and Chemistry has already its own peculiar methods of making gold, and has buried Alchemy with all becoming reverence in the promised land. It is further true that a vigorous imagination has sometimes anticipated the conclusions of inductive science. Thus, *e.g.*, Goethe conceived the idea that "the flower of a plant is just the highest development or transformation of its leaves; that all the parts of a plant, from the seed to the blossom, are simply modifications of a leaf." This idea was at first scouted by scientific men as the merest fancy of a poet; but it is now regarded as one of the fundamental truths of Botany. Nor let it be thought that this is mere coincidence. Indeed, in this special case, it turns out that the idea of the poet had been actually anticipated by a somewhat dim presentiment of Linnæus. And the fact is that, in multitudes of cases, the very process of discovery involves an exercise of the imaginative faculty. A discovery is not always the pure result of an inductive process; it is frequently the result of the verification of a theory. An observer carries on a series of investigations; he thus gathers together a number of facts; but, before he has completed his researches, his mind leaps from the known to the unknown—he forms a certain theory; he then proceeds to test this theory by special observations and experiments; and, if it fulfils all necessary conditions, he declares it verified. This is the natural history of many a discovery. Now, what is that "theorizing," which is the transition-stage in this process? A truly scientific theory—even if it be erroneous—is not a mere arbitrary guess; it is the imagination forming its ideal explanation out of those materials which have been provided by research, or out of abstract ideas of order and harmony which exist in the mind itself. And surely it is not a strange thing that the "creative faculty" in man should thus aid him in the study of the "creation" of God. Many instances might be adduced of such successful imaginings. The poet may well speak of "the fairy tales of science"—recognizing in them the workings of a power kindred with his own. Dr. Whewell, in his *History of the Inductive Sciences*, when speaking of the labours of Kepler, who was remarkable for his fertility of conjecture, gives it as his own belief that this method of theory followed by test has been usual, rather than exceptional, in the process of discovery. And Tyndall says that "Newton's passage from a falling apple to a falling moon was, at the outset, a leap of the imagination." Ruskin, too, refers to "the instinctive grasp which the healthy imagination has of possible truth"; and Dr. John

Brown, commenting on this word of Ruskin's, puts the matter well, when he says: "I believe there has been no true discoverer from Galileo and Kepler to Davy and Owen, without wings; these Nimrods of 'possible truth' have ever had, as their stoutest, stanchest hound, a powerful and healthy imagination, to find and 'point' the game."

All this is true of Invention, as well as of Discovery. In invention, the mind holds up before itself certain conditions which must be fulfilled, and conceives that which will fulfil these conditions. A host of possible plans may picture themselves successively in thought, before the advent of the one plan which is felt to solve the problem. This whole process manifestly involves an exercise of the representative faculty. Mere mechanical skill, working by arbitrary experiment, is never likely to produce any grand results. The greatest inventors have been men of imagination. Daguerre had his dream that the images which he saw in the camera could be made permanent; and he pursued his experiments with a zeal which was quite inexplicable to the matter-of-fact people about him. Even his wife consulted a medical friend on the symptoms of insanity involved in her husband's devotion to such a chimera of the brain! When Brindley, the engineer, proposed to construct his aqueduct over the Irwell, another engineer was called in, to give his opinion on the project. The "practical" man exclaimed: "I have often heard of castles in the air, but never before was shown the place where any of them were to be erected!" Robert Stephenson's tubular bridge existed in his own conception before it spanned the Menai Straits; and, whilst he was engaged in the great undertaking, he was haunted by visions of it even in the night. James Watt was, in his early days, a dreamy sort of lad, although so remarkable for mechanical dexterity. He loved to wander by himself at night amidst the wooded pleasure-grounds surrounding an old mansion that overlooked Greenock. He himself has left on record how his great invention was, in its main feature, the result of a sudden thought. He tells how he was walking one day in Glasgow Green, thinking of his experiments and failures, when all of a sudden the idea of a separate condenser flashed upon his mind. Now, what does this sudden "flashing" mean? Does it not mean that his imagination had been busy, creating out of the materials of former experiments all kinds of combinations and arrangements that might possibly lead to the results he had in view, and that now at last it had pictured the one arrangement of materials which he recognized as satisfying the conditions of the problem? It is indeed true that only a man of mechanical genius like Watt could have lighted on such a conception; just as it was only a great astronomer like Newton who was likely to imagine the law of gravitation. Of course, it is only out of the brain of Jove that Minerva can spring full-armed! But imagination is imagination still, although its achievements vary according to the direction given to it, and the materials placed at its disposal. We may add that, when Smeaton saw Watt's first model working, he admitted the excellence of the contrivance, but predicted its failure, on the ground that it was too complicated, and that workmen were not to be found capable of manufacturing it, on any large scale, for general uses! Here, again, is the objection of the "practical man," who proves himself less practical, after all, than the man of more fertile imagination.

V. The Imagination also plays an important part in the *practical business of the world.*

Not that in the routine of book-keeping, or in the making of a chair or table, or in the overlooking of a steam-loom, there is necessarily involved any exercise of the representative faculty. A bricklayer may be an imaginative man, and his imagination may be at work even whilst his hands are busy; but the act itself of laying one brick upon another becomes a thing of habit. But, in all the higher business of the world—in all work which demands a vigorous intelligence—the imagination is more or less prominent. The manufacturer is often an inventor. To the barrister, the physician, and the preacher, the practical uses of imagination are neither few nor small. Think, too, of the enthusiasm with which soldiers will fight for some old flag which imagination has surrounded with a halo of glory. Look at Napoleon studying his map on the eve of conflict, and picturing all probable and possible contingencies; for it has been well remarked of him that "he never blundered into victory, but won his battles in his head, before he won them on the field." And Napoleon himself said, "The men of imagination rule the world." Let us, however, consider here, more especially, the business of the statesman and the business of the merchant.

Many of the greatest statesmen have also been great orators; and the highest efforts of oratory are impossible to an unimaginative mind. The chief business of the statesman, however, is not to speak well, but to aid in the task of legislation and government. Now a man on whom this duty devolves had need be quick in conceiving probable results and possible complications. To be a really good diplomatist, he must be able to imagine the position of those with whom he is in treaty or correspondence. If he is a political leader, he has his men to direct, and his battles to fight, and needs the inventive skill of a great general. It ought not to be forgotten that our present premier, who has for so many years led and "educated" the Conservative party, is the author of *Coningsby* and *Lothair*. If, again, a statesman is bent on initiating righteous and beneficent measures, he has need of that imaginative sympathy which, as we have already seen, is such a valuable handmaid to justice and benevolence. In one of his speeches, delivered at Rochdale, Mr. John Bright has told an impressive story of the origin of his agitation against the Corn Laws. "In the year 1841, I was at Leamington, when there fell upon me one of the heaviest blows that can visit any man. I found myself left there, with none living of my house but a motherless child. Mr. Cobden called upon me on the day after that event, so terrible to me and so prostrating. After some conversation, he said, 'Don't allow the grief, great as it is, to weigh you down too much. There are at this moment, in this country, wives and children who are dying of hunger—of hunger made by the law. If you will come along with me, we will never rest till we have got rid of the Corn Laws.' . . . I recollect, at that time, I took to myself something of prophecy from the lines of one of our poets. When that day shall come, I thought, then

'Shall misery's sons and daughters
   In their lowly dwellings sing;

> Bounteous as the Nile's dark waters,
> Undiscovered as their spring :
> We will scatter o'er the land
> Plenty with a secret hand !'"

Now, who does not see in all this the workings of the imagination ? It is not merely that the politician cheered his heart by the words of the poet—we refer more especially to the vividness with which these two men realized in thought the misery they deplored, and idealized the happy change their joint labours might achieve. It is also a striking fact that the most brilliant budget-speeches of our times have been delivered by the author of the best budgets. What places Mr. Gladstone in the foremost rank of English statesmen is precisely this blending, in his mind, of imagination with judgment. In his budget you see the artist as well as the financier. You see the workings of his imagination, not only in the boldness with which he constructs some new scheme, but also in his impatience to get rid even of some petty tax which mars his ideal. "There are some statesmen," said Edmund Burke, "who are mere pedlars." The author of *Homer and the Homeric Age* is not one of these. He knows the power of ideas, and does not lose sight of abstract principles even amid the dust of the political arena. No doubt the Palmerstonian type of statesmanship is greatly preferred by many "practical" Englishmen. They could understand Palmerston better ; there was nothing "heroic" about him. Be it so ; but if by "hero" is meant one who imagines a noble ideal and strives earnestly and wisely to realize it, then the greatest "practical" benefactors of our race have been none other than its heroic men.

When Burke said that "he knew statesmen who were pedlars," he added that "he knew merchants who acted in the spirit of statesmen." No doubt, in much of our ordinary buying and selling, even the exercise of mind which is involved is almost mechanical; and, certainly, there are many men who have been successful in business without any vigorous exercise of the imaginative faculty. But it is also true that, given a certain amount of industry, perseverance, and specific knowledge of his business, every merchant is a gainer by possessing, in addition to these, a healthy imagination. This will give him greater fertility of resource in seasons of emergency. It will also enable him to combine more readily the various considerations which ought to weigh for or against any project; and he will be less likely to overlook any conditions necessary to the success of his schemes. We have taken James Watt as a type of the inventor; we may take Boulton, the Boulton of Birmingham, as a type of the merchant. Boulton's biographer says of him: "He had a genius for business. His power of imagination was such as enabled him to look clearly along extensive lines of possible action in Europe, America, and the East. He was almost as full of speculation as Watt himself, as to the means of improving the steam-engine." Here the word "speculation" is used in a good sense. And, assuredly, in merchandise as in philosophy, there is wise as well as wild speculation. To speculate means, literally, to "look out from a watch-tower." It is not to our credit, therefore, that in business life the word should now be used most frequently to denote a species of gambling in which the dice—sometimes "loaded" too—are shares and bales! To look out from a watch-tower, and to draw lots blindfold, are surely very different actions. Many of our greatest merchants have been "speculators," in the true sense. They have been honest men, hazarding no money but their own ; they have been prudent men, running no wild, mad risks ; but they have also climbed their " watch-tower," and, looking abroad upon the fields of enterprise, have formed their conceptions of the opportunities open to them. And the imagination which plans many a business scheme is essentially the same faculty which is at work in the poet's mind ; just as the electricity which brings to-day's telegrams to the counting-house is the same, essentially, as the lightning which plays against the background of the lurid cloud.

Thus, then, we have shown abundant reason why the man of most practical temperament may well honour the imaginative faculty. And from what we have said it is simply an inference of common sense that the due culture of this faculty should form a prominent part of education. Let us not be over-anxious to tell our children only such stories as have a " moral " in them. *Cinderella* and *Jack the Giant-killer* perform no despicable function in the development of mind. And be not over-impatient with your boy if he is a little " dreamy " ; or he may perhaps become, by and by, more " matter-of-fact " than even you could wish. If you cannot appreciate poetry yourself, be thankful if your children do. And there is many a good healthful novel—it need not be realistic either— which you may be glad to see in their hands. No doubt the imagination may be excessively developed, or injuriously directed : the " abuses of the imagination " might furnish matter for a separate essay. But indeed many of the most useful forces in the world may, under certain conditions, become the most destructive; their power to injure is often the measure of their power to bless. Imagination is a mettlesome steed, which sometimes throws its rider; but let a steady judgment hold the reins, and an instructed skill direct the course, and the mettlesome steed may do most practical service. We are only pleading that imagination may have its fair share of culture. We are not shut up to choose between Don Quixote and Sancho Panza. In Mrs. Browning's *Aurora Leigh*, the statistician and the poet have both to confess at last that they had each been taking but a partial view of life. The actual ought to be wedded to the ideal. Judgment and Imagination are as the warp and woof of all the most enduring fabrics that are woven in the "loom of time."

VI. We close this paper with a brief glance at the uses subserved by the Imagination *in the distinctively Christian life*.

The Bible itself, which does so much to nourish that life, cannot be thoroughly appreciated without the exercise of this faculty. Our minds picture to themselves the scenes which its histories describe. We animate and comfort our hearts by the poetry of the sweet singers of Israel. The writings of the inspired prophets are rich with the utterances of a sanctified imagination. The words of metaphor and simile were by no means strange to the lips of Him who was "heard gladly" by the "common people." The Christian who is tempted to speak of poetry as mere unpractical dreaming had better open his Bible again at the Psalms, the parables, or the Apocalypse.

But a still more noticeable fact here is that faith itself involves a certain exercise of the imaginative faculty. In faith the mind holds up before itself that which is not present to the senses. " By faith Moses refused to be called the son of Pharaoh's daughter "; he had his inward visions of a nobler destiny. And when we exercise faith in Christ, we picture to our minds who and what kind of being He is to whom we commit our souls. For realities may be imaged to our thought as well as shadows. The Christian may often be sustained and cheered by visions which have their groundwork in the revelations and promises of God. Paul and Silas could sing together at midnight, with their backs bleeding from the lash and their feet fast in the stocks; for within the bare, black walls of their dungeon there was an inner chamber brightened by a " light that never was, on sea or land." And the Christian may also stimulate his endeavours after a holy life by keeping steadily before his mind the ideal of what he ought to be. Hawthorne's beautiful story of " The Great Stone Face " may almost be taken as an allegory. The loving contemplation of Christ makes us Christ-like. " Beholding as in a glass the glory of the Lord, we are changed into the same image from glory to glory."

The imagination further plays an important part in the awakening and sustaining of Christian activities. The church is called to a noble crusade against the sin and misery of the world; and such a crusade, whilst it needs to be directed by practical knowledge, needs also to be conducted in a lofty and chivalrous spirit.

"It takes a high-souled man
To move the masses even to a cleaner sty;

> It takes the ideal to blow a hair's-breadth off
> The dust of the actual."

There is too much of the counting-house atmosphere about our church life and our religious organizations. There are not a few who pay their pew-subscriptions in much the same spirit as they would buy a ticket for a season's concerts. The minister must be paid for entertaining them on Sunday; or the minister is regarded as a pew-filling power, whose value is to be estimated by the number of people whom he can attract to hear him speak. Oh for a breath of healthful imagination in some of our churches, that our "young men might see visions, and our old men dream dreams," and that our church worship, church relationships, and church duties might be looked at in the light of the Great Day! Imagination may sometimes also guide as well as stimulate us in our endeavours to promote the cause of Christ. By enabling us to understand better those whom we are seeking to bless, it may teach us when to be silent and when to speak, and how to speak most effectively. When Paul stands up in the synagogue of Pisidian Antioch, he looks at things with a Jew's eyes, and reasons with his audience out of their own scriptures. But when he stands on Mars' Hill, he delivers a very different address; his text is no longer Jewish history, but the Athenian altar with its vague inscription; he becomes in thought as much of a Greek as he can; he quotes "one of their own poets," and his speech breathes of the true philosopher as well as of the evangelist. This "being all things unto all men"—without compromising truth —is one of the noblest, as it is also one of the most useful, exercises of the imagination. Our Christian life may well be thankful for such a valuable handmaid here on earth.

And we may be sure that "the vision and the faculty divine" will also have to do with our life in God hereafter. If even our bodily life is to exist glorified in heaven, we can have little doubt that there also our mental powers—and this among them—will reach a higher stage of development. We shall not cease to be finite beings in the world to come; there, even as here, the eye will not be able to take in all. Surely there will be pictures to create, as well as scenes to behold, where the materials for such creation will be so much more beautiful and abundant. And thus the human imagination—with all its powers sanctified—may subserve the most practical uses for ever, in enhancing the joy of the redeemed who stand before the throne of God, and gaze upon the heavenly glories imaged in the Crystal Sea.

THE USES OF THE IMAGINATION IN THE CHRISTIAN MINISTRY.

[A Presidential Address delivered to the Manchester Congregational Board of Ministers, January 8th, 1883; subsequently utilized, in part, in addresses to students at Manchester and Rotherham; and also at an Ordination Charge, in June, 1891.]

THE IMAGINATION, in its widest sense, may be defined as "the image-making faculty of the human mind." It may be described as that power which the mind has of holding up before itself pictures of what we ourselves have seen or felt, and also of making new combinations of elements the most simple and familiar. This "representative faculty"—as Sir William Hamilton calls it—belongs naturally to every sound human mind. In discovery and invention, in science and statesmanship, and, indeed, in all the higher business of the world, it plays an important although often unsuspected part. I wish now to offer a few suggestions as to the value of this faculty in our own distinctive work. Many crude and new-fangled ideas are abroad as to the methods which the ministers of the gospel ought to adopt, in order to achieve success. Now, I believe that, in the faculty of imagination, all Christian ministers possess a "wonderful lamp," which may not only give us light in our work, but by the very rubbing of which, so to speak, we may summon the most practical and valuable assistance. And I think we shall do well to make fuller and wiser use of this power, and of the aids which it can bring us, instead of listening too readily to the hawker's cry of "New lamps for old ones!" Sometimes, verily, a *hawker's* cry—the cry of men who would test ministerial labour and success by the methods of the shop and the standards of the market.

Consider, then, first of all, how greatly the Christian minister may be helped in his work of PREACHING by a right use of the Imagination.

The Bible, which is our text-book, is largely a book of *History;* and our appreciation of the scripture-narrative depends, to a large extent, on the vividness with which we realize in our own minds the characters which it portrays, and the events which it describes. Those of us who have read Stanley's *Lectures on the Jewish Church* must feel that the special charm and value of that book is largely due to the remarkable power of historical imagination which was possessed by the author. And there can be no doubt that our own ability to make appropriate and practical use of the Bible narratives in our sermons will depend in no small degree on the manner in which we present to our thought the characters and scenes delineated. It has become a fashion with some to decry such books as Conybeare and Howson's *Life of St. Paul;* the critics complain of a superabundance of geographical, historical, and other collateral details. But surely all such books are valuable, in so far as they help us to realize the circumstances in which the men and women of the Bible lived and moved. Even such a book as Dr. Abbott's *Philochristus*—although it is a kind of romance—may be useful to us in bringing some aspects of the gospel story closer to our vision. No telescope is to be despised which enables us to see more clearly events that are centuries distant from us. On the other hand, the telescope is of no avail without the eye. Employing, then, all our knowledge of Bible times and Bible history, let us use our imagination as a *seeing*, rather than an allegorizing faculty. There has been more than enough of an artificial allegorizing of scripture story; and there has been not a little *abuse* of the imagination in this direction. I am convinced that, in dealing with the narratives of the Bible —including the narratives of the gospels—our chief power as preachers lies, not in quaint conceits and fanciful applications, but in bringing home to the hearts and consciences of our hearers those lessons which flow simply and directly from a vivid realization of the actual experiences portrayed in the history. Whatever else and more the Bible may be, it is at least a human book—a book written by men, about men, and for men; and it demands to be treated with *human-ness*. The men and women of scripture are not to be dangled by us as marionettes before the eyes of our hearers. Elijah is but one of many who were "of like passions with ourselves." Our own heart, conscience, and experience, utilized by our imagination, are the best interpreters of Bible history. "As in water face answereth to face, so the heart of man to man"; and even if we know Greek well—which is possible—and Hebrew better—which is perhaps more doubtful—we ought nevertheless, in this *deeper* sense, to "consult the original," by reading the Bible in the light of human nature.

Again, the Bible is largely a book of *Poetry;* and our power to rightly interpret and handle its imagery depends, in no small degree, on the extent to which we cultivate our imagination. Not only have we in the Bible the poetical books, distinctively so-called, we have also poetry embedded in its narratives; and the prophets were, all of them, more or less poets. Now, to treat Bible poetry as if it were prose is one of the commonest exegetical blunders. And yet, how shall a man enter fully into the spirit of the Psalms unless there be somewhat of the lyrical in his own nature? How shall he rightly expound or apply the language of the Book of Job without some appreciation of its dramatic form and spirit? How shall he intrepret the glowing predictions of the prophets if he comes to them as a mere chronicler or statistician, or even if he applies his fancy to them, as a man might try to read a telegram in cipher? How can a preacher make his hearers feel anything of the purpose and power of the Apocalypse, if he treats that magnificent allegory of the church's struggles and victory as if it were a chronological chart in hieroglyphics? The remarkable notions of the "Anglo-Israelites," and the Great Pyramid-mongers, and those gentlemen who take it upon themselves to fix the precise date of the end of the world, may seem at first sight to be due to a misuse of the imagination. But, in reality, they are due rather to a suppression of that faculty. The poetry of prophecy is treated as if it were mere prose. Its "figures"—both rhetorical and arithmetical—are taken literally, or at any rate in a literal spirit. The fancy may indeed be used; but it is used prosaically and technically, much as a land-surveyor may sometimes exercise his ingenuity. These modern prophecy-mongers, with their fanciful conceits, remind one of the artificial poets of whom Keats wrote—

> "with a puling infant's force,
> They sway'd about upon a rocking-horse,
> And thought it Pegasus!"

And in this region, even learning is no adequate substitute for a healthy imagination. A mere pedant may move ponderously about amid the poetry of the Bible, like an elephant in a flower-bed. The crushed thyme, indeed, cannot help giving forth some of its fragrance; but alas for "the rose of Sharon, and the lily of the valley!"

Again, the Bible is largely a book of *Sermons* and *Letters*. I have said that the prophets were more or less poets; but they were mainly preachers. They had an immediate message for the men of their own day. We cannot, therefore, rightly understand or apply their sermons unless we throw ourselves back in thought into the circumstances in which they were placed. If we wish to re-preach Isaiah's message in England let us try to take our hearers back in thought to the Jerusalem of his day. In this way we can strip the message of its mere accidental, local, and temporal elements, and bring our hearers face to face with that "word of the Lord" which "endureth for ever." By thus bringing our lamp of imagination to the writings of the prophets, we see more clearly the connection subsisting between the predictions which they uttered and the principles to which they testified; and we can better understand that blending of Israel's greatest hope with hopes as to the proximate future, which is one of the peculiar features of Messianic prophecy.

The same thing is true with regard to the epistles of the New Testament. If we would rightly expound and apply these epistles, we must endeavour to realize for ourselves—and to make our hearers realize—the circumstances in which they were written. It is not enough that the message which they contain is translated from the Greek into the English language; we must endeavour to translate it further into the language of present circumstance and need. And one of the best helps towards applying the abiding principles enshrined in these letters is to make our hearers feel how they were originally applied by the writers themselves. It is, perhaps, difficult to interest our modern congregations in the Judaizers of Galatia, the ascetic Gnostics of Colosse, the Antinomians of the Epistle of Jude, or the wavering Jewish believers for whom the letter to the Hebrews was written; but I believe that, by a vivid exercise of the representative faculty, the thing can be done.

This healthy use of the imagination, which enables us to read the utterances of Scripture in the light of their original spirit and setting, will also help to prevent us from making an unfair doctrinal use of isolated texts. The "letter" which "killeth" is often first of all killed! If the whole spirit of a passage is taken out of it, through its being violently torn from its surroundings, there is little wonder that the text thus murdered should sometimes have its revenge by taint-ing the theological atmosphere. Metaphors, too, with all the poetry taken out of them, are dangerous tools in the hands of some theologians. Certain doctrinal statements, for example, concerning the Atonement and concerning Future Retribution, have sprung out of this unimaginative treatment of Bible-imagery. We smile at the old idea that, inasmuch as Christ "gave His life a ransom" for sinners, He must have paid this ransom to the devil, as being the tyrant who had held men captive; but may not some of our more modern notions be founded on a similar abuse of metaphor? The proof-texts of systematic theology have sometimes been only too like the specimens in a botanist's portfolio—lifeless and dry, and perhaps also wrongly classified and labelled. Even the Westminster divines would occasionally have been none the worse for letting their imagination play about some of their proof-texts. Thus, they tell us that the "civil magistrate hath power to call church-synods, to be present at them, and to provide that whatever is transacted in them be according to the mind of God"; and one of the proofs of this statement is that *Herod the king* " gathered together all the chief priests and scribes, and demanded of them where *the Christ should be born!*" I do not say that we may not legitimately and profitably use a text as a mere motto of discourse on this or that subject. But I think that we ought to do this in full recognition of its primary reference and meaning, and that we ought always to beware of attempting to build on isolated passages of Scripture an argument or a doctrine which they are inadequate to support. Let us especially be on our guard against dealing with the metaphors and parables of Scripture as if they were scientific expressions of spiritual truth. There must always be points of *difference*, as well as of *resemblance*, between a picture and the reality which it portrays. An artist's delineation of an "interior" may be painted in admirable perspective; but we do not therefore attempt to walk into his canvas! Neither ought we to handle similes as if they were the realities, or attempt to construct a scientific theology on the basis of analogy and metaphor. All parable is a creature of the imagination, and by the imagination it ought to be interpreted.

I have thus spoken of the help which may be given us by the imaginative faculty towards the right interpretation, citation, and application of scripture. But there are two other uses of the imagination in our work of preaching to which I would now specially refer. One of these is the power which this faculty gives us of lighting up our sermons by vivid and appropriate illustrations. I do not mean that we should emulate Butler's *Hudibras*, who

" could not ope
His mouth, but out there flew a trope."

Nor do I mean that we should ransack a "Cyclopedia of Quotations" in order to interlard our discourses with poetry, or that we should regard the mere beauty of a simile or the mere *arrestive* power of an anecdote as a sufficient reason for introducing it into a sermon. I fear that our "illustrations" sometimes throw more light on our own lack of imagination than on the special subject we may have in hand. They are sometimes more akin to the gilder's frame than to the artist's picture. But we all recognize the power which there is in really appropriate parable, simile, and metaphor;

and the value of the imagination in this direction is sufficiently obvious.

I would rather, therefore, dwell here on the power which we may acquire over the hearts and consciences of our hearers, through a vivid realization of their actual or possible condition. Nervous preachers have sometimes been advised to look from the pulpit upon the heads of their audience as upon "so many blocks!" The recipe, although it seems to have had the sanction of Luther, is of very doubtful value. It is certain, at anyrate, that in the *preparation* of our sermons, it is desirable to picture to our thought the circumstances and needs of the living men and women to whom we have to speak. And our minds ought to be busy, not only about their circumstances as perchance actually known to ourselves, but also about their *possible* condition—their possible ignorance, their possible temptations, their possible griefs, misgivings, and scepticisms, and even their possible sins. Mr. Froude, describing the preaching of John Henry Newman at Oxford, says of him:—"Taking some scripture character as a text, he spoke to us about ourselves, our temptations, our experiences. He seemed to be addressing the most secret consciousness of each of us, as the eyes of a portrait appear to look at every person in a room." Now, although we may not hope to become preachers like Newman, yet I venture to think that we might acquire more of this incisive, searching power in our practical appeals, if, in our preparations for preaching, we would allow our imagination to play more freely about the characters, the thoughts, and the lives of our hearers. It is for lack of this sympathetic use of the imagination that our conduct of controversy is sometimes so unfair and ungenerous, and our sermons are sometimes also so much " up in the air." We fire at random instead of taking aim—taking aim, I mean, not at individuals (for such "personal preaching" is likely to be as unprofitable as it is offensive)—but taking aim at certain perplexities of thought, difficulties of belief, states of feeling, habits of conduct, and phases of experience. This is perhaps *the* most important use of the imagination in our work of preaching. Power of illustration, technically so-called, is a minor affair as compared with this. And, whenever we do thus vividly realize the actual and possible condition of our hearers, those illustrations with which we seek to throw light upon our theme will probably be all the more natural and appropriate; for we shall be more content with the homely holding of the candle, and less ambitious of shooting rockets into the sky.

Passing now from our preaching to our CONDUCT OF THE DEVOTIONAL SERVICES OF THE SANCTUARY, it becomes obvious that the peculiar exercise of the imagination on which I have just been dwelling, is, in this region also, of the highest value. It is often said to be one of the advantages of a liturgy, that it keeps a congregation from being at the mercy of this or that minister. And there can be no doubt that one of the chief dangers of our free prayer does lie in the direction thus indicated. In order that we may lead the devotions of others aright, more is needed than a devotional spirit in ourselves. It may, indeed, be true that the spontaneous utterance in prayer of our own present feelings and special yearnings may sometimes, through its very freshness and naturalness, be peculiarly helpful to others. The touch of individuality in a minister's prayer is sometimes a stimulus to the devotional spirit of his congregation. But it is not always so. Instead of leading the prayers of others, may we not sometimes be only dragging their thoughts at the wheels of our own passing mood? "Common Prayer" is, after all, prayer in which an assembly can *unite*. If we only pray —however sincerely—in the hearing of the people, and do not succeed in getting them to pray along with us, we certainly fail in this most important and difficult region of our work. To guard against such failure, let us resort to the healthy outlook which imagination can give us. Let us seek to picture to our thought the various feelings and conditions of those whose devotions we are called to lead. There may be in our congregation the young and the old, the glad and the sorrowful, the perplexed and the restful, the rich and the poor, the cultured and the ignorant, the bereaved and the united, the despairing and the thankful, and many of these must be in a different condition from that in which we ourselves happen to be at the hour of social worship. Let a minister, by an effort of the imagination, draw near to the throne of the One Father, as a brother amid a band of brethren, all linked together by community of need in diversity of experience, and this will tend to prevent the stimulative individuality of his prayers from passing into an exclusive self-absorption.

And now, as most of us are not only ministers of the gospel but also pastors of churches, I should like, further, to say a word as to the importance of letting the imagination play freely around THE PASTORAL RELATIONSHIP. I sometimes fear that in our

Congregational churches both ministers and people are losing, to some extent, their sense of the sacredness and beauty of this relationship. The average duration of the pastorate amongst us is becoming lamentably short, and one of the causes of this is, I suspect, the lack of that mutual affection which ought to exist between minister and people. The transfiguring power of the imagination is a great quickener of affection. And let us remember that transfiguration is not necessarily illusion. Our so-called "practical men" are often just the men who miss some of the truest and sweetest realities of life. And when a minister's "flock" becomes to *him* a mere Sunday audience, and a people's minister becomes to *them* a mere Sunday lecturer, one chief charm and value of the pastoral relation is gone. I am not here confounding "pastoral work" with so-called "pastoral visitation." I am speaking of a certain attitude of mind and soul. I am well aware that some of the best "pastoral" work may be done from *the pulpit*. What I am pleading for is that it be done with the *shepherd-heart*. And as for "visitation," a pastor may regret that he has not more time to give to it; but I utterly fail to see why he should despise it. Why should a man grudge the touch of simple human-ness that lies in the homely call and the kindly inquiry? It may not, perhaps, be worth calling "pastoral work"; it may not be worth calling "work" at all; but, if he does it out of the shepherd-heart, it may be a valuable help towards the spiritual success of his labour. The Great Teacher did not disdain to accept the invitation to the house of the Pharisee, or to invite Himself to the house of the publican, and the very Cross of Calvary itself owes not a little of its spiritual power to the human-hearted life that went before it.

I believe that one of the crying needs of our modern Congregationalism is a higher estimate of the Christian ministry as a *vocation*. I fear that there are some of our seat-holders who pay their pew-rent in much the same spirit as they might subscribe to a season's concerts. I fear that there are even some of them who regard a minister as a kind of pew-filling machine, and who, if he does not succeed in this special function, begin to think of giving him "three months' notice." Brethren, we did not devote ourselves to the work of the ministry in order to be regarded as hired Sunday-entertainers, or as the salaried managers of a joint-stock company, limited. Be it ours to make this low estimate of our ministry an impossibility. Be it ours to "magnify our office." But let us take care that we do really *magnify* it. If a pastor regards himself as the only important unit in the management of church affairs, and regards his deacons as simply so many ciphers who come after him to swell his magnitude, there is little wonder if by and bye the ciphers should come in front of him, decimal-fashion, and reduce his importance to that of a fractional quantity. Let us sometimes place ourselves by imagination in the diaconate, and ask ourselves whether *we* should be willing to remain in such an office, if we were expected to do nothing but register the decrees, and carry out the plans, and perhaps even the whims, of one absolute ruler. Such an exercise of the imagination would perhaps help to give us the *tact* which, as pastors, we need, not the diplomatic tact of manœuvre and finesse, but the simple tact which disarms suspicion and distrust, because it springs from true Christian courtesy, and from a thorough respect for man as man.

Surely the true way to magnify the pastoral office is to give to it that touch of unworldliness and dignity which comes of cherishing high aims and unselfish affections. If we would teach *our* people what Christian pastorship means, we must love them. We must try to look at them as through the eyes of the "Great Shepherd of the sheep." Here, to idealize is to realize. We cannot see our work *as it really is*, unless we behold it in the eternal light. Our people must be to us, not mere occupiers of pews who appreciate *our* sermons, and minister to *our* success, but immortal souls, whose value we appreciate, and to whom we are called to minister. And I think it might be a good thing for all of us who preach the gospel if we would sometimes picture in imagination that coming day when the grand question for us will be, not whether we have built up a reputation, or "built up a congregation," but whether we have really tried to arouse and convert, to console and strengthen, to instruct and build up *souls*, by speaking to them the word of divine truth out of the fulness of a loving human heart.

BROWNING'S "PIPPA PASSES."

[Reprinted from *The Christian Leader*, July 23rd, 1891.]

ONE of the most striking poems written by Robert Browning is the drama which he has named *Pippa Passes*. Pippa is a young girl who works at the silk mills in Asolo, a little town not far from Venice. It is New Year's Day—her one holiday in the whole year; and she rises early with the hope that it will be a bright and happy day for her. She considers who are likely to be the four happiest persons in Asolo that day; and she resolves that in the morning, at noon, in the evening, and at night, she will, in turn, fancy herself to be each of these four. She will thus enjoy her New Year's Day to the full. Not that she envies those who are in happier circumstances than her own; for she believes that she is doubtless " as dear to God" as they are; and her New Year's hymn tells her that " all service ranks the same with God." But she will, for one day, indulge in the pleasures of Fancy, and imagine herself to be in the positions of " the happiest four in Asolo." And so, in the course of the day, she passes, in turn, the four houses where these four persons are; and, as she passes each of them, she sings a song. Hence the poem is called *Pippa Passes*.

First of all, in the morning, she passes the mansion of her employer—the old man who owns the silk mills. She fancies herself to be the young wife of this old man—living in wealth and luxury. She knows the gossip of the town—that this young wife has a lover; but little does she dream of the terrible tragedy which has just been enacted within that mansion. The wife's lover has murdered the old man, in order to get him out of the way; and now the guilty pair are trying hard to drown all remorse for the crime in the passionate utterance of their mutual love. Just then Pippa passes outside; and, as she passes, she sings her song:—

> "The year's at the spring
> And day's at the morn;
> Morning's at seven;
> The hill-side's dew-pearled;
> The lark's on the wing;
> The snail's on the thorn;
> God's in His heaven—
> All's right with the world!"

The guilty pair hear these words. The man cannot bear them. The contrast between the foul crime which he has just committed and this happy song sung in the fresh morning air by the simple-hearted girl, rouses all his better nature. The words, "God's in His heaven," keep ringing in the man's ears. The spell is broken. His eyes are opened to see the enormity of his crime. "That little peasant's voice," he says, "has righted all again." He turns away with loathing from the woman who has lured him to the deed of murder. He cannot bear the sight of her. He denounces and renounces her, and then kills himself through the remorse that has taken full possession of his conscience. Meanwhile Pippa has passed on, all unconscious of what has been going on within the house, and of what her singing has done.

Then again, at noon, she passes the house of an artist, and fancies herself to be the young and beautiful bride whom the artist has that day married. But, although Pippa knows nothing of the actual facts of the case, it turns out that the artist has been tricked into this marriage, through forged letters, by a rival artist who hates him. Now that he has brought home his bride, he discovers that she is simply an ordinary girl in humble life—very different from the ideal maiden whom the forged letters had presented to his imagination. He resolves to give her all that he has and leave her. But, just as he is forming this resolution, Pippa's voice is heard outside, singing a peasant's song about a page who loved a queen. This song, coming at the critical moment, alters the artist's resolve. Why should *he* not stoop where he expected to worship? This young bride, whom he has just married, really loves him; she has been simply a tool in the hands of others; and so he makes up his mind not to leave her, but to take her away with him to some distant island, and make her happy.

Then again, at evening, Pippa passes the house where a young man and his mother, who love each other dearly, are known to be talking together. Pippa, who is herself an orphan, fancies how delightful it must be to enjoy the tenderness of a mother's love. The young man is an Italian patriot, and has pledged himself to kill the Austrian despot. The Austrian police, unknown to him, are at this moment watching his movements; and, if he stays another night in the town, they will arrest him. His mother is seeking to keep him with her and to dissuade him from his purpose of assassination. He is almost beginning to waver under the influence of her pleading; but, just then, Pippa's voice is heard outside, singing a song about a good king who "lived long ago." The song reminds him, by contrast, of the tyranny under which his beloved Italy is groaning; his patriotic spirit is roused; and he departs, that very evening, on his mission. He has no idea of the immediate danger which he thus escapes: and Pippa passes on, all unconscious again of what her song has done.

Finally, Pippa passes, at night, the house where the bishop is visiting. It is the house of his dead brother; and he has come to look into that brother's affairs. Pippa thinks it must be best of all to be that holy man, living constantly in the light of God's love, and with the peace of God resting within his heart! As she approaches the house, the bishop is engaged in conversation with the steward of his dead brother. This steward is a bad man, and has done some wicked deeds for his late master. Amongst other things, he had, years before, put out of the way his master's niece—an infant whose life stood between his master and the inheritance of an elder brother's estate. The bishop, who has been secretly investigating these matters, and who supposes that this infant had been murdered, and that he himself is now heir to the estate, is determined to punish the wicked steward for his crimes. He tells him so. The steward then informs the bishop that his niece (who is none other than Pippa herself) was not murdered, but still lives, and that therefore she now stands in the way of the bishop's inheritance of the estate; but he offers to plot the girl's ruin, and get her out of the way, if only the bishop will let him leave the country with the ill-gotten gains of his past iniquity. For a moment it almost seems as if the bishop were tempted to listen to the villain's offer; but, just then, Pippa's voice is heard outside, singing of God's care for young souls. The bishop is roused; he sees how he stands on the verge of dallying with a terrible temptation; and, in his strong revulsion of feeling, he at once summons his servants, and orders them to arrest the steward on the spot. And now, all unconscious once more of what she has done, Pippa passes on and goes to her own humble dwelling. There, before retiring to sleep, she reviews her holiday: and she wonders whether it is possible that she should ever come "near" to any of those four persons whom she has fancied herself to be—come near to them, so as really to "touch" or "move" them, or influence their lives even in " some slight way ! "

Such is the story of this dramatic poem. It is a poem which shows more genius even in its idea and plan than in its execution: for there can be little doubt that, as a work of art, it would have been more effective if the story had been more clearly told, and especially if the songs sung by Pippa had been of a simpler and more popular character. The poet himself seems to have been conscious of a certain failure to realize his own conception; for, in his inscription of the drama to his friend, Mr. Sergeant Talfourd, he uses the significant words, " I dedicate *my best intentions* in this poem." The poem may be regarded as a kind of parable, illustrative of the fact that humble and childlike souls may often, without suspecting it, touch and influence the lives of others for good. Sometimes even bad men feel in their consciences the power of simple goodness. Sometimes, also, those who are wavering at a critical moment of temptation may be checked and turned aside from iniquity by some casual intercourse with an honest and guileless soul. Simplicity and unworldliness are spiritual forces as mighty as they are subtle. They generate an atmosphere which it does men good to breathe. Even Christian people are apt, in seeking to promote the kingdom of goodness, to lean too much on material resources— to assign far too much importance to earthly wealth and to ecclesiastical position and strategy. But it is character, in the long run, that tells. When a man's "heart is pure," he "has the strength of ten." When a woman is unselfish and unworldly—sweetly and simply and truly good—her influence is as a spiritual magnetism, drawing others towards goodness. To the mind of Christ the babe was a natural emblem of what He wished His disciples to be in spiritual character; and to those who are babes in spirit God gives power as against "His adversaries." Let us seek, therefore, to cultivate the childlike heart.

Let us also seek to keep our own souls open to the influences of childhood and of the childlike. It is not only through Bible and worship and sermon and sacrament that God works upon our hearts: He has also other and less direct methods of appealing to us. The human atmosphere in which we live is laden with divine and subtle influences which are seeking to penetrate us at every pore of our spiritual being. Let us never shut our hearts against any of these indirect appeals whereby God would move us to a higher life. Whatever tends to crush the evil lurking within us— whatever rebukes our worldliness—whatever tends to waken better thoughts and holier desires and purer affections—let us welcome as the very breath of heaven! Let us open our hearts to the influences of childhood, and to the lyric melodies of purity and unselfishness. "Out of the mouth of babes has God established strength": and we are none of us so strong in our conflict with sin that we can afford to despise any passing influences that may help us to "still the enemy and the avenger."

VASHTI.

[Reprinted from *The Manchester, Salford, and District Congregational Magazine*, July, 1883.]

THE one act of Vashti which is recorded in the Book of Esther—her refusal to appear before the king's guests, at the king's commandment—would be quite sufficient to give us the key to her character, if only we had been definitely informed as to the motive of her conduct. But this is just what we are not told. One thing, however, is clear; she must have been a woman of great courage. When we think how the women of an Oriental harem are treated as the vassals and toys of their husbands, we may well wonder at the daring self-assertion manifested by Vashti on this occasion of the royal banquet. She knew the man with whom she had to deal; she knew his passionate temper and revengeful cruelty; she knew that to disobey him thus, before his nobles, would be most mortifying to his pride; and yet she disobeyed him. Perhaps, indeed, she over-estimated her own influence over him; and knowing also his weakness, imagined that she would be able to manage him, after his wrath had spent itself. But, however this may be, she could not have thus defied the despot, unless she had been a woman of high spirit and unusual courage.

Whether, however, her tact was equal to her bravery, whether she was as gracious as she was high-spirited, and whether she had sufficient justification for her conduct, are points which are more open to question. It is often taken for granted that for Vashti to have appeared, under any circumstances, in the presence of these nobles and princes with her face unveiled, would have been an utter violation of the customs of her country, and therefore of the modesty of her sex. Even Josephus seems to have taken this view of the matter; for, with reference to this very incident, he speaks of the "laws of the Persians" as "forbidding their wives to be seen by strangers." Now, if this could be proved, if it could be shown that Ahasuerus was attempting to magnify his royal authority by placing his mere whim above those laws of modesty which were recognized by the whole community, we might well pay our tribute of unqualified admiration to the woman who had the courage to disobey the despot. But, on closer investigation, it does not appear that this was the case. It seems, indeed, that in modern Persia it is regarded as a violation of decorum for a wife to be seen, with unveiled face, by any man except her own husband. But this does not appear to have been the case among the ancient Persians. Doubtless, even then, their women were kept in a certain seclusion; we read of Vashti as giving a separate banquet to the women in the palace. But we read also of Haman as being present at a banquet which Esther had prepared for him and for the king—present, moreover, at her express wish and invitation. Haman, too, in boasting of this, says, "Yea, Esther the queen did let no man come in with the king unto the banquet that she had prepared but myself": from which it seems that he would not have regarded it as at all surprising if other men had also been invited. This, of itself, is enough to show that the seclusion of women in Persia was not then so rigid as has been often supposed. Then, again, Herodotus—writing about half a century after the death of Xerxes (who is now usually identified with Ahasuerus)—tells how certain Persian ambassadors, having come to Amyntas, the king of Macedonia, to demand his submission to Darius, were entertained by Amyntas at a splendid banquet. He tells also how, when they began to drink, one of the Persians thus addressed Amyntas:—"It is a custom with us Persians, when we make a great feast, to introduce our . . . . wedded wives, that they may sit beside us. Since, then, you have received us so hospitably, follow this our custom." Amyntas informed them that the Macedonian manners were very different, that with them it was the custom to keep the women separate from the men; but that, as the Persians were now his "masters," he would grant what they had requested. It does not appear, therefore, to have been considered an unbecoming thing in ancient Persia for women to appear in public, in the company of men. And this seems to be further confirmed by the attitude of the counsellors of Ahasuerus, when he asked them what ought to be done to Vashti "according to law." It is not, indeed, strange that these courtiers should have fallen in with the angry mood of the king by counselling the divorce of Vashti.

But, had Ahasuerus been demanding what was contrary to the universally recognized code of propriety, they would probably have condemned Vashti on the ground that the will of the king was above all law and custom, that *he* occupied an altogether exceptional position and had a right to demand an exceptional obedience. This, however, is not the ground on which they gave their decision. They say that the queen has set a bad example to *all* the wives of the empire, in deliberately disobeying her husband. They thus seem to imply that the king had asked nothing but what any other husband in Persia would have had a right to ask. It is surely improbable that even the courtiers of the despot would have advised the issuing of a decree against Vashti on this *common* ground of wifely disobedience, if they had been thereby risking a revolution in the social manners of the country. On these various grounds, we may conclude that the appearance of Vashti in a public assembly, at the wish of her husband, would not, considered in itself, have been any violation of the then recognized code of Persian decorum.

When, however, we proceed to inquire what were the motives of her refusal, we are left to conjecture. Possibly the clue to her conduct lies in the fact that, when the king sent for her, he was "merry with wine." Naturally enough she might shrink from appearing before a company of revellers. Plutarch tells us that it was a custom with the kings of Persia to have their queens seated beside them at their meals and banquets, but that, when they wished to riot and drink, they sent the queens away, and summoned the wives of inferior rank. Perhaps, therefore, Vashti regarded it as an indignity to be sent for at all, at such a stage of the banquet. On the other hand, the circumstances were peculiar. This was a state-banquet, and Vashti was asked to come in royal apparel, with "the crown royal" upon her head. Her queenly position, therefore, could not well have been compromised, nor would there seem to have been much danger of insult. But perhaps Vashti was offended because of the motive which had induced the king to send for her. He wished to show her face to the princes and nobles; and to be exhibited thus, merely as one of the beautiful treasures of the king, might well affront her sense of dignity. Or again, she may perhaps have resented the fact that the king sent the chamberlains to command her attendance, instead of himself doing her the honour of personally introducing her to this state-banquet. These are some of the conjectures that suggest themselves; and according as we might adopt one or other of them, our view of Vashti's character would of course be modified. In the absence of fuller information, we must be content to leave the question undecided. But certainly there does not seem to be sufficient evidence to warrant us in glorifying Vashti as a martyr in the cause of womanly modesty. Had her disobedience been prompted by a sensitive shrinking from the gaze of an excited assembly, it is doubtful whether the counsellors would have spoken of her conduct as a "despising" of her husband. Racine, in his drama of "Esther," speaks of "the haughty Vashti."; and it is quite possible that her act may have been inspired by an imperious pride rather than a modest dignity. We may well indeed sympathize with any woman who occupied the position of wife to a capricious, unreasonable, and selfish tyrant like Ahasuerus; she must often have had a "hard time of it"; and it may be that, on this occasion, she was placed in circumstances of peculiar difficulty. Nevertheless it is conceivable that a woman of greater tact and graciousness might have found her way out of the difficulty, without publicly humiliating her husband before the grandees of his kingdom. It is conceivable that she might even have consented to gratify this wish or whim of the king, and yet have done it in such a manner as to show that, on her part, there was no violation of modesty or dignity.

Without, however, pronouncing any definite judgment as to the conduct of Vashti, it may be remarked that there is always more or less danger of a high-spirited self-respect passing into pride, and losing influence through want of tact, forbearance, and meekness. To "stand on one's dignity," as it is called, is not always the most graceful of attitudes. True meekness, although opposed to pride, is quite compatible with self-respect; but meekness is a virtue which is still generally under-estimated. Then, again, the simple desire to please others—when we can do so without degrading ourselves or injuring them—is one of the most charming features of character. And the magnanimous and human-hearted forbearance which can make allowance for the weaknesses of others, and can deal with these weaknesses in such a way as to dissolve instead of crystallizing them, is an excellence of no mean order and potency. Yet it is precisely here that noble souls are often deficient. Their own ideal of life is so high that they are apt sometimes to treat the sins and faults of others with a hardness which is neither human nor divine. Their sense of self-respect is so keen that, in their revulsion from what is unworthy or insincere, they needlessly offend others, and lessen their own influence. Shakespeare's "Cordelia," for instance, is so disgusted with the hypocrisy of her sisters, and so impatient of her old father's foibles, that she needlessly courts martyrdom, and speaks with a dignified coldness which does not at all represent the depth of her filial affection.

> "I love your majesty
> According to my bond; nor more nor less.
> . . . .
> Sure, I shall never marry, like my sisters,
> To love my father all!"

This was certainly the language of a noble scorn—of a soul that would not stoop to purchase favour by insincerities; but it was not the wisest and most gracious way of dealing with the weakness of her fond and foolish father. It only irritated him into a childish rage, and really gave him a mistaken notion of the actual condition of her feeling towards him.

It is thus that the very nobleness of a woman's nature often places her in a difficult position, where, her moral instincts being offended, her self-respect is in danger of passing into pride, and of lessening the influence which meekness and patience might increase. The gospel of Christ has banished polygamy from Christendom, and protests against those vices which are the roots and fruits of the Oriental harem. The New Testament proclaims the spiritual equality of the sexes in the sight of God: in Christ Jesus there is "neither male nor female." But the New Testament also guards against the misunderstanding and perversion of this doctrine. Whilst abolishing the serfdom of the wife, it maintains the "headship" of the husband. It protests against the revolutionary spirit which would subvert the natural relations of the sexes, and abolish those finer shades of character which distinguish the feminine from the masculine type of virtue. It presents us with an ideal of marriage in which the authority of the husband is held in solution by the chivalrous tenderness of a protecting love, and the submission of the wife is elevated into an expression of reverence, trust, and modesty. It will be difficult even for modern progress to surpass this ideal, grounded as it is in the very constitution of human nature, and glorified by the genius of the gospel. We have not yet ceased to despise "effeminacy"; we have not yet begun to admire the "virago." It is indeed a sad spectacle to see a husband playing the tyrant over his wife, and taking advantage of her weakness, or her meekness, to treat her as a cipher or a slave. There is one spectacle, however, which is perhaps sadder still—to see a wife tyrannizing over her husband, ignoring his wishes and defying his authority, exposing his faults and weaknesses, and openly humiliating him in the presence of his guests and companions.

But what is a Christian woman to do, when she is married to a tyrannical, sottish, foolish, or ungodly husband? Alas! what? It is one of the hardest problems in Christian ethics, and in practical Christian behaviour. It was a problem which met the apostles of Christ on the very threshold of the church's history. Often it happened that the wife became a Christian, whilst the husband remained an unbeliever. What was the wife to do? The apostles could only answer in general terms, laying special emphasis on the spirit she was to cultivate and manifest. She was, of course, to do nothing, in deference to her husband, which would violate the dictates of her own conscience. But, within this limit, she was to show all possible patience and meekness. She was counselled not to leave her husband, unless in extreme cases. She was reminded that she might perhaps be able, under God, to save him by her influence. But, oh! it is hard work—this struggling after the Christian ideal of marriage-duty from only one side of the relationship. There is many a poor wife who would be only too glad to "reverence her husband"; but how is she to reverence a tyrant or a sot? How is she to yield herself to the guidance and counsel of a man who is constantly revealing his folly or his worldliness? Well, one thing at least—if she is an Englishwoman—she can do. She can remember that she married of her own free will, and that duty does not cease to be duty merely because it becomes difficult. And she can remember also that, if her husband has sadly changed, Christ is still the same, and that her duty to Christ remains the same as ever—to govern her temper in presence of provocation, to cherish the spirit of forbearance and forgiveness, and to prevent her self-respect from passing into pride. But ah! it is hard, uphill work: and there is many a maiden who might save herself from the struggle and the misery, if only she would resolve to marry no man whom she cannot respect and love, and whose character and principles she cannot thoroughly trust.

STOICISM.

[Written November, 1877; revised September, 1885.]

"I have learned in whatsoever state I am, therein to be content" (αὐτάρκης).—Philippians iv. 11.

WE have here an instance of that Baptism of Language, as we may call it, which naturally follows in the wake of Christianity. The word translated "content" means literally "self-sufficient" or "self-sufficing," and it was a favourite word with the old Stoic philosophers. According to the teaching of the Stoics, the "wise man" was he who was independent of external circumstances, who was indifferent to pleasure and pain, who was above being moved by things over which he had no control, who, amid all events prosperous or adverse, kept himself perfectly calm, and who in every emergency was "sufficient for himself." The man who set his heart on anything outside of himself was a slave; he was at the mercy of the varying accidents of life. But the man who had mastered his own desires, who had thoroughly conquered his own nature, and who found his satisfaction within himself,—this man was free and lord of all things. "It is shameful," said the Stoic Seneca, who was himself a rich man, "it is shameful to depend for a happy life on silver and gold. Apply thyself rather to the true riches." And the Stoic Epictetus, who was himself a slave, represents some one as asking, " How is it possible, if I have nothing, if I am naked, homeless, foul, without a slave, without a country, to spend my life in happy calm ? " And Epictetus replies with a lofty dignity—" Lo ! God has sent *me* to show you in fact *how* it is possible. See, *I* have no country, no home, no wealth, no slaves, no bed, no wife, no children, nothing but the sky, and the earth, and one sorry cloak, and what is lacking to *me ?* "

There was indeed a noble element in this old Stoic philosophy. At a time when the masses of men were sunk in selfish gratification, when the philosophy of thousands might have been summed up in the maxim of a degenerate Epicureanism, " Let us eat and drink, for to-morrow we die ! " it *was* something to find men declaring that the true object of human life was not wealth, or fame, or pleasure, but to " live according to nature," to submit without cringing to the inevitable, to have a mind independent of the mere accidents of life, and capable of meeting all events with a self-sustained serenity. There was at least in all this a protest in favour of the inherent dignity of the human soul. There was something grand in a man saying to himself, " I refuse to be made miserable with envy and discontent ; I will not be dependent on the gratification which comes from things outside of myself ; I have a power of will within me which makes me lord of myself and of my circumstances ; I can shape my thoughts ; I can crush my desires ; I can form my own estimate of things ; I can gird myself to endurance ; I can maintain the calm of my spirit; I may be in poverty, or disease, or pain, and I may not be able to obtain deliverance from these things, but one thing I *can* do—I can cease to wish for deliverance. I can be a wise man, and, without murmuring or whining, can bear the part allotted to me in the great scheme of universal nature."

Now, the Apostle Paul was doubtless familiar with this ideal of Stoicism. Seneca lived at the same time as Paul. Tarsus, where Paul was born, was a great centre of philosophy, and the home of several well-known Stoic teachers. The apostle's celebrated speech on Mars' Hill at Athens shows that he must have known something of Greek philosophy; and the words, "For we are also his offspring," on which Paul laid so much stress, are a quotation from Stoic poetry. And we can readily conceive that the nobler elements of this Stoic school would find an echo in the brave spirit of the apostle. We can see, too, that the man who began life as a Pharisee of "the straitest sect," accustomed to self-denial and familiar with self-complacency, and who afterwards cast in his lot with the persecuted Nazarenes, and found in his new faith an inward compensation for all outward hardship, was in a position to estimate aright the Stoic ideal of "the wise man" "sufficient for himself." The nobler side of this ideal would appeal to Paul's bravery and unworldliness, whilst his own experience would give him a keener insight into its dangers and its weakness. No doubt he felt that what was good and true in Stoicism could easily be taken up into the gospel; or, to speak more correctly, was already included in the Christian doctrine and the Christian ideal. And so here, writing from his prison-lodging, in that very city of Rome which was the home of Seneca, Paul does not hesitate to use the favourite word of the Stoics, "I have learned, in whatsoever state I am, to be *sufficient for myself.*" But, even as he adopts the word, he baptizes it into the name of Christ; he lifts it into a higher atmosphere; he explains the sense in which he *is* "self-sufficient" —" I can do all things in him who strengtheneth me." "*In him who strengtheneth me*"; here is the idea which Seneca would have spurned. The Stoic did not need strengthening from without; in and of himself he was strong.

Now, precisely here lay the radical weakness of Stoicism, the resolving of all wise character and life into strength of will. It would not, indeed, be true to say that this philosophy was a stranger to religion and to religious motive. Many allusions to "God," or to "the gods," are to be found in the writings of the Stoics. Thus Seneca says, "No man is good without God," and he speaks of men as the children of God. And again he says: "It is best to endure what you cannot mend, and without murmuring to attend upon God, by whose ordering all things come to pass." Epictetus even calls upon men to join him in singing hymns of praise to God. He exhorts men to act worthily of their noble birth as the offspring of God. And, in language which might well shame many of us who call ourselves Christians, this poor heathen, who was both a slave and a cripple, says: "Dare to look up to God and say, Use me henceforth whereunto Thou wilt; I consent unto Thee; I am thine. I shrink from nothing that seemeth good to Thee. Lead me where Thou wilt, clothe me with what garments Thou wilt. Wouldst Thou that

I should be in office or out of office, should live at home or in exile, should be rich or poor? I will defend Thee for all these things before men!" Surely the Spirit of God was at work in the soul that could feel like this! May we not even say that the Unseen Christ was "strengthening" the heart of this poor slave, although he himself would have repudiated the idea that he needed any such help. There is surely, in such language, the *germ* of a religious faith, which, had it only been fully developed, might have burst through and shed the hard husk of Stoical self-sufficiency, and blossomed into the self-sufficiency of the Christian apostle.

But the fact is that, in the writings of the Stoics, there are many contradictions, many things which are out of harmony with the fundamental principles of their philosophy. We must judge of Stoicism by its central spirit, its general tone, its natural fruits. The great aim of the Stoic was to secure calmness and freedom by sheer force of will. He gloried in his strong will, which enabled him to crush his own emotions, to trample upon his own desires, and thus to make himself indifferent to all pleasure or pain. Thus his very piety tended to increase his pride. If the fact that God was ordering all things helped him to be calm, still he found his satisfaction not so much in the thought of God's wisdom and goodness as in the thought of his own calmness. He became as a little god to himself. He even ventured to say that the wise man was equal to God in goodness. The Stoic was in many respects a philosophical Pharisee, and, like all Pharisees, he became more or less inhuman. He professed to "live according to nature," but he violated *his own* nature in the process. His determination not to care about either pleasure or pain was itself unnatural. His endeavour to reach perfect calmness by sheer force of will led him to kill his natural affections. He refused to be pitiful, and he regarded it as a mark of weakness to grieve over the death of a friend. Penitence for his own sins, or indignation at the vices of others would have been too disturbing an emotion. He sought also to root up his natural desires, lest he should be made unhappy through their not being gratified. Thus, in order to prevent his nature from being swept and tossed by storms, he made it narrower and shallower. That he might be enough *for* himself, he made himself smaller, whilst at the same time he became, in his own estimation, larger and grander. Thus the self-sufficiency of the Stoic made him proud, self-centred, hard, inhuman, with his power of will developed at the expense of all the rest of his nature. And we need scarcely wonder when we hear that some of the most eminent of the Stoics died by suicide, overcoming by strength of will the instinct that clings to life, and thus securing for themselves by their own hand the impassive calm of death!

How different from all this is the "self-sufficiency" of Paul the Christian apostle! He, too, regarded it as an unworthy thing that a man should be the mere creature of circumstance. He, too, regarded it as a most desirable thing that the human soul should have an inward peace and satisfaction not dependent on mere outward things. He, too, saw the grandeur of courage and of patient endurance. He, too, felt that a child of God ought to have within himself that which could sustain him amid difficulty and trial. He, too, recognized the fact that a man might be made nobler and stronger by the drill and discipline of life. Paul, in short, felt that the Christian might reach that inward freedom and true peace and noble self-control which fascinated the mind of the earnest Stoic. But how did Paul propose to reach this ideal? how did he himself, in point of fact, make such progress towards reaching it? Not by the way of *pride*, but by the way of *faith*. Not by throwing himself back simply on himself, but by throwing himself upon God. He became a freeman by becoming the willing "slave" of Jesus Christ. His self-reliance sprang from his reliance upon a Higher Power—" our sufficiency is of God." He had a strong will, but it was not made strong at the expense of his conscience or his heart. He was not afraid of noble emotions. He was not ashamed to be pitiful and tender: he did not imagine that a holy anger was inconsistent with true wisdom. "Who is weak, and I am not weak? who is offended, and I burn not?" His epistle shows how his heart went out in love towards his friends in Philippi. He did not "make a desert" in his nature, and "call it peace"! He did not seek to root up his natural affections or desires in order to secure an unnatural calm. Here is his recipe for the true peace—" In nothing be anxious; but in everything by prayer and supplication with thanksgiving let your requests be made known unto God. And the peace of God, which passeth all understanding, shall guard your hearts and your thoughts in Christ Jesus." Not by crushing his desires, but by laying them in prayer before a wise and loving Father, did Paul find rest from anxious care. Nor did he make light of human sympathy.

"Do thy diligence to come shortly unto me," he writes to Timothy from his lonely prison. And we can see from his epistle how his heart responds to the sympathy of his Philippian friends. Neither did Paul cultivate indifference to pleasure and pain, or despise the ordinary comforts of life. From his prison he sent for his "cloke, and books, and parchments." Earnestly he besought that his "thorn in the flesh" might be taken from him. To King Agrippa he said, "I would to God, that not only thou, but also all that hear me this day, were both almost, and altogether such as I am, *except these bonds.*" True, he learnt to "glory in tribulation" to "take pleasure in infirmities"; but this was not because he was insensible to the pain they brought, but because he felt that good came out of tribulation, that Christ was perfecting strength in weakness, that "all things work together for good to them that love God." What the wisdom and goodness of God withheld from him he was content to be without. He subjected his body also to a watchful self-discipline; but he was the resolute opponent of an inhuman asceticism. Thus the "self-sufficiency" of the apostle was not inconsistent with natural desire, or humility, or penitence, or tenderness, or sorrow, it was simply a noble and manly independence springing from his dependence upon God, a lofty freedom from the tyranny of circumstance, born of his faith in God, and his union with Christ, and his recognition of the true wealth and the true aims of an immortal nature. "In whatsoever state" he was, Paul was "self-sufficing," simply because God was sufficient for him, and Christ was with him and in him, "strengthening" him both to do and to bear.

And *this* is the only true " self-sufficiency " for any human creature. Do not let us dream that Stoicism is dead. In all ages there have been men who have taken refuge in it amid the ills of life. They may have known nothing of philosophy, but practically they have been Stoics. The hard, proud, unsympathetic, and perhaps cynical, spirit of surly independence is with us still to-day. And, more than that, there is now rising in England a school which is in some points akin to the old Stoicism. Men stand up and tell us that they can do without any leaning on a personal God, or any hope of immortality, that prayer is absurd and repentance useless, that a wise man frees himself from all such superstitions, and can front the universe of mystery in the strength of his own reason and his own will. Well, it looks all very grand, and such an attitude has its fascinations. It is no doubt a grander thing for a man to stand up and defy an avalanche, than for a man to flee at "the sound of a shaken leaf"; but whether it is much "wiser" is another question. Is it not a far wiser thing to recognize and confess the limitations, needs, and cravings of our own nature? The simple fact is, that man is not a god. He comes into the world a dependent creature, and a dependent creature he remains. In a thousand ways he must go *out of himself* for the satisfaction of his nature! He is not even able to keep himself alive, far less to meet the higher needs of his being. It is a truly grander, as well as wiser, thing to face the naked facts of our own nature. Stoicism fails because it is not true to nature and to fact. The gospel of Christ comes to us, *just as we are*, with a message that meets our *needs*. It speaks to us as dependent creatures;

it recognizes our natural cravings; it speaks to our hearts and to our consciences, as well as to our wills; it comes to us as sinners needing forgiveness; it tells us of Christ the Saviour; it tells of God, the Perfect Father; it points to a glorious heaven; it bids us live with the humility and dignity, the trust and patience, the simple sincerity and the high aims that become children of God. To believe this gospel and to live in the light of it, to recognize our own weakness and to cling to God and Christ for strength, *this* is the way to the only independence which becomes a dependent creature, and to that living and blessed peace which is neither the impassive calm of torpor, nor the haughty serenity of pride.

CYNICISM.

[Reprinted from *The Christian World Pulpit*, December 6, 1876.]

THE Cynics were a sect of philosophers among the Greeks, founded by Antisthenes, who, on account of his snappish, snarling propensities, was frequently called " The Dog "; and probably enough it may have been on account of this that his school of philosophy was called the *Cynic* or *Dog* school. He was stern, proud, and unsympathetic. He taught that all human pleasure was to be despised. He was ostentatiously careless as to the opinions, the feelings, and the esteem of others. He used to appear in a threadbare dress, so that Socrates once exclaimed, " I see your pride, Antisthenes, peeping through the holes in your cloak ! " His temper was morose, and his language was coarse and indecent. His disciple, Diogenes, even " bettered the instruction," living, it is said, in a tub, and peering about the streets with a lantern in the daytime, in search, as he alleged, of a man ! It was part of his system to outrage common decency, and he snarled and growled even more bitterly and insolently than his predecessor. It is from this old school of philosophy that we derive the term cynicism ; and we commonly apply it, nowadays, to that mood or habit of mind which looks out upon mankind with cold and bitter feeling, which finds little or nothing to admire in human character and action, which systematically depreciates human motives, which rejoices to catch men tripping, which sneers where others reverence, and dissects where others admire, and is hard where others pity, and suspects where others praise.

It would appear to have been some such mood as this through which the Psalmist had been passing when he said " all men are liars." With him, however, the mood seems to have been but transient. For a time his soul was darkened by its baleful shadow—all human goodness eclipsed for him, and his own human sympathies and affections frozen. But only for a time. He does not seem to have cherished this cynical mood. On the contrary, he seems to have been conscious of its wretchedness, and to have retained the power to pray against it. I daresay there are not a few of us who have tasted somewhat of the bitterness of cynicism, or who at least have experienced certain moods of feeling which have given us a glimpse of what cynicism is. For surely that man or woman must be exceptionally blessed who has been able to pass through disappointment and sorrow with temper ever sweet and disposition never soured, and who, although confidence in individuals may have been shaken, has nevertheless always preserved a genial and trustful outlook on humanity. Most of us, however, have failed, I fear, to manifest such grace, and must have known what it is to have our sympathies and affections temporarily soiled and curdled in times of vexation and disappointment. Well is it for us when such a mood is merely a passing one, when we recognize and feel its bitterness, and when, like the Psalmist, we retain the power to fight and to pray against it.

The great danger is lest the mood should pass into a habit—lest we should nurse it until it becomes a chronic attitude of mind, and we begin to lose the taste of its bitterness, and to take a morbid pleasure in indulging it. Distinguish, however, between *cynicism* and *satire*. No doubt the cynic is often satirical; satire is just the kind of weapon that comes ready to his hand. But the same weapon may be wielded by very different hands, and in very different causes; and satire may often be employed by men who are anything but cynical. There is such a thing as genial satire—the light and even humorous play of irony or sarcasm around some venial fault, or some peculiar excrescence of character. Then there is also the satire of moral indignation, which applies the stinging lash to manifest vices, or pours the vials of scorn on some detestable meanness, in order to make the shameless ashamed, or to infuse a healthy contempt of vice into the souls of those who are still uncontaminated by it. The old Hebrew prophets knew how to wield this weapon; and even in the pages of the New Testament it finds its fitting place. In fact, all such satire as this—whether of the genial or the vehement type—is often used by men who are passionate admirers of human excellence, and who are not only warmly attached to individuals, but also earnest lovers of their race. Whereas it is the very characteristic of cynicism that it lacks earnestness. It knows nothing of a noble scorn. Its satire is neither genial nor vehement. Even its humour is always sardonic. Its very bitterness, although intense, is unimpassioned. It is a kind of acrid gelatine. The fully-developed cynic prides himself on his indifferentism. Remorselessly he dissects and analyzes human character and action; for, like Iago, he is "nothing, if not critical"; but his criticism has no useful end in view; he is not seeking to make others wiser or better. He is scarcely earnest enough even to care about his success in stinging and wounding! It is simply his way to pick faults and to sneer. We find the culmination of this cynicism in Goethe's "Mephistopheles"; and, indeed, the word "devil" itself means "accuser"—the slanderer of God and man.

You will sometimes meet with a young man who has got into this indifferent, scoffing, carping, bitter habit of mind. He prides himself on having "seen life," when what he has seen has rather been—death! He fancies he knows men and women, when, in fact, a whole world of noble manhood and womanhood lies outside the range of his vision and experience. He judges of humanity from his own shallow nature and his own frivolous companionships. Burrowing like a mole underground, he sneers at the very idea of the stars. Feasting himself like a dung-fly, he cannot believe that there are any creatures that really prefer the flowers. No man is a hero to him; he seems to have lost the capacity of admiration. No woman wakes a pure and passionate love in his breast. To his eye disinterestedness, patriotism, philanthropy, missionary zeal, are only phases of selfishness. Point him to the sun; he will tell you of its spots. Point him to some exquisite statue; he will show you the flaw in the marble. Point him to a noble character; he will put some fault under his microscope. This is the spirit of cynicism; and it works terrible havoc in a man's soul. It kills enthusiasm; it kills tenderness; it kills self-sacrifice; it kills even self-respect; it also kills religion. For "he who loveth not his brother whom he hath seen, how can he love God whom he hath not seen?"

There can be no doubt that wounded vanity, and disappointed ambition, and trouble coming upon an intense egotism, are fruitful sources of the cynical spirit. A vain man is naturally exacting. He expects from others recognition, admiration, and deference; and if he does not secure the appreciation which he fancies is due to his abilities or merits, he may begin to rail at the blindness and stupidity of the world. An exacting nature, also, is apt to suspect the genuineness of an affection or friendship which is not always showing the amount of attention demanded and expected. The "milk of human kindness"—curdled somewhat at the outset by a selfish vanity—is still further soured when that vanity is wounded. A selfish ambition, too, when disappointed, is apt to leave the spirit embittered. Some of the most snarling and carping critics are men who have failed to reach the fame they coveted. And then, again, even the ordinary calamities of life, coming upon an intense egotism, will sometimes plunge a man into the cynical mood. That mankind *in general* should be subject to disease or to misfortune is not so strange to him; but that *he himself* should be thus visited surprises and chafes him. He feels as if a man of *his* importance ought rather to escape the troubles that fall on ordinary mortals. True humility will often save us from bitterness of feeling. "Let us not think more highly of ourselves than we ought to think, but let us think soberly." Who are *we*, that we should expect to escape " the ills that flesh is heir to " ? Who are we, that we should expect to be set free from the common discipline of toil and sorrow ? Who are we, that we should be so exacting in our demands on the time and attention and admiration of others ? Who are we, that we should ask so much and give so little ? Nay, but let us cherish a modest estimate of ourselves—this is a grand safeguard against cynicism, and helps to preserve the sweetness of the spirit in times of disappointment and affliction. A humble recognition, too, of our own defects and faults will tend to keep us from harsh and censorious judgments of our brethren, and from all scornful and bitter railing at the weaknesses of humanity.

The man who finds nothing to admire in others thereby reveals the shallowness of his own nature. A soul—and especially a young soul—that has no " hero-worship " in it, of some sort or other, thereby writes itself down as ignoble. The cynic who is constantly depreciating the actions and suspecting the motives of others is certainly paying no compliment to himself. A man does some deed that has a noble and worthy look about it. You know nothing whatever of the man ; but you must, forsooth, begin with bitterness to insinuate that his action may not be so disinterested as it looks—that it springs, probably, from some selfish or sinister motive ! What does all this mean but that you find it hard to believe in nobleness ? And what does this, again, mean but that you yourself are incapable of such disinterested conduct ? You may, indeed, quote your knowledge of the world and your experience of human nature; but is not your knowledge of *yourself* more to the point? If you yourself were really capable of such virtue, would you be so ready with your sneers and suspicions? You may have met with some men who are "liars"; but, if you yourself are thoroughly honest and truthful, why should not another man be as honest as you? Why should you rail at mankind because you have been occasionally deceived? Because one woman may have slighted you, or one man proved faithless to you, is that a reason for setting down all men and women as heartless or treacherous? Keep *your own* heart sound and true. Nobleness believes in the possibility of nobleness, and delights to recognize it. Get into the habit, then, of looking out for excellences of character instead of picking out flaws and magnifying faults. "Charity rejoiceth not in iniquity, but rejoiceth in the truth."

Cultivate also the habit of putting the most generous construction on human actions. If an action can be ascribed to two possible motives, why should you ascribe it to the lower? You must know, from your own personal experience, that your own conduct would often be utterly misunderstood, if it were thus judged. You must know that your "will" is often better than your "deed." You must know that you often think kindly of others and feel kindly towards them, when a number of circumstances come in to prevent your expression of your feeling. And why, then, should you not believe that, even when others appear to be forgetting or neglecting you, they are not, after all, so selfish or so unsympathetic as they seem? This is another safeguard against cynicism—the habit of dwelling on the nobler features of human character, and of putting the most generous construction on human conduct. "Charity believeth all things, and hopeth all things."

Let us seek to look at all men as through the eyes of Christ. This is the grand antidote to the cynical spirit. The grand secret of loving and caring for and bearing with others, lies in looking at them through the eyes of Him who is their Redeemer and ours. Christ "tasted death for *every* man." He so loved even the unworthy, that He was willing to shed His blood for them. When He "ate and drank with publicans and sinners," He saw the possibilities of goodness and of blessedness that lay beneath all the vice and misery. He had His word of stern severity for the respectable, self-righteous Pharisee; but you never find Christ railing bitterly or scornfully against mankind. For the fallen He had a heart to pity and a hand to help. His love detected the elements of goodness that lay smouldering in the ashes. They tell us that "Love is blind"; but be sure that hatred or even indifference is far blinder. Love may sometimes be blind to faults, but it has a quick eye for excellences. It has a quick eye, too, for the possibilities of character, for the ideal that lies within the actual, for the perfect statue that may yet be chiselled out of the marble. You cannot see *the best* that is in any man or woman until you look through the eyes of love. And therefore, if at any time we begin to feel the chill of the cynical mood creeping over us, let us place ourselves anew by the side of Christ, and try to feel a little of what He feels as He looks down on our weak, struggling, tempted, sorrowing humanity.

Yes; and let us try to look *even at the cynic* as

through the eyes of Christ. The Lord cares even for him, and pities him. His scornful bitterness is, indeed, a sin; but it may, perhaps, have its palliations. Perhaps his father and mother were very, very different from yours; perhaps the home of his childhood was darkened by moroseness and gloom; perhaps, in later years, he has been tried by sharp disappointment or even cruel treachery. And now, it may be yours to show him that "all men" are *not* "liars," that there is a sweeter and nobler side to human nature; and thus, by your forbearance and kindliness, you may, perhaps, do something to thaw his icy bitterness, and help him even yet to recover faith in love, human and divine!

SENTIMENTALISM.

[Reprinted from *The Christian World Pulpit*, January 10th, 1877.]

SENTIMENTALISM may be described as a lop-sided development of human nature, in the direction of mere taste, fancy, or feeling. It is not to be defined as an absolute excess of sentiment. It is rather sentiment not duly balanced or bridled. Even an ounce-weight, placed in one scale, will make the other scale "kick the beam," if there be nothing in it. A single horse will sometimes run away with an inefficient driver, when another driver will hold two, or even three horses in check. And often a sentimental person has really far less feeling than another whose nature is more uniformly cultured and more thoroughly disciplined. Indeed, as a rule, the sentimentalist is rather shallow and superficial, even in the region of emotion. His feelings may be more quick and lively, but they are not so deep and far-reaching. It is not that he has necessarily more sensibility, but he has less self-control. When the intellect is undisciplined, the conscience undeveloped, and the will weak, then sentiment, not being duly balanced, is apt to become sentimentalism. There is a relative—although not an absolute—overplus of feeling in the nature. Emotion comes to be cultivated for its own sake, just for the luxury of indulging it. An exaggerated value is attached to impulse as a guide of conduct. And this sentimentalism in fancy and feeling leads naturally to sentimentalism in word and action. There is apt to come in also an unhealthy self-consciousness, which is not unlikely to produce a kind of affectation. So that a sentimental person may sometimes be found in a moral attitude more graceful than genuine, or making speeches more gushing than sincere.

Now, this *tendency to insincerity* is one of the dangers of sentimentalism. When even virtue comes to be looked at merely on the side on which it appeals to the taste or the emotions—when its sterner aspects are disregarded—there arises the temptation to say not what we feel, but what we imagine it would be becoming to feel, and to turn our conduct into a kind of dramatic action which is to produce a certain effect on the feelings of the spectators. The endeavour comes to be to make of our conduct a moral picture, and not simply to live a true and good life. Thus words of sympathy are spoken, not so much out of real feeling for the sufferers, as because it is such a pleasant thing to be a comforter; and help is given to those who are in distress, not so much because of any anxiety to relieve them, as because benevolence is such a beautiful and becoming virtue!

But, even when there is no such insincerity or affectation, sentimentalism has still its dangers. It often *inflicts injury on others* through its incapacity to brace itself to necessary but unpleasant action. You would not admire a surgeon who should prefer to let his patient die rather than inflict the pain necessary to save life. Yet there are some who would allow society to be cursed by scoundrelism and savagery rather than inflict the needful punishment on our criminals. There are those, too, who can scarcely pass a beggar on the street without giving alms, and who are so quickly moved by any tale of distress, that in order to relieve their own feelings, or to get rid of a disagreeable importunity, they will put their hand into their purse. It would probably be a far truer kindness to say "No"; the chances are that, by this indiscriminate almsgiving, they are only nourishing imposture, idleness, and debauchery; but they cannot give themselves the trouble of investigation or the pain of refusal, and they do not like to figure, even in their own eyes, as apparently hard-hearted. Turning away from a beggar does not make a pretty picture! They forget that, if they really wish to be benevolent, there are many cases of genuine distress which they might search out and relieve; but all this sorrow which is "out of sight" is "out of mind"; whereas the seeming trouble, which proclaims itself aloud, touches their susceptible feelings. Thus the sentimentalist becomes the natural prey of the impostor, and really injures the parasite that feeds on him. Then, again, there are parents who, in their selfish fondness for their children, shrink from subjecting them to salutary discipline. The "little pet" must have everything he cries for! Why, he will scream, and stamp, and kick if he is crossed; and a screaming and kicking child does not make a pretty picture! If the "little darling" is to look like an angel, he must be kept pleased! And so self-will, and bad temper, and greediness, and insolence to servants are allowed to go on unchecked; and the poor child, it may be, grows up to make himself and others miserable—the pampered and selfish victim of a sentimental nurture.

But not only is sentimentalism dangerous through the injury which it thus inflicts by pampering, flattering, and corrupting others; it is also dangerous *to the sentimentalist himself*. The man whose sensibilities are keen, and yet unbalanced, is specially open to incursions of temptation on the sensuous side of his nature. His moral fibre is relaxed. He allows his feelings to over-ride his judgment. He loses power of rebuke, remonstrance, moral indignation. He yields good-naturedly to others at times when he ought rather to assert himself. All this is dangerous. When a ship is crowded with sail, and will not answer to her helm, her condition may be most perilous. And have you not known young men of lively emotions—genial, pleasant, and kindly, but deficient in common-sense and moral sense—whose excitable temperament has driven them on the rocks? Perhaps, however, the danger here is greater for women than for men, because in a man's life there are more generally other interests, lying outside the range of emotion, which tend to balance the sensibilities. But take the case of a girl of susceptible temperament, with perhaps a constitutional tendency to hysteria. Let this girl be constantly reading trashy novels, full of romantic incidents and sentimental conversations; and to this let there be added late hours, exciting dances, and stimulating wines, and verily you are laying a train of gunpowder that is only too ready for the match! I enter into no wholesale denunciation of novels, or dancing, or wine; but I say, Let us take care what we are about in the education of our daughters. All this heightening of the sensibilities—this one-sided cultivation of the emotional nature—so that ordinary life comes to look dull and prosaic, and there is engendered a longing for romantic episodes, and a picturing of pleasant and pretty situations—all this is full of peril. At the least, it is apt to beget a sentimental neglect of those " proprieties " which are often as the floating beacons that indicate the sunken rocks. Sometimes it leads to a self-indulgent flirting which inflicts cruelty on another heart and life. Sometimes, on the other hand, a sentimental ideal—unbalanced by conscience—will lead even to immoral self-sacrifice. And a young woman, who begins with a morbid longing to figure as the heroine of a pleasant romance, may end by turning her life into a veritable and painful tragedy!

Then again, *in the religious life* sentimentalism is also fraught with danger. It is true, indeed, that religion without emotion—without the thrill of awe, the throb of gratitude, the yearning of aspiration, or the glow of tenderness—is a poor, empty thing. But, on the other hand, when religion is viewed as consisting altogether in certain frames of mind or states of feeling, when it is separated from practical life, or when religious emotion comes to be cultivated for the mere luxury of indulging it, then there is danger. To value religion merely for its beauty and pleasantness, merely for the appeal which it makes to the taste or the imagination, is not the way to become "strong in the Lord and in the power of His might."

You remember how Christ likens the susceptible but shallow temperament to the thin layer of soil in which the seed springs up quickly, but, finding no depth of earth, cannot strike down its roots, so that the plant is scorched and withered by the sun. Thus is it with some whose feelings are touched by an eloquent sermon, a crowded audience, or a sweetly-sung hymn. They are captivated by the pleasant and beautiful aspects of divine truth, and so they even " receive the word with joy"; but by and bye, "when persecution ariseth because of the word," or when they find that faithfulness to Christ will involve self-denial and self-discipline, then "they are offended." No; it by no means follows, because your heart beats more rapidly, or your tears flow more readily under the preaching of the gospel or the singing of a hymn, that therefore you are more religious than your calmer neighbour. It may, perhaps, only show that your nerves are weaker, or your nature more emotional. We shall see what you are *to-morrow*, at business and at home—in honesty, and purity, and kindness, and self-control! Translate your emotions into deeds. If we regard religion as a thing of mere feeling, then, when our moods fluctuate, or when we are somewhat roughly awakened by the stern realities of life, we are apt to lose our faith. It is one thing to sing sentiments about the Christian armour, or confidence in the heavenly Father, or victory over death; it is another thing altogether actually to fight down selfishness—to trust God when your expectations are shattered and your home desolate—or to be calm and hopeful at the very gates of death. And, indeed, one great danger of sentimentalism in religion is the danger of reaction into morbid despair. If we make too much of our own feelings, then, when from some cause or other feeling is low, we are apt to think that religion is gone. Whereas, God is still with us; and we are still to cling to Him, even in the darkness, and to serve Him by bearing and doing His will.

What shall we say, then? Shall we, because of these dangers of sentimentalism, resolve to despise sentiment? Shall we seek to crush impulse, to deaden sensibility—to kill emotion? No. The culture of the feelings is part of a true human education. Imagination and emotion naturally and rightly play a most important part in the conduct of life. Your cold, hard, calculating man can never reach the heights either of goodness or of usefulness; and his passionless calculation may sometimes lead him far astray. The whole charm and power of certain words and deeds often lie in their being spontaneous. A man of noble impulse will often feel, as by an instinct, what is the right thing to do, long before the phlegmatic calculator can reason it out. A man, moreover, is sometimes lifted high above dangerous rocks of temptation, and carried right over them, on the swelling tide of a pure emotion. A noble scorn of what is mean and base, a considerate tenderness for the rights and feelings of others, will often be our best defence against the devil. What a different career King David's might have been, if only, at the crisis of his life, his soul had been filled with the same healthy sentiment of chivalry which led him to refuse the draught of water, brought from the Bethlehem-well at the risk of his comrades' blood! Life would be a poor thing, and virtue a cold, bloodless thing, without pure impulse, and tender generosity, and the play of the imagination about our duties and relationships.

The true way, therefore, to guard against the dangers of sentimentalism is not to eradicate sentiment, but to balance it. The feelings are to be educated; but the other elements of our nature ought to be educated also. Even *physical* training is, from this point of view, not to be despised. Sentimentalism finds a congenial soil in weakened nerves; and muscular exercise will sometimes help to throw off unhealthy fancies. Then the *will* also ought to be trained to habits of resoluteness and decision. Self-will, indeed, is a curse; and a strong will, in the absence of sensibility, may work tyrannically and cruelly; but, considered in itself, a strong will is a blessing, and gives power of self-control. Then, the *intellect* also ought to be educated. A well-instructed and well-disciplined mind is an admirable balance to the emotions. Let our girls, after they leave school, still devote some time, if possible, to systematic study, to mathematics, or language, or science, something that will really discipline the powers of thought. Our religion also ought to be intelligent. The Bible ought to be read and studied. We ought to be able to "give a reason for the hope that is in us," and our actions ought to be guided by judgment, and not merely by impulse. Finally, the *conscience* ought to be educated into sensitiveness and strength. This is the grand protection against sentimentalism. We need feeling, to help us in the doing of that which is right and good; but the all-important matter is to have a well-trained moral sense, pointing us ever in the direction of practical duty, rebuking us when we neglect it or come short of it, bidding us test our feelings by our deeds, and ask ourselves whether we are really "keeping" and obeying the "word of God."

MEEKNESS.

[Re-written 1889.]

OUR word "meek" seems now-a-days to need redeeming. Whatever the reason may be, the word does not hold the place which it used to hold in the Christian vocabulary. We rather fight shy of it as a term of praise. To speak of any one—especially of any *man*—as being "meek," seems now-a-days to carry with it a certain flavour of disparagement, not to say of contempt. Whilst the "grand old name of gentleman" holds its own as a designation of honour in universal estimation, there are not many "gentlemen" who would thank you for calling them "meek" men! No doubt this is partly owing to the conventional meaning of the word "gentleman" as it is commonly used in society. Conventionally—and indeed etymologically also—the gentleman is not so much the man of gentleness as the man of gentility— the man of good birth and good breeding. There is many a European "gentleman," who, if you were to say that he is *not* a gentleman, would at once proceed to vindicate his right to the name by demanding the opportunity of killing you in a duel! Meekness and gentleness are qualities of heart—graces of character:

but there are many people who attach far more importance to what they call "good birth," than to being "born of the Spirit." I suspect that, in the popular depreciation of meekness, there is a certain Pagan element which has not quite risen above the worship of mere force. Meekness is not one of the Carlylean virtues. It has too quiet and tame an aspect for many minds: it neither roars like the thunder, nor flashes like the lightning: they would fain have something more pronounced in manifestation: they do not perceive the spiritual strength that underlies it.

There is doubtless, however, another reason for the disparagement of meekness. Like many other virtues it has its counterfeits, which are not really admirable, and which lead men to mistake its true character. Christianity is mightier than Paganism; but a real Paganism may be a sturdier thing than a sham Christianity. The pride of obvious self-assertion naturally secures more respect than the "pride which apes humility." There is a bastard meekness which is associated with a flaccid and invertebrate character—lacking individuality, and marked by moral timidity. It is this namby-pamby mildness, which has no moral or spiritual pith in it, that men often mistakenly call "meekness," and despise accordingly. But this is not the meekness which is so often commended in the Bible. The word needs to be redeemed to its true and proper use. There needs to be, on the one hand, a better understanding of what meekness really is; and, on the other hand, a higher appreciation of genuine meekness as a quality of noble and godly character.

True meekness stands opposed, not to self-respect, but to pride. Christ claims us as the children of the Eternal God. The gospel takes the poorest believer and lifts him, here and now, as into "heavenly places," and sets him in front of a glorious immortality. He may never be admitted into the society of the rich or great of this world; but, every day, he may find admission into the presence-chamber of the "King of kings," and may come forth from that chamber to the humblest toil, with a face brightened by the smile of God. He may be despised by many on account of his poverty; but the gospel speaks to him as an "heir of God, and joint-heir with Christ," and reminds him that "the sufferings of this present time are not worthy to be compared with the glory which shall be revealed." The man who "learns of Christ," and who realizes these lofty privileges and promises, acquires a certain dignity of character and action. Such a man will not readily become the mere tool of others. He bears the "yoke of Christ"; and "to his own Master he standeth or falleth."

A genuine meekness cannot be incompatible with such self-respect as this. Meekness is not mere pliability. It is not a refusal to think and act for ourselves; it is not a thoughtless subjection of our spirits to any external influence. To be meek is not to be a mere "nose of wax." The truth rather is, that where there is no self-respect there can be no exercise of meekness. Meekness is just that quality which prevents self-respect from passing into pride. Look at the life of Him who said, "Learn of me; for I am meek." See with what dignity He carried Himself, even when He was "led as a lamb to the slaughter." Think of the dignified calmness with which He spoke to Caiaphas, and the dignified silence with which He met the questions of Herod. See how Pilate quailed before Him in the judgment-hall, and then tried to banish this feeling of awe by reminding himself of his own authority, as he threatened Jesus—"Speakest thou not unto *me?* knowest thou not that I have power to crucify thee, and power to release thee?" How majestic, in its simple dignity, was the calm reply of the thorn-crowned King!—"Thou couldest have no power against me, except it were given thee from above: therefore he that delivered me unto thee hath the greater sin." All this may surely teach us how compatible is the true dignity of self-respect with a genuine meekness. But observe that, in all this attitude of Jesus, there was no tinge of pride. The danger with *us* is lest self-respect degenerate into pride. And there is special danger here. For, of all vices, the vice of pride is probably the most attractive to every nature that is not grossly sensual. One great temptation of the intellectual, the refined, the brave, and even the upright, is to pride. And yet, of all vices, pride, when full-blown, is perhaps the most deadly. Nor is it difficult to understand why men who despise the vices of sensuality, avarice, and vanity should nevertheless fall into pride. Sensuality tends to degrade a man into a mere animal. Avarice makes a man the slave of a thing. Vanity is a petty subserviency to the opinion and admiration of others. But there is a certain grandeur of aspect about pride. Pride makes a man a little god to himself. Whether others admire him or not is a matter of little importance to him; he is his own worshipper. Enough for him that he is—*what he is!* To be above others—to be above depending on others—to be able to look down from a height on the weaknesses, ignorances, and petty vices of others—to be self-poised on a pinnacle of self-recognized greatness; *this* has an aspect of rock-like strength, and many a man is captivated by it. Others may not appreciate his greatness; but he has the satisfaction of knowing that they are fools. Some may regard him with scorn; but he schools himself into indifference to their scorn by cherishing towards them a contempt which perhaps he is too proud to express. If his enemies should begin to persecute him, he wraps himself up in a mantle of stoical endurance, and finds his satisfaction in proving to them that the citadel of his will lies beyond the power of their hate. In all pride, even in its earlier stages, there lurk the germs of this contempt for others. The pride of intellect despises the unlearned mob; the pride of refinement despises the vulgar herd; the pride of courage and strength despises the weak and timid; the pride of self-righteousness despises the fallen and the outcast. And you can see how this vice is as deadly as it is seductive. For man is made to respect himself in virtue of his relationship to that God on whom he is ever dependent. But, in proportion as he becomes self-centred, he loses the sense of his dependence on the Almighty. It was pride that hardened the hearts of those Pharisees to whom Jesus said, "The publicans and the harlots go into the kingdom of God before *you!*"

Although meekness is quite compatible with self-respect, it stands in opposition to all this haughty isolation, and self-sufficiency, and contempt for others. And surely it is possible to preserve our own individuality—to avoid all fawning and sycophancy—to reverence the voice of our own conscience, and yet at the same time to cultivate a universal charity, to cherish a sense of the value of every human soul, to recognize our own ignorance and sinfulness, and to remember our utter and constant dependence upon God. The man who lives thus is truly meek; and indeed we might almost define meekness as self-respect blended with humility.

Again, true meekness stands opposed not to courage but to self-will. The faith inspired by the gospel of Christ tends to raise us above the fear of man, and of the consequences which may follow the doing of our duty. Many a Christian, naturally timid it may be in temperament, has manifested a wondrous courage in confronting the opposition of wicked men. The battle of Righteousness must be fought in this world; and it needs men who can " endure hardness as good soldiers of Jesus Christ." Meekness must not be confounded with cowardice. Yea, there is even a certain self-assertion which is not inconsistent with meekness, and to which a man is sometimes forced, in his advocacy of the right. The Apostle Paul expresses this strongly when he says to the Corinthians, "I am become a fool in glorying; ye have compelled me." He means that he is half ashamed of having to speak so much about himself, of having to vindicate his claims to their respect and affection; but the blame, he says, must rest with them, and not with him. They have been listening to the accusations and insinuations of his detractors, and therefore, for the sake of his influence, and for the cause of the gospel, he *must* defend his own reputation. And it often happens that a man, who naturally and modestly shrinks from obtruding himself on the notice of others, finds that his own personality has become so identified with some righteous cause, that duty requires him to make his presence and position recognized and felt. All such self-assertion as this may be quite compatible with the truest meekness. And yet, at the same time, meekness is, in its own nature, more akin to self-negation than to self-assertion; so that, even whilst recognizing self-assertion when necessary, meekness gives to it a peculiar tone and aspect, delivering it from parade, bravado, and rudeness, and investing it with courtesy, calmness, and dignity.

Meekness, then, stands opposed, not to courage, but to self-will. It is written of Moses that he was "very meek"; and surely we do not regard as lacking in courage the man who stood before the proud king of Egypt and demanded the release of the oppressed. But the very secret of his courage lay in *this*, that he was not acting in self-will, but in obedience to the will of God. And a greater than Moses—the "meek and lowly" Jesus—whilst bearing brave witness for the truth, and boldly confronting Scribes and Pharisees, could say, "I am come, not to do mine own will, but the will of him that sent me." He who, in obedience to the Father, went forward to all the shame and agony of the Cross, refused to cast Himself down, in self-willed presumption, from the pinnacle of the temple. Meekness and self-will are directly antagonistic. The man who has no other reason for his action than that he himself has planned it, who overrides the feelings and wishes of others simply because he has formed a resolution from which he is too stubborn to depart, whose courage is simply a determination to execute his own despotic will, such a man has yet to learn the most elementary lesson in meekness. It lies in the nature of meekness to yield rather than to resist; and it delights to yield when self-respect, prudence, or duty do not counsel resistance. Christian meekness, whilst recognizing our own will as legitimate governor within our nature, desires at the same time that it shall govern as a manager that is a servant, the servant of God and of the Lord Jesus Christ. "Take my yoke upon you, and learn of me; for I am meek."

Further, true meekness stands opposed, not to the rebuking, but to the revenging of injury. It is no part of Christian duty to submit, without protest or rebuke, to wrong and injustice. Our own self-respect —the welfare of society—nay, even the true welfare of the offender himself—may all demand that we do *not* overlook iniquity. The meekest of men may feel it to be his duty, sometimes, to punish crime. It is an utter mistake to suppose that meekness dries up the springs of moral indignation. Why, the more gentle a man is in his own nature, the more indignant must he be at all cruelty and oppression. Here, again, let us "learn" of Jesus. He who brake not "the bruised reed," and quenched not "the smoking flax," charged His enemies, face to face, with their malicious designs. "Ye are of your father, the devil, and the lusts of your father ye will do," are words which came from the lips of *the meek and lowly One*. True, there were also occasions on which He bore injustice, cruelty, and mockery in silence; but these were occasions when silence was the most emphatic rebuke—the most effectual protest. And even so, by quiet and passive endurance of injury, *we* may sometimes rebuke more powerfully than by any words. Yet meekness is not always thus silent. Did Jesus lose His meekness when He openly rebuked the officer who smote Him? "If I have spoken evil, bear witness of the evil: but, if well, why smitest thou me?" Or, if it be alleged that Jesus, being sinless, is no example in this matter to *us* who are ourselves sinners and need forgiveness, then, surely, we may at least cite His own injunction to His disciples: "If thy brother trespass against thee, *rebuke him;* and if he repent, forgive him." The reason why an offender is not brought to repentance may sometimes be just because we have not met his offence with a meek and earnest "rebuke," but with a proud and somewhat sullen silence. So far, indeed, is silent endurance from being always a sign of meekness, that it is sometimes a method of exacting a petty revenge. Now *this* is what meekness is most certainly opposed to—the revenging of injury. The revenge you take may be on a petty or on a grand scale; but whether it be murder with a knife, or only a sulky sullenness, it is antagonistic to the spirit of meekness. Nay, there may even be no sullenness: an offence may be met simply with a designedly exasperating coolness, and yet, if there be ill-will in the heart, God discerns beneath all the outward aspect of meekness the latent spirit of revenge. Meekness is generally calm; but there may be more real meekness in the most passionate invective than in the torpid calmness of moral indifference, or the forced calmness of a calculating malice. Christian meekness carries in its bosom the spirit of forgiveness; its ultimate design is not to inflict pain. It will sometimes warn, sometimes reason, sometimes be silent, sometimes openly rebuke; but, in every case, its desire and aim is to save and bless by reaching, if possible, the conscience and the heart. "Brethren, if a man be overtaken in a fault, ye which are spiritual, restore such an one *in the spirit of meekness;* considering thyself, lest thou also be tempted." The meek man will not forget that he himself is "compassed with infirmity"; and, as he carries about with him a spirit of forgiveness, his severest rebukes will be designed to produce that penitence which desires and receives forgiveness.

Let us, then, seek to redeem this word "meekness" to its true and proper use; and especially, let us seek to appreciate and to cultivate the grace of character which the word expresses. We can never cultivate this grace by any mere affectations. Let there be no mock-humility—no insincere depreciation of ourselves—no false modesty which leads to a shirking of obvious duty—no mere mannerism which hides a stubborn will beneath the guise of seeming mildness, or conceals the spirit of revenge behind an air of meek and injured innocence. On the other hand, let us beware of the Pagan worship of mere strength. Let us beware how we overestimate the value of physical might, or of intellectual energy, or of mere force of character, apart from its moral quality. If we would cultivate a true meekness let us cultivate a genuine humility, and a genuine unselfish love. These are the twin roots from which the beautiful flower of meekness springs. Let us cherish a humble sense of our utter dependence upon God, and a penitent sense of our own sins and failures. Let us cherish a real regard for our fellow-men, by looking at them as through the eyes of Christ. More "sitting at the feet" of Christ—more appreciation of His character—more subjection to His authority—more communion with His Spirit: *this* is what we all need.

THE DANGERS OF EXPERIENCE.

[Reprinted from *The Manchester, Salford and District Congregational Magazine*, October, 1887.]

THE value of experience is proverbial. We have all heard that "experience teaches fools," and that "a man at forty years of age is either a fool or a physician." But we do not hear so often of the dangers of experience. Many men who have reached or have passed middle life are rather apt to flatter themselves that the years which are said to "bring the philosophic mind," have brought nothing but gain to them, so far as their own character is concerned. They are apt to fancy that their experience has simply produced greater maturity of judgment, given them a wider knowledge, delivered them from the illusions of imagination, put them on their guard against deceitful appearances and uncalculating impulses, and led them to conduct their life with more caution and self-control. Certainly it would be a strange thing if we could spend many years in a world like this without learning some lessons of practical wisdom. But, on the other hand, it may be well for us to remember, as the years roll on, that the wisdom of experience is not necessarily an unmixed gain—that, indeed, our very experience of life brings with it temptations and dangers peculiarly its own.

It will surely be acknowledged, to begin with, that some kinds of experience may be bought far too dearly. Not only may it be the case that the experimental knowledge obtained is not worth the initial cost; it may also be the case that the cost itself involves a permanent disability. There are men priding themselves on their knowledge of life, who are simply "glorying in their shame." They have been burrowing in filth, and they know what it is; but the taint of it may abide with them to the end of their days. They have learnt by experience what it would have been better for them to have learnt only by hearsay, or perhaps still better never to have learnt at all. Their experience may have opened their eyes in one direction, but it may have blinded them in another. Their moral instincts and spiritual sensibilities may have been dulled: and their special experience, with its special knowledge, may have robbed them of the benefits and blessings of an experience which would have been a wider, richer, healthier, and sweeter thing. The selfishness which is reckless of the injury done to other lives in the process of self-culture, cannot possibly produce the highest type of character. The rake who prides himself on having "seen life" may find it all the more difficult to "see God." The unscrupulous man who has reached the goal of his ambition may find that he has missed a far nobler goal. We must ask what a man loses, as well as what he gains, in the gathering of his special experience. Goethe once said that he was bent on "building the pyramid of his existence as high as possible into the air": did he forget that, after all, a pyramid may be only a big tomb?

But it is not only when experience is too dearly bought that it brings its own special dangers. We may gain much knowledge of human nature and human life without any self-degradation,—knowledge which may even be forced upon us in the necessary intercourse of the world; and yet this very knowledge brings with it temptations which may issue in the deterioration of our character. Men speak of the moral dangers which beset ignorance; but is it not the case that the healthy instincts of an inexperienced innocence are often a moral safeguard? Is it not sometimes also the case that an impulsive courage which is ignorant of danger succeeds in achieving what prudence, in full view of the risk, would scarcely have ventured to attempt? Thus the disadvantages are not all on the side of ignorance. Experience may beget an over-cautious timidity. Experience also furnishes a man with tools and weapons which he is tempted to use as mere instruments of selfishness. This temptation is one which especially besets men in middle and later life. The knowledge which gives a man an advantage over his neighbours, gives him also the opportunity of making an unfair or ungenerous use of that advantage. Experience may often prevent a man from being tricked; but it does not prevent him from being tricky. Youth is naturally generous, impulsive, and uncalculating, and is not usually given to manœuvre and diplomacy. It is the man of experience who usually excels in finesse, and in a kind of tact which may be closely allied to cunning. It is the man of experience whose knowledge of human nature enables him to play upon the prejudices and weaknesses of others so as to promote his own selfish ends. It is the man of experience who is able to lay traps for the unwary—to make bargains which are apparently generous, but which are really to his own advantage, and to tempt the ignorant into paths of sin and shame. There are human spiders who know well how to weave their web! And there are few things that degrade our nature more than the habit of looking upon our fellow-men, not as brethren to be loved and helped, but as instruments to be used for our own pleasure or profit. This is one of the greatest dangers of experience. For surely of all temptations one of the most dangerous is the temptation to become tempters or tricksters of our fellow-men.

Another danger of experience is the tendency which it sometimes produces towards a distrustful and even cynical habit of mind. The little child is naturally trustful; and the same may be said of every ingenuous and honest soul. The man who is himself conscious of pure motive and kindly feeling naturally looks out on the universe with faith. But it is impossible to live long in the world without having this faith severely tested. The mysteries of Providence—the afflictions which we ourselves have to endure, or which we observe in the lives of others—test our confidence in God. The knowledge which we acquire as to the possibilities of human nature in the way of vice, hypocrisy, and deceit, tends to lower our confidence in our fellow-men. Perhaps we ourselves have trusted those who have betrayed us. Such experience is apt to beget an over-suspicious habit of mind, which leads us to blunder in our estimates of the character and conduct of others. Instead of putting the best possible construction upon their actions—which is often the true construction—we may begin to indulge in groundless suspicion as to the motives of the most seemly deeds. This is very likely to be the case if we allow ourselves to become soured by our experience of disappointment, injustice, or unkindness. And it is still more likely to be the case if we have also had some painful and humiliating experience of our own moral weakness in the presence of temptation. Indeed, a man of wide experience who is also thoroughly selfish, is almost certain to become both cynical and sceptical. His experience of human life and of Divine Providence, interpreted by his knowledge of himself, makes it hard for him to trust either man or God. But even an honest and unselfish nature sometimes finds it difficult to combine a generous faith with the wise prudence which is forced upon us by our growing knowledge of human life. So, too, our hope of human progress is apt to be lessened, not only by our own failure to respond adequately to the good influences which have surrounded us through so many years, but also by the comparative failure of our endeavours to elevate and bless others. Enterprises of beneficence, which looked very promising for a time, have not been so successful as we expected. It is, indeed, one of the problems of life, how to preserve the earlier spirit of trust and hope amid the knowledge and wisdom born of maturer experience. And it is because this problem is too hard for many, that they begin, in middle life, to degenerate in character. They leave behind them the generous impulses, the energizing hopes, and the resolute courage, of youth. They cease to exercise their imagination in the practical conduct of life. They lose sight of the ideal in character and action. They seek to achieve practical successes by unworthy compromises. They allow their aspirations and inspirations to be chilled and frozen by their experience. They settle down into a hum-drum, prosaic, and even worldly habit of mind; and herein lie their weakness and their danger. Hence it is that men who have passed safely through the temptations of youth—having been borne over them on the high tide of generous emotion—sometimes fail and fall in middle life. They pride themselves on their freedom from illusions. They fancy that they see things as they really are, because they are walking " by sight," and not " by faith "!

How are we to meet and overcome these temptations and dangers of experience? By seeking to live in the light of that Son of God who once lay as a little child in the manger at Bethlehem. By all means let us learn those lessons which experience can teach us; but let us regard experience as simply one teacher in the school of Christ. Let us see to it that, first and foremost, we are Christ's scholars. He is the Great Teacher; and He employs other teachers besides experience, to whom we shall do well to listen. Imagination, conscience, intuition, faith, love; these have something to say to us. Above all, let us keep " in touch " with Christ Himself; let us sit at His feet and learn of Him. The Child of Bethlehem, as He grew in years, " grew in wisdom"; but He never lost the child-heart. He trusted His Father utterly; and He ever maintained that loving spirit which believes the best possible, and hopes the best possible concerning men. He "knew what was in man"; and He used this knowledge, not for His own aggrandisement, but for their welfare. He believed that the lowest of men were capable of redemption, and were worth redeeming. Let us, then, keep close to the world's Redeemer, that we may keep the ideals of life before us, and keep fresh within us that spirit of trust and hope which is born of a pure heart and a generous love. Thus shall we rise above the temptation to acquire experience at the cost of self-degradation. Thus also shall we rise above the temptation to use our experience as the mere handmaid of selfishness; for we shall catch the spirit of Him who "came not to be ministered unto, but to minister, and to give his life a ransom for many." And thus, too, shall we rise above the temptation to bury our hopes for mankind in a cynical distrust of God and of humanity; for we shall cling to Him who is the Revealer of God and the Redeemer of humanity, who has already by His gospel and His Spirit wrought so mightily in the world, and who, as the "bright and morning star," is the pledge and prophecy of "the perfect day."

THE CONCEALING POWER OF LIGHT.

[Reprinted from *The Manchester, Salford and District Congregational Magazine*, November, 1879.]

WE talk of the "curtain of the night," but the day has its curtain also. The sun conceals a far larger portion of the universe than he reveals. In showing us the earth, he hides the heavens. How much knowledge we should have missed but for the teachings of night! The wonder and awe with which we look up into the starry firmament—the visions which we have of an immensity peopled by myriads of worlds—these would have been lost to us through the concealing power of a perpetual day. It is not that darkness is, in itself, a revealer. We could have no knowledge of the starry firmament but for the light which comes to us from the stars themselves; nor could we have rightly interpreted the revelations of the night, unless we had also been instructed by the teachings of the day. It is light, and not darkness, that is the revealer; and yet light may become a concealer also, when, by its nearness, or glare, or glory, it hides other lights from our view.

This concealing power of light is a fact which

has its analogy in other regions than the physical. God is the one ultimate source of all truth; but truth shines in upon our minds through very diverse channels. Thus it becomes quite possible for us so to live in the light of this or that truth as that other truths of great importance may be practically hidden from us. A man may be so fascinated by one department of knowledge as to overlook some other department which might prevent him from falling into erroneous inferences. He may be so dazzled by the light of some new instruction as to forget old lessons which he had formerly been taught. It is well, therefore, to be on our guard against this tendency, and to welcome those teachings of history and providence by which this tendency is naturally corrected.

The history of Asceticism furnishes us with a striking illustration of the concealing power of light. The wonderful revelation of God in Christ—the nearness and glory of the spiritual world—the tremendous issues of the future life—the possible nearness of Christ's appearing—so took possession of some in the early Church that they completely lost sight of the value and importance of earthly duties and relationships. They were indeed "children of the day"; but they were almost blinded by the excessive radiance of the sun. Having come "out of darkness into God's marvellous light," they lost sight of old truths, in the surpassing brilliancy of the new. We, looking back on that night of Paganism, can see that it had its starlight. We can see that many of the early Christians might have been saved from the errors of a false spirituality and an inhuman asceticism, if only they had recognized the fact that the gospel did not despise or reject anything that was true and good in the old civilization. God was teaching men through the Greek, appreciation of nature and of human faculty; and through the Roman, appreciation of law and duty, of manly courage, and of domestic ties; but when the gospel flooded the world with its light, there was little wonder that many lost sight of those old teachings in the surpassing glory of what was special and peculiar in the new revelation.

And it is in this way that errors have often arisen in successive ages of the church's history. Heresies have sprung up in many instances simply because men *would* live exclusively in the light of one set of truths, or of one aspect of the truth. Thus there have been those who have dwelt so exclusively on the doctrine of Christ's divinity, that it has banished from their sight the reality of His human nature, and led them to speak of Him in such a manner as to remove Him to a distance from the sympathies of men. Whilst, on the other hand, some have been so fascinated by the vision of Christ's perfect humanity, that they have lost sight of His superhuman glory. Then, again, there have been those who have been so blinded by the dazzling radiance of the divine Sovereignty, that they have lost sight both of the responsibility of man and the compassion of God, and have spoken of the "Faithful Creator" as if He were the destroyer, rather than the redeemer, of our race! Whilst, on the other hand— and this is rather the danger of our own times—there are those for whom the glorious light of the universal Fatherhood and love of God has practically shut out of view the reality of the Divine wrath, the significance of Christ's sacrifice for sin, and the awful fact of future retribution. Now, in all such cases, it is not that there is an error in the radical doctrine mainly insisted on, but that this doctrine is so emphasized, to the exclusion of other important truths, as practically to lead to erroneous inferences and conceptions. One safeguard against this evil lies in the fact that extremes usually provoke re-action. Neglected truths generally re-assert themselves, and sometimes with an excessive emphasis proportionate to the degree in which they have been neglected. In this way men get what is somewhat analogous to the alternations of day and night; they get both the revelations of the sunlight and the teachings of the stars. But another safeguard lies in the cultivation of a habit of mind which (so to speak) *turns itself round* towards the various sources from which light comes to us, which never refuses to recognize facts, which is on the outlook for any truth that may even lie embedded in error, and which does not forget old lessons amid the effulgence of new revelations.

One would suppose that this habit of mind might commend itself especially to men of scientific spirit. And yet there are many of our men of science who are not sufficiently on their guard against the concealing power of light. The marvellous discoveries of modern science—the new views which it has given of physical laws and forces, and of the possible origin of the human species—have so dazzled and fascinated the minds of some, that, for the time being, they have altogether lost sight of a spiritual world. They see no spirit in man, no God in the universe. They see matter and force; protoplasm and evolution; and that is all. Looking up into the starry firmament, they behold it flooded with the light of modern astronomy, and do not see the "glory of God." Looking at the human conscience in the light of their doctrine of development, they have no vision of a moral lawgiver or a future life. What is all this but living exclusively in the light of one set of truths, forgetful that there are other revelations than those of physical science? What such men need is some *alternation* of their thoughts, a turning away of their minds at times from the light of science, that they might receive the truth which shines from other luminaries, that they might look out, with Moses and Isaiah and Paul and John, into the infinitudes of the spiritual universe, and see the light which comes from the conscience, affections, intuitions, and yearnings of man, and from that Christ who is "the root and offspring of David, and the bright and morning star."

Truth is also sometimes hidden from men by the glare of familiarity or the sunshine of prosperity. Often we do not appreciate all the excellences of a friend until the night of bereavement darkens down upon us. The "fierce light" of familiarity is apt to bring his faults into undue prominence, and hide from us some of the quieter and less obtrusive aspects of his character. But, when the light of his personal presence is gone from us, the stars begin to come out one by one, and many a good deed, long ago forgotten, shines out once more in our memory. Often too it happens that, whilst men are bathed in the sunshine of prosperity, they lose sight of the heavenly realities. They love "the garish day"; and the truths of the eternal world grow dim to their vision, pale and spectral as the moon, when we see it in the daytime. But by and bye there comes some revolution in their circumstances; the sunshine of prosperity departs for a season; and then, it may be, in the night of their sorrow, the heavenly lights begin to shine out in all their clearness. True, the sunlight of our joy tells us of the goodness of our God; and, when our life is bathed in gladness, we may well look up with gratitude to the heaven from which it comes to us. But still, for creatures such as we are, so prone to keep our eyes fixed on earth, it may be well that there should be, in our experience, the alternations of day and night, of prosperity and adversity. Blessed are we, if, when the night of our trouble comes, we do not, by our own sin and unbelief, draw across our sky a thick cloud which seems to blot out the very stars. But even then the hidden stars are not really blotted out: "the truth of the Lord endureth for ever."

THE EVANGELISTIC POWER OF CHRISTIAN CHARACTER.

[Chairman's Address to the Lancashire Congregational Union, March 6th, 1889. Reprinted from *The Lancashire Congregational Calendar*, 1889.]

CHRISTIAN BRETHREN,—We live in an age of work and worry. All around us is the hum of industry, the whirl of machinery, the stress of competition. Men are eager to obtain rapid results of their toil. They are so accustomed to excitement in business that they cannot do without it even in recreation. Our whole atmosphere seems to be saturated with the locomotive spirit. How can Isaac go "out to meditate in the field at the eventide," when he has just received a telegram to the effect that Rebekah is arriving by the 7.15 train? It is quite proverbial that we are living "at high pressure"; and I fear it cannot be denied that the bustling activity of our times is largely accompanied by the feverishness of anxiety, and the unrest of impatience.

Now, it is only natural that these characteristics of the age should influence, to some extent, the Christian church. We must acknowledge also with thankfulness that it is, so far, a gain to the church, when

Christian men of business bring into the management of its affairs the industry, energy, and practical skill which they manifest in commercial life. Many of the enterprises of religion and benevolence are being conducted with an activity and zeal which evoke our admiration. We may well rejoice to see men as earnest in doing good to others as in making money for themselves—as eager for practical results in evangelistic work as in mercantile pursuits. The Christians of to-day are bent on doing something, and they do it. A new order has arisen within the modern church—an order designated "workers." We live in an era of religious organizations, conferences, committees, and "guilds." Our home and foreign missionary societies are large "concerns," managed by boards of directors, among whom are to be found some of our ablest men of business. In the church, as in the world, our ears catch the hum of industry and the clank of machinery, and our eyes see abundant tokens of practical sagacity. This, of itself, is not to be regretted. Christ commends the servant who *trades* diligently with the talents which he has received. And surely it is matter for rejoicing whenever "the sons of the light" are as wise in all their righteous stewardship for the Righteous Lord, as "the sons of this world" are wise "for their own generation."

On the other hand, however, it must be admitted that there are some dangers and drawbacks associated with these features of modern church life. I have said that our age is one of worry, as well as of work; and it cannot be an unmixed gain to the church, if, along with the spirit of practical industry, it imports also the spirit of unrest and impatience. Christian activity cannot be too earnest, but it may be too bustling, too fussy, too eager for immediate results. There are Christian "workers," who, like Martha of Bethany, are "cumbered about much serving," and like Martha also, lay the blame on Mary, rather than on themselves. Then, again, it may be a very good thing for our church life to have infused into it the industry, energy, and sagacity of our commerce; but it does not follow that the church gains by an accompanying infusion of ideals—or rather of un-ideal notions—generated in the factory and the market. Business-habits of industry and of skilful adaptation of means to ends are one thing; business-ideas of barter and bargain, of hire and service, of labour and success, are quite another thing. And, just as the *church militant* has been too often "militant" in another sense than that of fighting "the good fight of faith," so the *church mercantile* (if I may use the metaphor) is sometimes "mercantile" in another sense than that of diligently trading with the Master's talents in the Master's service.

In our own busy centres of manufacturing and commercial industry we are specially prone to import business ideas into regions where they are altogether incongruous. Of course there are business details connected with the external affairs of our churches, which are best managed by business-methods, and according to business-notions. But it is another thing to attempt to shape the whole tabernacle of church life "after the pattern shown us" in the workshop or the exchange. Then we are apt to become impatient of the processes of spiritual growth. The Christian minister comes to be regarded, not so much as a sower of good seed, which, when it falls into good ground, may be expected to produce a good harvest, but rather as the manager of a factory or a joint-stock company, who, if he is to be worth his salary, must show rapid and definite results of his skill and toil. When the ecclesiastical atmosphere becomes saturated with these commercial ideals, men begin to talk as if the unconverted could be spun and woven into Christians, or the impure bleached into purity, or the avaricious dyed into generosity! They begin to talk as if it were only necessary to set in motion a certain kind and amount of religious machinery—with all the newest improvements in church organization and evangelistic method—in order to secure certain spiritual results. They begin to talk as if our theological colleges ought to be able, without fail, to "turn out" every student as a "finished article," duly calendered and ticketed for the ecclesiastical market. They begin to talk as if the fidelity and ability of Christian work could always be gauged by its success, or as if such success could be measured by statistical tables. Fortunately, there are many of our men of business who have too much piety and common-sense to intrude commercial notions and standards, after this extreme fashion, into the kingdom of God. But it is not always an easy thing to pass from the atmosphere of the counting-house into the atmosphere of the church, with full recognition of the distinctive processes of spiritual life, the peculiar conditions of spiritual work, the befitting instruments of spiritual enterprise, and the essential qualities of spiritual success. And I venture to think that, amid all that is excellent in the business industry and practical sagacity of our Lancashire Christianity, one of our special dangers lies in over-rating the value of religious and philanthropic machinery, and in underestimating the transcendent importance of the Christian spirit as embodied in Christian character. Charity-organization is a good thing; but it may sometimes cramp the spirit of benevolence. It belongs naturally to the "quality of mercy," that

> "It droppeth as the gentle rain from heaven
> Upon the place beneath,"

and, although it may be very desirable to gather some of this rain into reservoirs, yet I fear we sometimes lay ourselves open to the sharp satire of "Aurora Leigh"—

> "If we give,
> Our cup of water is not tendered till
> We lay down pipes and found a Company
> With Branches."

I fear, also, that we are sometimes too anxious about religious machinery, whilst we are comparatively careless about motive power. It is possible, moreover, to under-rate some of the more subtle kinds of spiritual energy. The kingdom of God has its magnetic and vital forces, which work none the less surely or mightily because they work often without noise and "without observation." One of these subtle forces is the power of Christian character *as such*. We sometimes talk as if the evangelization of the world depended entirely on direct effort, consciously put forth towards that end. We talk as if mankind were to be converted to God, simply and solely through such agencies as Bible societies, tract societies, missionary societies, church-aid societies, Sunday school teaching, and evangelistic services. We are constantly appealing for more workers, and for more money, to carry on these various agencies. Far be it from me to say that such appeals are unnecessary. I do not think that the Christian church is doing anything like the amount of work which it ought to do, or giving anything like the amount of money which it ought to give. It is most needful that direct and strenuous efforts should be constantly put forth for the extension of the kingdom of God. It is especially needful, in order to the evangelization of the world, that the Christian evangel should be preached. But it is also true, nevertheless, that there are aspects of the kingdom of God, in the light of which its progress resembles, not so much the diligent extension of a business, or the aggressive re-conquest of usurped territory, as the growth of a seed into a tree, or the hidden fermenting of leaven in a mass of dough. Quite as much as we need direct effort, and more than we need money to aid such effort, do we need the subtle and indirect influence of the Christian spirit. This, I think, is what we are tempted to overlook, amid the eager and somewhat bustling activities of our modern church-life. And this, accordingly, is the point on which I wish now to lay special emphasis—*the evangelistic power of Christian character.*

Brethren, God requires us to *be* something as well as to *do* something. The most energetic activity is no substitute for the spirit of godliness and goodness. Indeed, what a man *is* determines the quality of what he *does*. God looks at the motives of our conduct. The influence, too, of our words and deeds upon our fellow-men depends largely upon the character which lies behind. A gift may sometimes be more like a blow than like a kiss. The same words, spoken by two different men, may produce very different results. Truth, of course, is truth, by whomsoever it may be uttered; and if men believe the truth and act upon it, they will certainly reap the benefit of their faith and action. A patient may benefit by following the strict regimen prescribed by his physician, although the physician himself may be suffering from the same ailment, and may decline to submit himself to the same restrictions. The influence of the gospel, therefore, does not necessarily depend on the character and conduct of the preacher. "Some, indeed, preach Christ even of envy and strife; and some also of good will. . . . What then? only that in every way, whether in pretence or in truth, Christ is proclaimed; and therein I rejoice, yea, and will rejoice." On the other hand, it is undeniable that the power of truth is often lessened, or even nullified, by the character of the man who utters it. To an eloquent preacher, whose life was very inconsistent, it was once said: "When I hear you in the pulpit, I wish you were never out of it: when I see you out of it, I wish you were never in it!" If a minister is known to be ambitious, or despotic, or bad-tempered—if he is in the habit of glorifying himself and depreciating the gifts of his brethren—it cannot be expected that his exhortations to humility or gentleness should come home with the same power to his hearers. Men are not always logical. They do not always distinguish between the preacher and his message. The very truth of God is apt to lose its influence over them when uttered by one whom they cannot respect or trust. Especially is this the case when there is a mercenary taint in the character of the preacher. Of course, there are some niggardly souls that are always ready to suspect the presence of covetousness in the Christian ministry. They find it difficult to believe that anybody can think less of money than they themselves. But this only makes it the more desirable that all pastors and evangelists should shake themselves absolutely free from mercenary motives. "The Lord," it is true, "did ordain that they which proclaim the gospel should *live of* the gospel"; but it is still more desirable that they which proclaim the gospel should *live* the gospel. The truth is a thing to be done, as well as to be spoken. Christian character has an eloquence peculiarly its own. Like the firmament, it has "no speech nor language"; its "voice cannot be heard"; and yet its "words go out" into the world. A speaker of the truth, who is also a doer of it, is doubly eloquent; but, if he is not a doer of the truth, he may undo by his deeds the good which he does by his words.

As it is with the preacher so is it with all Christian "workers," so-called. The spiritual influence of their work is likely to be either helped or hindered by the spirit which they themselves manifest, both in their Christian labours and in their ordinary life. If they are consumed by selfish rivalry and jealousy—

if, like "King Bramble," they are more anxious to be prominent than to be useful—if they are too self-willed and touchy to co-operate with their brethren, they must not be surprised that such "dead flies" spoil the fragrance of their "ointment." Or, if their daily life is grossly inconsistent with their evangelistic zeal, they may do far more harm in the world than if they had never enrolled themselves in the ranks of Christian workers. Who can calculate the amount of evil that has been wrought by self-seeking philanthropists, by immoral Sunday school teachers, by religious orators who have electrified their audiences in public with their unction, and electrified their acquaintances in private with their temper, by tract distributors who have distributed slanders as well as tracts, and by praying Pharisees who have "devoured widows' houses"? There are not a few unbelievers who could trace their present infidelity to the shock received by them when some prominent member of the church, whom they had honoured, was proved to be living a life of hypocrisy. To lose confidence in some trusted man or woman may be the first step towards losing faith in the reality of Christian goodness; and this, again, may be the first step towards losing faith in the Christian gospel. Any bearer of the gospel who by his immorality begets cynics is likely thereby to beget unbelievers also. On the other hand, the man whose own life betokens a Christian spirit does thereby commend the gospel which he is seeking to promote. Thus, the evangelistic power of Christian character is shown by the manner in which it gives greater efficacy to evangelistic work.

But this is not all: it is not nearly all. Christian

character—even apart from its connection with distinctively Christian work—is a Christianizing force. It is, in and of itself, one of the mightiest agencies used by the Spirit of God; and it is mighty in proportion to its simplicity and purity. Christ Himself is "The Light of the world," not only in virtue of what He taught, but also—and even more—in virtue of what He was and is. The light which comes from Christ is pre-eminently "the light of *life*."

> "And so the Word had breath, and wrought
> With human hands the creed of creeds
> In loveliness of perfect deeds,
> More strong than all poetic thought."

So, too, when our Lord said to His disciples, "Ye are the light of the world," He does not seem to have been referring specially to the truth which they might preach. "Let your light shine before men, that they may *see your good works* and glorify your Father which is in heaven"; such words point rather to the light which shines from character. And again, when He said to them, "Ye are the salt of the earth," He must have been referring chiefly to the influence of their spirit and life; for He added, by way of warning, that the salt is "good for nothing" if it "have lost its savour." It is surely also a significant fact that, in those epistles of the New Testament which are addressed to churches, there are comparatively few exhortations to special effort for the spread of the truth and the conversion of souls, whilst there are many exhortations to a holy character and conduct. The apostles seem to have been chiefly anxious that all Christian converts should beware of relapsing into the heathenish or the worldly life, and should carry the Christian spirit into their ordinary duties and relationships. The apostles, moreover, laid emphasis on this, not only for the sake of the converts themselves, but also for the sake of the kingdom of Christ. They looked upon each church as a centre of Christianizing influence, in virtue of the new life which its members were living. Doubtless they took it for granted that every true Christian naturally desires the extension of the kingdom of God; but they also knew well that one of the most potent forces towards such extension was the simple manifestation of the Christian spirit. The general tenor of apostolic exhortation throughout the New Testament clearly shows what transcendent importance was attached by the first preachers of the Cross to the virtues and graces of the Christian character, as a practical testimony to the power of the gospel, and as an evangelizing force in human society.

It is also to my mind a very striking fact that, throughout the Gospel narratives, we do not find the slightest indication that Christ ever gave any special instruction to children. We know that the Great Teacher loved the little ones. It is natural to suppose that He sometimes spoke to them on religious subjects. It certainly seems as if it would have been a great help to *us* to have had a specimen of the manner in which He talked to the young about God, and sin, and goodness. But surely we may venture to say that, if it had been part of Christ's plan and usual method to win the children for His kingdom by direct appeals to their tender hearts and consciences, we should have had some record of such addresses. Now, may not the explanation of this somewhat strange blank in the Gospels lie simply in the great importance attached by Christ to parental training and influence? May He not have felt that, when once He got parents to enter into the kingdom of God, their children would be likely to grow up into loyal citizens of that kingdom? The little children might well be allowed to play at marriages and funerals in the market-place, if only He could get the men and women to give up playing at the game of Religion, and to make their relation to God an earnest and spiritual reality. He saw that, if the fathers and mothers of the land would repent and believe His evangel, their new character and life, produced by their faith and discipleship, would become an evangelistic force in the training of the rising generation. It is true, indeed, that those who are "born again" are "born of the Spirit," and "not of blood," nor of the mere "will of man." But the Spirit of God works through the instrumentality of spiritual truth and spiritual life; and these are present in the influences of Christian parenthood. We make much—and rightly—of our Sunday schools; and yet we ought not to forget that, historically, the occasion of their origin was the parental neglect of children. I do not deny that it may be a healthful thing for the children even of Christians to gather in the Sunday school, as in a children's sanctuary, and there to join in worship and receive instruction, specially adapted to their capacities. But who would think of comparing the influence of the Sunday school—in depth and permanence—with the influence of a truly Christian home? And it is a serious question whether the Sunday school system, whilst partially covering parental deficiency, has not also to some extent weakened the sense of parental responsibility. It is a strange and sad fact that there are multitudes of men and women who passed through our Sunday schools when they were young, and who, now that they are parents, are sending their children in turn into these same schools, but who themselves rarely or never enter our places of worship. I do not say that they have derived no benefit from their early religious instruction; for to keep outside of all churches and chapels is not necessarily to hold aloof from God and Christ. But I do fear that, in the case of many such parents, the sending of their children to Sunday school is the one act of homage which they pay to Christianity, and that this act is substitutionary rather than representative. By this act many of them would fain exonerate themselves from the duty of setting before their children the example of a sober, righteous, and godly life. Is this process to go on from generation to generation? Are the hopeful children of unhopeful parents thus to grow up continually, in such large numbers, into the unhopeful parents of hopeful children? May it not be the case that we have been too hopeless about the parents? May it not be the case that we would do more for the children, if we did more to arouse a deeper sense of parental responsibility? As it is, the periodic and direct efforts of the Sunday school are too often counteracted by the indirect but constant influence of character in the home. No doubt, even in spite of all this, a large amount of good is done, otherwise the work were a Sisyphus-labour which it would be folly to continue. By all means, let our Sunday school efforts be prosecuted with still greater zeal and spiritual earnestness. But let us also look facts in the face. Let us not imagine that the Sunday school can ever be an adequate substitute for the influences of Christian parenthood. It is in these influences that the marvellous power of character is often most signally revealed.

The light of Christian life is, indeed, like the sunlight, dynamic. There is movement in it—the movement of the spirit of Christ. Many souls are even unconsciously influenced by its subtle energy. They are often far more indebted to it than they dream. It has purified to some extent the very atmosphere which they have been breathing since their childhood. The fact is, that men cannot well escape altogether from the influences of Christian life. They may turn away from the truth when it is presented to them in the form of solid doctrines, and yet be captivated by the truth as it is held in solution in character and fills the air with perfume. They may be stirred into resistance by direct arguments, rebukes, and appeals; but they are not so likely to fortify themselves against the fragrance of "love, joy, peace, long-suffering, kindness, goodness, faithfulness, meekness, and temperance." Christian character embodies and illustrates the Christian evangel. Being produced under the *impress* of the gospel, it also *expresses* the gospel after its own fashion; like the phonographic cylinder, which gives back—whilst it retains—the message that has been charactered upon it by the living voice. The man who has been reconciled to God through Christ does, by his filial response to the divine love, bear testimony to the divine Fatherhood. His trust *in* God gives glory *to* God. In his unmurmuring resignation to the divine will, his very silence becomes eloquent. His sympathy with righteousness is a tacit rebuke of unrighteousness. His integrity in business is a practical condemnation of the trickster. His generosity shames the avaricious and niggardly. His peace of conscience and his spirit of forgiveness both make the divine pardon more credible. His humility, meekness, and patience help men to believe in the Christ of the Gospels. The divine "statutes" are his "songs"; and the lyric melodies of his cheerful obedience may sometimes—like the singing of the maiden in Browning's "Pippa Passes"—touch and move the hearts and consciences and lives of others, without his intention or his knowledge. Wonderful, too, is the activity of the passive virtues. There is an energy in them, which radiates from them, and stirs men's souls in secret. There is often far more spiritual force in patient waiting or suffering than in active doing. Well might Paul say to the Colossians: "Strengthened with all *power* unto all *patience*." And the force that is present in godly patience is all the more powerful over others because it is non-aggressive. True meekness also is mighty. There is the spiritual force of self-control at the heart of it. And "the meek shall inherit the earth." Pride and ambition may have many proximate victories, but the ultimate triumph is with meekness. The "Lion of the tribe of Judah" is the "Lamb that was slain." The Cross of Christ is the divine magnet, which not only attracts men to itself, but also, when they are thus attracted, makes their own characters magnetic. And, just in proportion as Christians manifest a genuine humility, meekness, patience, and self-sacrifice, do they thereby bear witness to Christ and His Cross, and put forth an evangelistic power.

Was not this, indeed, largely the secret of the rapid progress of the early Church? The Christian gospel was illustrated and confirmed by the Christian character. That character was itself a "holding forth of the word of life." When we read, in the Acts of the Apostles, the description of the first church in Jerusalem, we can scarcely be surprised when we read also that such a church received "daily" additions. Men were naturally fascinated by the simplicity, the freshness, the gladness, the brotherliness, the unworldliness of the new life. The late John Stuart Mill, speaking of the manner in which so many Christians of the present day fail to shape their conduct in accordance with "the maxims and precepts contained in the New Testament," has remarked that, if this had been the case with the early Christians, "Christianity never would have expanded from an obscure sect of the despised Hebrews into the religion of the Roman empire. When their enemies said, 'See how these Christians love one another' (a remark not likely to be made by anybody now), they assuredly had a much livelier feeling of the meaning of their creed than they have ever had since." And he adds: "To this cause, probably, it is chiefly owing that Christianity now makes so little progress in extending its domain." This is caustic criticism; but, instead of merely resenting its severity or its exaggeration, let us seriously lay to heart whatever of truth there may be in it. We cannot for a moment doubt that, if "all who profess and call themselves Christians" were manifestly actuated by the Spirit of Christ in their ordinary life, a mighty impetus would at once be given to the evangelization of the world. Think what an additional force would be lent to missionary work in heathen lands, if all immigrants into those lands from so-called "Christendom" were godly, honourable, pure, and unselfish in heart and life. Think what a spiritual power the churches of Lancashire would become to-morrow among the people of Lancashire, if all the members of these churches were, in anything like a marked degree, exhibiting the mind of Christ, in their domestic, commercial, political, and social life. Doubtless all true Christians are "epistles of Christ"; but they are not always very legible as such. Too many of us, alas! are sadly like those manuscripts called "palimpsests," on which was originally written some portion perhaps of sacred scripture, but which have since been written over with some inferior literature. The Christian character in us has been rubbed into dimness, and the worldly character has been written on the top of it. If only the *autograph* or *style* of the Divine Master were easily recognizable in the life of every disciple, what an evangelistic power there would be in the "epistles of Christ!"

I plead, therefore, brethren, for a more adequate estimate of the value of Christian character as a Christianizing force. Amid all the energetic activities of our modern church-life, let us give a more proportionate attention to the cultivation, in ourselves and others, of the Christian spirit. Let us seek to grow in virtues that are robust. We may have broader views of life and duty than our Nonconformist ancestors; but I doubt whether we are as sturdy in our integrity, as loyal to our convictions and as willing to make sacrifices for conscience' sake. Let us seek also to grow in graces that are beautiful: for beauty has its divinely-ordained uses; and there are those to whom the flowers of a garden are even more beneficial than its fruits. It is not always the so-called "practical" man who really renders the most practical service to humanity. Let not Christian "workers" despise their fellow-Christians who, in "the trivial round and common tasks" of life, are quietly serving God and man in the spirit of love. Whilst Dorcas is busily making garments for the poor, Eunice may be doing quite as good work for the kingdom of God, through the influence of her character on her son Timothy. And let those of us who are pastors remember that it is not only when we are preaching the gospel to the unconverted that we are doing evangelistic work. Every time we succeed in deepening the piety of Christian hearts, in strengthening the roots of Christian virtue, in adding some new touch to the beauty of a Christian home, in stimulating believers to a conduct more worthy of their high calling, we are thereby increasing the volume of evangelistic force in the world. And let all of us who are seeking the extension of the kingdom of Christ be careful to employ only such methods as are in harmony with the Spirit of Christ. The Lord looks, not only at the ends we have in view, but also at the means we use. "The end" does *not*, of itself, "justify the means"; and when the means are unworthy of the end they may only hinder its accomplishment. There are unevangelical ways of preaching the gospel; there are methods of raising money for the cause of Christ which tend to choke and defile the springs of Christian liberality; there are ways of seeking to make Christianity the religion of a nation which are out of harmony with the very genius of Christianity. As members of the "church militant," we ought to bear in mind that the true "weapons of our warfare are not carnal, but spiritual"; and, as members of the "church mercantile," we ought to bear in mind that, in trading with the Master's talents, the true methods of *such* commerce are not carnal, but spiritual. Even in our church-life,

> "The world is too much with us; late and soon,
> Getting and spending, we lay waste our powers."

We should have more power for good in the world, if we were more unworldly and more restful in spirit. We discard indeed—and rightly—the monastic ideal of the saintly life. But that ideal was, after all, only the perversion of a great truth. Unworldliness of character *is* one of the mightiest of spiritual forces. We have talked so much recently about "religion in common life" that we are in some danger of forgetting that common life is not, of itself, religion. There is no religion in the counting-house, unless a religious man is at the desk; there is no religion in the smithy, unless a religious man is at the anvil. It is true that on the very "bells of the horses" may be inscribed, as it were, the words "Holiness unto the Lord"; but we must remember that the bells cannot consecrate themselves. Let us carry the spirit of religion into all the business of the world; but let us not bring the spirit of worldliness into the aims or methods of the church. Our Lord Himself was willing even to be defeated, in order that He might win the victory; and, if we would do our best towards conquering the world for Him, let us, as individuals and as churches, strive and pray that we may walk more closely in His steps, along that road which Thomas à Kempis has so well named "the King's highway of the Holy Cross."

ON THE DUTY OF GIVING PLEASURE.

[Reprinted from *The Christian Leader*, February 9th, 1882.]

WE venture to think that many of us do not sufficiently recognize the Christian duty of giving pleasure to others. In reading the apostolic maxim, "Let every one of us please his neighbour, for his good to edification," we are apt to emphasize the second clause rather than the first. The apostle enjoins a duty, and suggests its limits; and we are apt to plead the limitation as an excuse for neglecting the duty. There are even some cantankerous and churlish people with whom the fact that anybody greatly desires anything seems to be a sufficient reason for withholding it. They like to play the rôle of a disagreeable destiny. It increases their sense of power. They appear to be afraid lest people should be too happy. There are others, again, whose one aim in life is to get—not to give—pleasure; and they grow so peevish and discontented when their exaggerated expectations are unfulfilled, or their exacting claims are disregarded, that they become fountains of bitterness instead of joy.

In family life, too, there are some parents who,

from a perverted ideal of duty, rob their children of a great deal of that happiness which is the natural heritage of childhood. In their culture of the "olive plants," the pruning-knife is ever in their hands. This policy is as mistaken as it is inhuman. A child to whom pleasure is doled out, as if it were a medicine labelled "poison," is apt to have his nature stunted and impoverished on the very threshold of a life which may yet demand all possible energy and hopefulness. To make a child happy is often one of the best ways of helping him to be good. And when he sees that his parents are glad to give him pleasure, he will be the more ready to trust them when they think it best to deny him what he desires.

It is indeed true that children ought to be trained with a view to the coming duties and trials of life. When you are building a ship which is by and bye to be launched into the deep, and which may have to face many a storm, you wisely build her with a view to her future. But still you build her thus *in the dockyard*—high, and dry, and safe. In the physical training of children, there is surely a medium between coddling and neglect; the child that is well-nourished and well-clad may thus be built up into a physical robustness which shall be able by and bye to endure hardness. And, similarly, in the moral training of children, there is surely a medium between the enervating and foolish indulgence of every whim, and that repressive rigour which frowns upon the natural cravings and pleasures of childhood. A boy may be turned out into the world hardened and cowardly through the rough

R

training which was intended to make him hardy and brave. And, whilst we very wisely train even young children into habits of self-denial, we must not forget that there is a great difference between self-denial and denial by others. An unnecessary harshness is only likely to breed selfishness in children. Having received but little pleasure from others, they may go forth into the world only to please themselves.

And, as it is with children, so is it often with those also who are of maturer years. By trying to give them pleasure, we may help them to a higher life, and may, perchance, save them from unbelief, cynicism, or despair. We may also do something to remove the prejudices of the narrow-minded, by showing them that we do not wish needlessly to wound their feelings. Truth is none the less powerful for being spoken and acted out in the spirit of love. Our Christian liberty will be none the less attractive when it is seen that we are not enslaved even by our own freedom. No doubt the very law of love itself limits the duty of pleasing our neighbour. A pure love has its eye mainly fixed, not on the delights of loving, but on the object of its affection. If we really and deeply care for another, we shrink from giving him a mere temporary pleasure which will end in pain. We are to please him "for his good to edification": we are not to lose sight of the up-building of his character into moral and spiritual robustness and grace. There is such a thing as a self-sacrifice which really injures those whom it seeks to benefit, by feeding and pampering their already swollen selfishness.

On the other hand, we ought to remember that it is

the withholding—not the giving—of gratification that *needs to be justified.* Every Christian ought to be, as far as possible, a fountain of happiness to others. Christ, our Lord, "pleased not Himself." He came to give "beauty for ashes, and the oil of joy for mourning." And the world is full enough of pain and sorrow, without our doing anything needlessly to increase it. Rather let us, whenever we lawfully can, seek to lighten the burdens of others, by the manifestation of a simple kindliness which may help to lift them above those temptations that appeal to despondency, and may also help them to believe in a love that is far deeper than ours.

UNWASHEN HANDS.

[Reprinted from *The Manchester, Salford and District Congregational Magazine*, January, 1884.]

IT may seem to some sanitary enthusiasts a strange declaration that "to eat with unwashen hands defileth not the man." But we must remember that those traditional ablutions of the Pharisees which drew forth this utterance from Christ were part of a religious ritual. Had their custom of washing their hands before every meal been a mere custom of cleanliness, comfort, or decency, the Pharisees would not have found such serious fault with Christ's disciples for omitting it, nor would Christ have spoken of it as He did. But to see these men giving themselves airs of superior sanctity on the mere ground that they washed their hands more scrupulously and frequently than their neighbours—this the Holy Redeemer could not bear. He saw through all the outward and ceremonial "cleanness" of these Pharisees into their very souls; and to His eye the men were as "whited sepulchres." To His earnest outlook on the universe this substitution of a hand-basin for repentance, and of the washing of cups for the cleansing of hearts, seemed a childish playing at religion. Nay, more : this elevation of petty, formal, and often superfluous punctilio to the front rank of religious virtue was, in the estimation of Jesus, a dangerous and deadly snare. And so He says plainly and boldly: " Not that which entereth into the mouth defileth the man; but that which proceedeth out of the mouth, this defileth the man." Christ is speaking, of course, not as a physiologist, or as a sanitary reformer, but as a religious teacher. From a religious point of view—and this was the point of view of the Pharisees also—Christ affirms that what a man speaks with his mouth is of far more consequence than what he eats with his mouth. A man may eat a little dust with his food, and be none the worse in the sight of God; but foul words are a very different matter, for they reveal a defiled condition of the heart, and their utterance tends also to make the man worse than he was before. Christ, moreover, extends this same principle to other things than words—to everything, indeed, that comes "out of the heart." He wished His hearers to understand distinctly that the purity or impurity of a man in the sight of the Holy God depends primarily on the state of the man's soul. To bear this grand spiritual truth constantly in mind is the best antidote against all exaggeration of the value of ritual in religion.

It might, however, be asked how, in front of such sins as gluttony and drunkenness, Christ could say, " Not that which entereth into the mouth defileth the man." Is not a man really defiled in the sight of God by excess in eating and drinking? Yes; but to the eye of Christ even such sins were primarily sins of the inner man. They were simply outward manifestations of a certain inner condition. It is not the mere physical act of eating or drinking, considered in itself, that constitutes the sin; but it is the fact that this excessive indulgence is the voluntary act of a creature who has lost due control over his appetite. The spiritual nature surrenders itself to the dominion of the animal; and the higher characteristics of manhood disappear in the overmastering lust of physical gratification. It is this—and not merely "that which enters into the mouth"—that constitutes the essential "defilement" of gluttony and drunkenness.

But still it might be asked: Are there not laws of physical health written by God on the very constitution of the human body? Is not cleanliness one of these laws? And is it not the fact that squalor and filth tend to breed disease and pestilence, and to produce conditions favourable to immorality and licentiousness? Does it not, then, seem strange, in the face of such facts as these, that Christ should speak unconditionally of physical ablution as if it were a matter of indifference in morals? The answer to this question is—as I have already hinted—that Christ is not speaking of physical cleanliness, as such, but of ablution as a religious ceremonial. There is no indication in the Gospels that Jesus had any sympathy with an asceticism which despises the body and tramples on its legitimate claims. Had a sect of religious devotees come to Him, giving themselves airs of superior sanctity —as, indeed, some of His own professed followers have done—on the ground that they never washed their skin, the probability is that He would have spoken to them even more indignantly than to the Pharisees. He who said to His disciples, "The life is more than meat, and the body than raiment," could not have regarded it as a matter of indifference whether men ate wholesome or unwholesome food, and whether they lived in dirt or in cleanliness. He who Himself washed His disciples' feet showed that He did not despise the basin and the towel in their own proper place. The works also which He wrought as a Healer of disease show how He valued physical health, and regarded the human body as worthy of attention and care. Christianity indeed has created a physical branch of practical religion, distinct from mere ceremonial or symbolic ritualism, and standing also in direct antagonism to the licentiousness of Nature-worship. "Know ye not," says Paul, "that your body is the temple of the Holy Ghost?" Where men and women are willingly and lazily living in dirt and foulness, there we generally find immorality also. There is a true sense in which even physical uncleanness cometh "out of the heart"; the inward defilement precedes as well as succeeds the outward. But Christianity, especially when joined with physiological knowledge, naturally begets a rational physical religion, grounded in that self-respect which Christian faith inspires, and in a desire to obey those laws of health which are recognized as the laws of God.

On the other hand, it must be said that it is quite possible to over-estimate the value and importance of physical cleanliness. The gospel of soap and whitewash—like the gospel of abstinence, and the gospel of art and culture—may be over-preached. I do not think that Jesus would have endorsed the popular maxim that "cleanliness is next to godliness." There are many things much more closely allied to godliness than a clean skin or a clean house. An aesthetic materialism may have its perverted ideal of human life, as well as a religious asceticism. The tenant is, after all, of more importance than the house; the spirit is of more importance than the body. The young men of Imperial Rome who used to spend hours in the baths were not remarkable for either morality or bravery. The modern Japanese seem to be nearly as licentious as they are fond of bathing. The washtub is not the "laver of regeneration." No amount of soap will give what the Bible calls "clean hands." The fact is, that physical cleanliness does not necessarily lead on to moral purity.

But whilst it is quite possible to exaggerate the value of physical ablution, it is impossible to overestimate the importance of having the heart cleansed by faith and godliness. And I think it would be well for us to cultivate our taste—our love of beauty, order, and purity—more on the moral and spiritual side. We look into the mirror, to see if our face needs washing; but how often do we look into the "perfect law of liberty," to see what "manner of men" we are? What a good thing it would be if we could have a "Spring-cleaning" of the family life, as well as of the family rooms! There are many people whose physical sensibilities are much more delicate and fastidious than their moral tastes. There are some souls that have little or no sense of smell. They are not much disgusted by the foul odours of vice, nor do they much perceive the fragrant and delicate aroma of the finer graces of character. It is not surprising that a lady should shudder at the thought of a sweep sitting down on her drawing-room couch; but we have a right to be surprised that the same lady should invite a rake to sit there and talk with her daughters. There is many a so-called "gentleman" who is exceedingly dainty with regard to the food he puts into his mouth, but who is not always so fastidious with regard to the words which come out of it. Let us seek, then, to cultivate our moral and spiritual tastes and sensibilities, so that we may more earnestly long after purity of heart, and may recoil with greater disgust from all dishonesty, licentiousness, and malignity.

Let us consider, too, the spiritual danger which lurks in physical refinement and delicacy, when it is unassociated with a sympathetic heart. It is a hardening thing to allow physical squeamishness to override the call of duty and the instinct of compassion. What should we think of a woman who could stand by and see an infant suffocated in a shallow, dirty ditch rather than defile her white fingers and her dainty dress? And yet this is just an extreme instance of the hardened selfishness which may be wrought by the disproportionate and unmoral culture of physical refinement. When manual labour is regarded as degrading because it soils the hands—when domestic servants are treated as if they belonged to another species, because they have to do with the dustpan—when the poor are despised and forgotten, because so many of them live in squalor—when the very duties of the sick-room are shirked, in spite of the claims of suffering—we see what can be done by a physical fastidiousness which is unregulated and unbraced by conscience and affection. Yes, there are many things far worse than "unwashen hands"; and one of them is a hard, cold, selfish, inhuman heart.

CHRISTIAN HOSPITALITY.

[Re-written February, 1887.]

HOSPITALITY is a virtue which is not peculiar to Christianity, but which, like other virtues that existed before the coming of Christ, was adopted and ennobled by the spirit of the gospel. In the New Testament it is enjoined that the Christian bishop or pastor, *especially*, should be "given to hospitality," and Christians generally are exhorted to its exercise. We should try to understand clearly the distinctive characteristic of a virtue on which so much stress is laid, especially as in our modern society some misapprehension prevails on the subject. In order to clear the way let us consider what hospitality is *not*; and then we shall be better prepared to consider what hospitality *is*.

Christian hospitality is not the feasting of our neighbours in the expectation that they will feast us in return. There is a great deal of this in modern society. People meet at each other's houses to spend a few hours happily together in eating and drinking, conversation and amusement. Those who invite expect to be invited in turn. It is very much a matter of mutual benefit. The bargain is not expressed in so many words, but it is understood. Thus a round of pleasant gatherings is secured, and there is nothing that is blameworthy in any such arrangement. It may be a very pleasant and quite a legitimate arrangement for those who can afford it. Such gatherings may be most recreative and refreshing if conducted by right-hearted people in a right and fitting manner. But let us call things by their right names. This mutual feasting and entertaining of friends and acquaintances may be very pleasant and very lawful; but it is *not* what the New Testament means by "hospitality."

Neither is Christian hospitality the feasting of our neighbours in a spirit of vain-glorious display. There are many people who do not exactly follow the method I have just named; they *do* invite to their houses those from whom they do not expect any invitation in return; but it is that they may dazzle them with a show. They are vain, perhaps, of their house, their furniture, their plate, their dinners, and they are pleased to have their vanity gratified by the admiration of their guests. I am not speaking here of the rich only; this spirit of ostentation may be found in almost all ranks of society, at any rate it is often found amongst those who are far from wealthy. Sometimes you will even find people, in foolish vanity, trying to rival each other in the *relative* splendour of their entertainments. Now, of course, we must not forget who it was that asked why the alabaster box of ointment had not been "sold and given to the poor!" We must beware of all churlish and indiscriminate censure of what we may call "luxury." A costly entertainment may sometimes be—as the alabaster box of ointment was—an expression of deep reverence, or of grateful respect, or of warm affection, and, as such, it may be worthy of commendation. But all feasting of guests in a mere spirit of vanity and ostentation;—this is, you may call it what you will, but this is *not* Christian hospitality.

Still less is Christian hospitality the feasting of our neighbours at other people's expense! This may seem to be a truism; but truism or not, it demands special notice in these days. We have all heard of men who have been living in splendour, feasting and being feasted, exceedingly "hospitable" according to some men's notions; and then all of a sudden there has come the crash, and it turns out, perhaps, that widows and orphans have been robbed, that tradesmen's accounts are unpaid, and that creditors have really supplied these so-called "hospitalities." I have the utmost sympathy with honest men who suffer from commercial disaster; but I ask, Why should a dishonest man have any praise for liberality? We have simply no right to be charitable or generous with that which is not our own. Let us all understand clearly that to pay our lawful debts is a prime duty of the Christian life. The world refuses to believe in the kind of "saint" who makes his "faith" a substitute for simple honesty, and who is too "heavenly-minded" to attach importance to such a sublunary consideration as the paying of his bills! And the world is right. Never be so foolish as to run into debt merely because some people may suspect or accuse you of niggardliness. If you do, these are the very people, I daresay, who will first raise against you the cry of extravagance. When a man knows that he is feasting his neighbours at other people's expense, he is not a man given to "hospitality"; he is rather, in plain language, a man given to *theft*.

But, further, Christian hospitality is not necessarily feasting at all. It is scarcely creditable, I think, to our modern society that when the word "hospitality" is mentioned, the first, and almost the only, idea which occurs to many minds is the idea of feasting! Understand, therefore, that you may show true hospitality to a man without giving him anything whatever to eat and drink, and most certainly without feasting him. On the other hand, you may spread before a man the most abundant and delicate feast, and yet not have a particle of true hospitality in your heart. Hospitality may be associated with feasting, but it is not necessarily so. Hospitality is a virtue to be practised by the poor as well as by the rich, and no doubt many of the Christians in Rome to whom Paul wrote his epistle belonged to the humbler and poorer classes. Hospitality, like every other true virtue, is primarily of the soul. Of course, where the hospitable spirit exists, it will reveal itself in action; but this action does not necessarily take the form of feasts and entertainments.

Let us now consider, more positively, what hospitality is. Our English word is derived from a Latin word which means, sometimes a *guest*, sometimes a *host*, and sometimes a *stranger* or foreigner. There is another Latin word, apparently connected with the same root, which means, sometimes a *stranger*, and sometimes an *enemy*. From this other Latin word we get our English word "hostility." It is a curious circumstance that the words "hostility" and "hospitality" can thus be traced back to the same root. But the circumstance is easily explained when we remember how naturally a *stranger* may pass into either a *guest* on the one hand, or an *enemy* on the other. It was a sacred duty in the olden times to protect and befriend a helpless stranger. So, too, the Greek word translated "hospitality" in Paul's Epistle to the Romans, means literally, "the love of strangers." No doubt the word came to have a wider significance, but this radical meaning of the word is exceedingly suggestive. It suggests that true hospitality springs from genuine kindliness of heart. It has more to do, you observe, with affection than with eating and drinking, for the literal meaning of the word is "the *love* of strangers." If there is no kind or degree of love, therefore there is no hospitality. There may be ever so much feasting and entertaining; but, if it be all done in the spirit of selfishness, to obtain admiration or to acquire power, there is no hospitality.

Then, again, the New Testament hospitality was primarily "the love of *strangers*." "Be not forgetful," says the writer to the Hebrews, "to entertain strangers; for thereby some have entertained angels unawares." And it is easy to see why so much stress should have been laid on this virtue in the early Church. The men of the world knew quite enough about feasting their friends, and being feasted in return. But the disciples of Christ were to show the spirit of their Master by caring for the stranger when he came amongst them, for the man who had no "friends." And the Christian was to feel—wherever he might travel—that when he came amongst Christian brethren, he came amongst those who would take a kindly interest in his welfare. Immediately preceding the injunction to hospitality the apostle exhorts the Roman Christians to care for "the necessities of the saints." But there was one class of saints in Rome for whom Paul wished them to care in a special manner—those Christians who were *strangers* in the great city. From all quarters of the world Christians would come to Rome, either to transact business, or to settle permanently there. It would seem that *Phoebe*, a member of the church at Cenchrea, who was the bearer of this epistle to the Roman Christians, and who is commended by the apostle to their Christian regard, was visiting Rome on some matter of business. Now, it was surely most desirable that all such Christians coming to the metropolis of the world, and often bringing with them a "letter of commendation" from the church to which they belonged, should meet with real sympathy, and not be left alone in the solitude of a crowded city where there was no familiar face to be seen. It was most important that they should be made to feel that Christian "brotherhood" was a *reality*, that it was something to be enrolled in the ranks of those "called to be saints." To show kindness to such strangers implied a spirit of unselfish love. It was this same unselfishness to which Christ exhorted His hearers, when He told them to "bid" to their feasts, not those who could "bid them again," but those, rather, who could "never recompense them." A man, to be truly "hospitable," must catch somewhat of this spirit. Not, of course, that, in every case, hospitality implies that the person to whom we show kindness is, literally, a "stranger." But it is well for us to remember this root-idea of the word, that the distinctive kindness of hospitality is kindness done for love's sake, without thought of recompense or return, a kindness which is ready to manifest itself towards those who are, as yet, outside the circle of intimate friendship.

It follows from this root-idea of hospitality that, as I have already hinted, it may manifest itself in a variety of ways.

The disciples in Rome were exhorted to be kind to the stranger. Suppose, then, a stranger comes to the great city. Suppose they are assured of his integrity and Christian character. Is it only meat, and drink, and lodging, that he wants? Why, these are perhaps the very things that he does *not* need at all! What he needs most—away from all his friends, and in the midst of that city-solitude—may be the kind look, the kindly word, the sympathetic grasp of the hand, the occasional hour of friendly converse. Is it not obvious that, if they really care for the stranger, they will be able to show their interest and sympathy in many little ways? And, on the other hand, if there is nothing of this real sympathy, they might feast the stranger in one Christian house after another, but there would be no true "hospitality" in their hearts or in their homes. But Paul expects and exhorts them to cherish and manifest an actual benevolence. He does not, indeed, enter into details. He does not think it necessary to tell them that, when a stranger comes into their Christian assembly on the Lord's Day, and happens to take a seat which one of them is accustomed to occupy, they are not to be so inhospitable as to turn the stranger out of the seat he has taken! Paul did not think it necessary to enter into such particulars. He exhorted them simply to cherish the spirit of love to the stranger; and he knew that, if only this spirit was in their hearts, it would find its natural outcome in kindliness and courtesy, and would manifest itself in a variety of ways.

Do not suppose, then, that, because you are poor and cannot afford to give feasts and entertainments, you are therefore excluded from the exercise of this Christian virtue. The poor may often show kindness to the stranger. Ay, and it is often the poor who are really kindest to the poor. They know their ways, their wants, their sorrows, their difficulties, and when and how they can best step in for their relief. There are always those around us, who have few friends or none at all, to whom we can be "hospitable," if we will. We may not be able to feast them. But we can speak kindly words to them, and show some interest in their welfare, and perhaps give them counsel or assistance that may be useful to them.

Hospitality, then, is not a virtue which is easy for the rich, and difficult for the poor. Hospitality may be shown by the wayside, as well as at the fireside—by the sick-bed, as well as at the festive board. Kindness to strangers may be shown by visiting *them*, as well as by asking them to visit *us*. Kindness to strangers may be shown by giving them a pleasant hour of social intercourse, which may cost *us* but little, and may refresh *them* much. And I think that those of us who *can* afford to show a certain amount of hospitality in our own homes would do well to ask ourselves whether we are utilizing our houses and our home-life as much as we might do for the benefit of the friendless. Young men often come up into a large city like this, who, because of their very loneliness, are exposed to many temptations; and sometimes a little pleasant society and an occasional evening of cheerful recreation might be a real help and protection to them. Of course, such hospitality must be exercised with common-sense and ordinary prudence, or we may sometimes find that, in "entertaining strangers," we become only too soon "aware" that we have entertained—not *angels!* Nevertheless, I cannot help believing that, if we were less exclusive and more unselfish—if we had less worldly pride and more Christian love—we might, many of us, by taking a little trouble, and exercising ordinary discretion, and contenting ourselves with simple entertainment, do far more to brighten the lives of the lonely and the friendless by admitting them to share the benefits of a genuine hospitality.

We may also call to mind that the word "hospital" comes from the same root as the word "hospitality." The very same spirit of *kindness to the stranger* which found expression in the ancient virtue of hospitality, and in some of the social ceremonies and obligations of Pagan life, has, in Christendom, expressed itself, amongst other ways, in the institution of hospitals for the sick and infirm poor. Such institutions spring naturally out of the very *genius* of the gospel, which points to One who preached glad tidings to the poor—who healed all manner of diseases by His mighty power—who showed His sympathy with the helpless and friendless—and who exhorted His disciples to live as true children of the God of Love. Poverty has hardships enough of its own to face; but poverty and sickness combined are likely to bring with them a crushing burden. Let us seek to do something towards the alleviation of such burdens. Those who are being nursed and cared for at our various medical charities may be strangers to us; but this is simply one reason why we should show them kindness in their need. "If ye love them," said Jesus, "that love you, what thank have ye? . . . And if ye do good to them that do good to you, what thank have ye? for even sinners do the same." The spirit of sympathy with the mind of Christ, who has revealed to us the One Father in heaven, naturally leads us to extend our kindness beyond the circle of our own kindred and friends. And the hospital is as a "guest-chamber," in which the united benevolence of a community may, through the agency of the physician and the nurse, perform the part of "host" to the sick poor. It is, therefore, no mere play upon words—it is etymologically and ethically true—that to support our "hospitals" in the spirit of genuine kindliness towards human beings who are strangers to ourselves is one form of Christian "hospitality."

MINISTERIAL SUCCESS.

[Chairman's Address to Ministers' and Deacons' Association, June 16th, 1885. Reprinted from *The Manchester, Salford and District Congregational Magazine*, July, 1885.]

I.

CHRISTIAN BRETHREN,—We are met here as a body of Congregational ministers and deacons. It will therefore, I think, not be inappropriate if I venture to say a few plain words on the subject of "Ministerial Success." By ministerial success I mean success in our ministerial functions; and by our ministerial functions I mean our functions as ministers *and* deacons. I use the word "ministerial" here in an inclusive sense. The word "minister" is Latin, and the word "deacon" is Greek; but they both mean the same thing—a "servant." As "ministers" and "deacons"—distinctively so called—we may have different duties to fulfil; but we are all "ministers" in the wider sense of the word. Our offices are offices of ministry—of service. We are all called to serve Christ by serving in a special manner the church of Christ. Let us, then, consider the subject of success in these special departments of Christian work.

"Success" is a word which has different meanings to different minds. In estimating success much depends on the hand that holds the scales, and on the kind of weights that are used. In ordinary life he who is popularly called "a successful man" is sometimes, in the deeper sense, an utter failure. What is called "getting on in the world" may sometimes be, in the eyes of the angels, a very retrograde movement. Success, too, is a relative term. A manifest gain is often purchased too dearly at the cost of a hidden loss; and, when the balance comes to be struck at last, it is found to be on the wrong side. An athlete may train his muscles into greater strength at the cost of weakening the vital energy of his heart. A merchant may succeed in some questionable speculation; and this very success may tempt him to his ruin. A statesman may grasp the prize of his ambition, but it may possibly be with the sacrifice of his nobler nature. The world is prone to measure success according to the present and the visible, without taking into calculation the ultimate and the hidden. And we must acknowledge that the church is sometimes too prone to adopt those standards of measurement which are current in the world.

What, then, is ministerial success? It is success as a minister. And a minister, as we have seen, is a servant—a man who serves Christ and Christ's church. Our first conclusion, therefore, must be that ministerial success is success in service. In this region, however much a man may get for himself, he does not succeed, unless he serves others in the spirit of love. He may get plenty of wages of a certain kind; he may get much applause; he may get a high reputation for ability, or industry, or sanctity; he may get even slavish deference from others; he may get his own will and way in the church: but if he has not been really helpful to his fellow-men—if he has done nothing to promote the purposes of Christ—he has had no ministerial success. Doubtless a man may serve by ruling well. The sceptre may be a badge or instrument of service, as really as the spade or the broom. The governor of a province may serve both his king and his fellow-countrymen by wise and firm administration. Paul speaks even of the civil magistrate as a "minister"—or deacon—"of God." But to succeed as a mere "lord over God's heritage" is not to succeed as a servant of the church. A servant bent on promoting his own interests may succeed in doing so; but this does not make him a successful servant. A servant succeeds *as* a servant when he accomplishes the work which his master gives him to do. A preacher may be popular, and a deacon may be influential, but it does not necessarily follow that they are successful as ministers of Christ. One of our English satirists has said that "a daw's not reckoned a religious bird because it keeps a-cawing round a steeple"; and certainly ambition does not become a holy thing by choosing a pulpit or a vestry as the sphere of self-aggrandisement. To climb the ladder of mere selfish ambition is not even to engage—far less to succeed—in Christian service. "Ye know," said Christ to His apostles, "that the rulers of the Gentiles lord it over them, and their great ones exercise authority over them.

Not so shall it be among you; but whosoever would become great among you shall be your minister (literally, your *deacon*); and whosoever would be first among you shall be your servant; even as the Son of man came, not to be ministered unto, but to minister, and to give his life a ransom for many." There are few words of the New Testament that pass into music like these. And yet, notwithstanding all the sweetness of their divine melody, how often do we fall back into the old Pagan notions of greatness, and allow our ears to be deafened by the clanging cymbals and the big drums of popular applause! Brethren, let us seek to remember that "ministerial success" is, primarily and essentially, success *in service*.

Passing now from these general and inclusive considerations to our more distinctive functions, I would first of all seek to emphasize the fact that a successful preacher or pastor is one who succeeds in accomplishing those ends for which his special office exists. This proposition is of the nature of a truism; but, like many other truisms, it is often practically forgotten. If a statesman were sent out as an ambassador to a foreign country on a special mission, you would not say that he was a successful ambassador if he failed in accomplishing the object of his mission, however much he might succeed in other directions. He might charm people by his manners; he might win golden opinions in many quarters; he might have a special liking for the study of natural history, and might perhaps bring home interesting specimens of the *fauna* and *flora* of the country which he had visited; he might write a fascinating book of travel;

but all this would not make him a successful ambassador. In like manner, the Christian preacher is an "ambassador for Christ"; and he is successful as a preacher only in proportion as he succeeds in accomplishing the objects of preaching. And what are these objects? To persuade men to be reconciled to God in Christ, and to help in maintaining and deepening the religious life in those who are already thus reconciled. One preacher may be more gifted as an evangelist, and another as a pastor or teacher; one may be more successful in those appeals to the conscience and the will which issue in conversion; another may be more successful in comforting the sad, and strengthening the weak, and maturing Christian character by placing it on the basis of a wider Christian intelligence. These are the high functions of the Christian "ministry," distinctively so called; it is essentially a ministry to the human spirit; and, unless spirits are touched and profited, the minister is unsuccessful. As a skilful speaker, or even as a fervent orator, he may succeed in charming men by his eloquence, and securing their admiration. He may be even popularly ranked along with certain actors and singers as being able to "draw a house"! Or, as a diligent student, he may succeed in furnishing his own mind with stores of Biblical knowledge, and may acquire a reputation as a theologian. Or, as an organizer, he may succeed in setting up certain kinds of machinery for Christian work, and in keeping that machinery in motion. Or, as a pastor of genial temper, courteous manners, and kindly spirit, he may succeed in winning the personal affection of his flock. But the Christian ministry, as such, has not been instituted for the purpose of eliciting admiration, or of acquiring knowledge, or of organizing ecclesiastical machinery, or of winning personal affection. The possession of eloquence, or learning, or administrative faculty, or genial courtesy, may indeed be most useful to a pastor or preacher as a means towards the accomplishment of that special work to which he is called; but unless the means are used with a view to this end, and unless this higher end is in some measure attained, he is not a successful minister of Jesus Christ. He may build a fine chapel; he may build up a congregation; he may build up a reputation for himself; but unless he builds up human souls—unless he touches the very spirits of men, and influences them in the direction of godliness and virtue—he fails. A preacher of worldly spirit may secure many of the objects of his ambition; but what of that if he does nothing to promote within the hearts of his people any of those characteristics over which Christ pronounces His beatitudes? On the other hand, a preacher may not have the faculty—or perhaps not even the opportunity—of gathering a large congregation; he may sometimes be compelled to wonder whether his church-treasurer is fully alive to the fact that he has a wife and children to support; he may not be one of those men concerning whom "vacant" churches inquire whether he is "movable"; he may never have published a volume of sermons, and his name may never appear in the columns of denominational journals; he may have none of that un-Pauline *finesse* which would enable him to "become all things to all men, that he might by all means save "—himself; and yet it is quite possible that he may be most successful as a true spiritual helper of human souls. He may be "unknown, and yet well-known"; he may be "poor, yet making many rich"; he may be sending forth into the world "living epistles"; and he may have the sympathetic tact and unworldly wisdom which only Christian love can give. Even if he is not instrumental in converting many souls, or in adding many names to the roll of church-membership, he may nevertheless be a successful shepherd of men—he may be an "ensample to them that believe, in word, in manner of life, in love, in faith, in purity." He may not perhaps be a "worker" in the sense of being industrious everywhere except in his study; but he may be most diligent in acquiring religious knowledge and in trying to impart it to others, and so he may be "a workman that needeth not to be ashamed, handling aright the word of truth." He may not regard it as his function to speak as a "prophet" of God; he may be content with the humbler task of expounding and enforcing the words of prophets and apostles; but by his ministrations in the sanctuary and in the home he may be keeping souls from going back into sin and worldliness, he may be reviving good resolutions and banishing oppressive thoughts, he may be awakening fresh interest in those Scriptures which "are able to make" men "wise unto salvation," he may be helping Christians to "fight the good fight of faith." He may often do more good to men than they themselves know. He may often send his hearers away, pondering the truth rather than admiring his ability. We do not usually go into ecstasies over our ordinary meals; but, if they nourish us, that is the important thing. The work of a pastor who really "feeds the flock of God" cannot be measured by any statistics of pew-rents or even of church-membership. No minister can be called unsuccessful if his preaching is a nourishment, and his life a refreshment, and his memory a fragrance.

Turning now to the special functions of the diaconate, I would remark, first of all, on the curious fact that we scarcely ever hear of "an unsuccessful deacon"! We are familiar enough with the inquiry concerning this or that minister, Has he been successful in his pastorate? But we should almost think it a strange thing to hear the question put concerning this or that deacon, Has he been successful in his diaconate? And when a church is not prospering outwardly—when its members and adherents have been diminishing instead of increasing in number—and even when its finances are not in a flourishing condition—it seems to be commonly taken for granted that, if any of the office-bearers of the church are to blame for this state of things, it must be the minister, and not the deacons. I confess that to my own mind such a conclusion does not appear to be of the nature of an axiom. I can conceive it to be quite possible that both the outward and the spiritual prosperity of a church might be greatly hindered by the dispositions and actions of its deacons. That we should so seldom hear of an unsuccessful diaconate is, therefore, a phenomenon of Congregationalism which I would respectfully submit for investigation, but which I do not now attempt to analyse or explain.

For the present I content myself with emphasizing the fact that a successful deacon is one who succeeds in accomplishing the ends for which his special office exists. Those "seven" men whom we usually regard as the first deacons of the Early Church were appointed in order to allay certain disputes which had arisen with reference to the administration of the church's alms. Thus their office was created in order to maintain the unity and concord of the church; and their distinctive function was to "serve the tables" of Christian beneficence, and thereby to set the apostles free for their own special work. The diaconate, as it exists amongst Congregationalists to-day, may be fairly regarded as of close kinship to the original institution; although, perhaps it may be viewed as also practically taking the place, in some measure, of that plurality of elders which seems to have been customary in the early churches. Looking back, then, to the original purposes of the office, and looking also at the exigencies of our modern Congregational churches, the functions of our deacons may thus be summed up:— To foster the spirit of unity and concord in the church; to care for its poorer members; to make arrangements for the maintenance of its ordinances and institutions; to manage its financial and other secular affairs; to enable the pastor to give himself more fully to his own distinctive work; and, generally, to form, along with the pastor, a council for promoting the interests and objects of the church. Such being the special ministry of the diaconate as it now exists amongst us, a deacon has "ministerial success" precisely in proportion as he succeeds in rendering this kind of service. The maintenance of peace within a church depends not a little on the spirit of its diaconate. A deacon may be ever so influential, but he cannot be called a successful deacon if he does nothing to prevent or allay unbrotherly murmurings or strifes,— far less if he makes himself the leader of a clique. Stephen and his colleagues would have failed to accomplish the purpose for which they were elected if they had not succeeded in healing the breach between the Hebrew and the Hellenistic Christians. Then, again, with regard to the helping of the poorer members of a church, I sometimes think that this is a branch of service which does not usually receive the attention to which it is entitled. It is not desirable that we should go back to the Communism of the Apostolic Age; but it is most desirable that we should retain the spirit of sympathy and brotherhood of which that early Communism was the impulsive and enthusiastic expression. Do not many of us know of cases in our churches which are not exactly cases for a "poor-fund," technically so-called, but in which timely assistance—not necessarily pecuniary—might, if judiciously and delicately rendered, greatly lighten the burden of anxiety and hardship? I would call that man a successful deacon who could direct the beneficence of Christian brotherhood into such channels as these, who would keep his eye on those members of the church that are struggling with misfortune, and would seek to devise the means of rescue or of assistance. It is a work which requires a large heart, a sound judgment, and a delicate tact, and which would bring with it a blessed reward.

Then, too, in relation to the ordinary finance of the church, I would call those deacons successful who can get at men's purses through their consciences and hearts, and who do not dry up the very springs of Christian giving by dealing with the maintenance of Christian ordinances as if it were a matter of mere commercial equivalents, or by treating a Christian pastor as if he were a mere salaried official. And, once more, he is a successful deacon who is able by his counsels to promote the highest interests of the church, and who helps to set a faithful pastor free from such work or such anxiety as would cramp and hinder him in his own distinctive ministry. Doubtless the ideal deacon, as he exists in the pastoral imagination, is rarely met with in reality. Perhaps he is about as rare as the ideal pastor who seems to exist in the imagination of some deacons;— the pastor who diligently studies the Scriptures, and as diligently visits his flock, and as diligently takes part in "public work"—who is at once a patient thinker, an accomplished scholar, and a practical organizer—who excels both as an evangelist and as a teacher—who has a special gift for speaking to the young, and also for interesting the cultured— who keeps himself "abreast of the thought of the age," but has not the slightest sympathy with heretical opinions—who prepares his sermons with the utmost pains, but never uses a manuscript in the pulpit—who, in addition to his other duties on the Sunday, frequently visits the Sunday school— who increases the congregation by his eloquence, and the membership by his spiritual power—who has an educated ear for music, but never interferes with the choir—who has a refined, eager, sympathetic temperament, and yet a constitution so robust that he never breaks down through overwork, or suffers from nervous depression! Perhaps, I say, the ideal deacon may be as rare as this ideal pastor. And yet I will venture to affirm that many of my brethren in the pastorate will thankfully and gladly acknowledge, along with myself, that we have often been greatly encouraged and aided in our work by the sympathy and counsel of men who have sought to fulfil, conscientiously and heartily, the duties of the diaconate.

One word more before I close. Let us beware of regarding the ministerial success either of a pastor or of a deacon as the criterion of his fidelity or worth. Let us remember that in this region success cannot be commanded. To have to deal with the freewills of men is a very different thing from managing the machinery of a factory. Cotton cannot, in stubborn self-will, refuse to become calico; but sinners may refuse to be converted under the most earnest preaching of the gospel. Even to deal with servants whom you can dismiss is a very different thing from dealing with brethren whom you have to persuade. If the clerk in a counting-house refuses to obey orders, his master can send him away; but if seat-holders decline to increase their subscriptions at the appeal of a deacon, what is the deacon to do? or, if the members of a church will not lay to heart the exhortation of their pastor, what is the pastor to do? There were places where even Christ did not succeed during His earthly ministry. Paul was persecuted at Iconium, and stoned at Lystra, and mocked at Athens. And it is possible for a modern pastor even to thin his congregation by his firm and uncompromising allegiance to the truth. By all means let us desire and aim at true success in our ministry as pastors and as deacons; but let us remember that it is "a very small thing to be judged of man's day," and that, in "the day of the Lord," we shall be judged, not according to our *success*, but according to our *fidelity*.

MINISTERIAL SUCCESS.

[Address read at a Devotional Meeting of the Manchester Congregational Board, on March 2nd, 1891.]

II.

IN the course of our recent discussions on the position and prospects of our Congregational churches, we have naturally been led to ask whether we ministers are, in any large measure, to blame for a state of things which we acknowledge to be far from satisfactory. Is there anything in our characters, our conduct, our methods, our general spirit and attitude, which tends to repel men unnecessarily? Can we do anything to increase our spiritual influence so as to make it more attractive?

Now, here, I would not forget that there is a certain *repulsion*, as well as *attraction*, in the magnetism of Christian character and Christian truth. It is quite possible for a minister to make his congregation smaller by earnest preaching, and by faithful dealing with the consciences of his hearers; he may drive away, or keep away, some who would like him better if he were to "prophesy smooth things." It is also possible that a congregation may sometimes be increased by meretricious attractions which are not altogether in harmony with the genius of the gospel.

It does not follow that by becoming holier and more Christlike we shall necessarily become more attractive to all around us. Christ Himself repelled, as well as attracted, men. His "fan was in His hand." His teachings sifted His audiences. After some of His sayings "many of His disciples went back and walked no more with Him." We read, it is true, that "the common people heard Him gladly," especially when He "turned the tables" on those ecclesiastics who tried to puzzle and entrap Him. But we must not forget that it was the same "common people" who, not long after, took the side of those very ecclesiastics against Jesus, and clamoured for His crucifixion. Jesus was "popular" at the first, but He became unpopular as His aims and methods became more fully known. The people were charmed and fascinated by His *human-ness*, especially as it stood contrasted with the pedantry of the Scribes and the self-righteousness of the Pharisees. But His spirituality repelled them. They were "out of touch" with that. He yearned to win the masses of the people, and to draw them into the kingdom of God; but He would not "play the demagogue" even to secure their sympathies. And He Himself said—"It is enough for the disciple that he be *as* his master, and the servant *as* his lord." It does not follow, therefore, that a minister or a church will necessarily grow in immediate popularity by becoming more Christlike. The reverse is, doubtless, sometimes the case. Christian enterprise and endeavour may sometimes have less of visible and proximate success, in proportion as it becomes more unworldly in its spirit and methods, discarding unworthy manœuvres, compromises, and catchwords, and cultivating "the simplicity and the purity that is toward Christ." I know that I am treading here on delicate and dangerous ground—*delicate* ground because of the differences of opinion which exist as to what are and what are not legitimate methods of attracting the people to our churches; and *dangerous* ground because we may be tempted to indulge in a spirit of self-complacency and to overlook the extent to which our lack of success is due to defects in our own character and work. I hasten, therefore, to say that *in the long run* our spiritual influence as ministers will be powerful and lasting in proportion as we enter into fellowship with " the mind of Christ," and cultivate His spirit of unselfishness and unworldliness. It may be a paradox, but it is a fact, that many people are repelled from our churches *both* by the excellences *and* the inconsistencies of Christians. Sometimes a church would prove more attractive to outsiders if it were *either* more worldly *or* more unworldly than it is. There are two reasons why many people dislike the " parson ": the one is that they think the parson is a much better man than they are; the other is that they think the same parson is not nearly so good a man as he ought to be! Worldly minds are not at home in an atmosphere of unworldliness; and yet there is something in unworldliness which appeals to their better nature, and they are quick to detect the signs of a worldly spirit in those who, by their very vocation as Christian ministers, are pledged to discard that spirit.

There can be no doubt that holiness, blended with humility and human-ness, is ultimately the greatest spiritual force amongst mankind. I have referred to the fact that the *proximate* issue of Christ's character and teachings and life was an apparent failure; but He Himself, looking through and beyond the Cross to the *ultimate* result, said, "I, if I be lifted up from the earth, will draw all men unto Me." He felt sure that, in the long run, unworldliness and self-sacrifice would *tell*. And we also may be sure that, whatever may be our proximate and visible success—or whatever may be our seeming failure—our ultimate spiritual influence as ministers will depend, other things being equal, on the degree in which we receive this "mind of Christ."

Let us, therefore, seek to rid ourselves of all mere worldly and selfish ambition. May it not be that, in our lamentations over the condition of our churches, there is a "touch"—perhaps even more than a *touch* —of wounded vanity or wounded pride? What is the main secret of our regrets? Is it because the principles we cherish are not more widely appreciated? Is it because so many of our fellow-men are robbing themselves of blessings which they might receive if they would come into sympathy and communion with the Christian church? Or, on the other hand, is it *chiefly* because *we ourselves* are not as successful as we should like to be—because *our* efforts are not more appreciated—because *our* influence is not more extensive—because the comparatively poor results which seem to follow our endeavours do not bring us much outward honour and glory? Let us examine ourselves; and, if we find that we are too much governed by these lower and more selfish considerations, let us seek to cultivate a higher and holier ambition.

The Greek word meaning "to be *ambitious*" occurs three times in the New Testament; and it is somewhat singular that on each occasion it is used in a *good* sense. Paul, who uses it, must have been familiar enough with the evils wrought in the world by the spirit of ambition; but it seems as if he wished to *Christianize the word,* and to cast into a Christian mould that natural "love of honour" which so often finds its outcome in the restless, selfish strivings of an ambitious worldliness. To the Romans he speaks of himself as being "ambitious to preach the gospel"—especially where he would not be "building on another man's foundation." Paul "loved honour"; but it was the honour of being an "ambassador for Christ"—the privilege of bringing the divine message of salvation to the souls of men. He craved honourable distinction; but it was the distinction of being willing to face *dis*honour for the sake of the truth. Then, to the Corinthians he speaks of being "ambitious to be well-pleasing" to the Lord. Paul did not crucify his natural love of approbation; but he directed it into a safe and holy channel. He felt that it was "a small thing to be judged of *man's* day"; for he was looking forward to "the Day of *the Lord,*" whose searching light would reveal "the secrets of the heart." Once more, Paul exhorts the Thessalonians to be "ambitious to be quiet, and to do their own business." *Ambitious* to be *quiet!* There seems to be almost a touch of irony in the expression. But the apostle meant it seriously enough. He meant that the Thessalonians should give up the restless excitement which was leading them to despise their ordinary, commonplace work, and that they should make it a point of honour to live a life of quiet, steady, diligent fulfilment of duty.

Here, then, are three phases of Christian ambition which we preachers and pastors may well cultivate. Let us be "ambitious to preach the gospel"—faithfully, earnestly, and lovingly, as it ought to be preached—to preach it with the *primary* object of saving, and blessing, and helping the souls of our hearers, whether they be many or few. Let us never forget that it is an honourable and weighty task to address even a small audience on things divine and eternal. Let us also be "ambitious to be well-pleasing to Christ." To please men, and to secure their favour and adhesion, is a poor affair, if we are not seeking such ends and pursuing such methods as Christ approves. And then, again, let us be "ambitious to be quiet, and to do our own work" to which we have been called. It is not always the most prominent work that is the most useful. It is not necessary to make a great noise in the world in order to promote that kingdom which "cometh not with observation." Let us seek to be more resolutely attentive to those duties which bring no special promotion or applause. We can make it a point of honour not to be greedy of honour. We can cherish a spiritual dignity which shall pour contempt on our own pride. We can be ambitious to rise above the restless cravings of a mere worldly ambition. Sometimes we are apt to think too much about our own influence, or too eagerly anxious that the spirits should be subject to *us*. Ought we not "rather to rejoice that our names are written in heaven"—to think less of our own personal power and visible successes, and to think more of the honour of being enrolled as *soldier-citizens of the kingdom of God?*

My one point, then, this morning, is that, if we would exercise more power in the world for good, we must discard all mere selfish and social, and even ecclesiastical ambitions, and cultivate more earnestly the holy ambition of growing in Christian goodness, and doing our simple duty. There are some things which we secure more easily by not being too eager and anxious about them, and I suspect that spiritual influence is one of these things. You remember the old fable of Orpheus—how he had nearly regained his loved Eurydice, but in his eager impatience looked back to see if she were really following him, and then lost her for ever! There is such a thing as losing our influence by turning our eyes too much upon it. When we can say of any man that

> "He never turned his back, but marched breast forward,
>   Never doubted clouds would break,
> Never dreamed, though right were worsted, wrong would triumph,
> Held we fall to rise, are baffled to fight better,
>   Sleep to wake,"

then we know that such a man is sure to have exercised spiritual power over others. When any man marches steadily forward towards the upper light and air, keeping his eye fixed on godly character and simple duty, he may well leave his influence to take care of itself, or rather God will take care that his influence *shall* follow him.

THE RELIEF OF CONSTRAINT.

[Reprinted from *The Manchester, Salford and District Congregational Magazine*, July, 1882.]

IT is sometimes a great relief, in practical life, to feel that we are simply shut up to a certain belief or to a certain course of action. It is this that often gives to the scientific investigator a positive and justifiable assurance as to the conclusions at which he arrives. In the earlier processes of investigation many possible results may be present to his thought; but, as test succeeds test, one hypothesis after another is rejected, and the issue is gradually narrowed until, by some final and crucial experiment, he is constrained to adopt a certain conclusion. Thus also a statesman, whilst theoretically it might seem as if several courses of action were possible to him, may nevertheless feel, at a given crisis, that he is shut up to one course, and that all others are meanwhile excluded from the sphere of practical politics. So, too, in ordinary life, we may sometimes be halting between two opinions, finding it difficult to determine which of two views has the preponderant evidence in its favour, when suddenly some fact of which we had been ignorant comes to our knowledge, and immediately one of the two scales kicks the beam. Or again, we may be hesitating between several possible courses of action; we feel ourselves overburdened by the responsibility of choice; and the gravity of the issues involved may make decision the more difficult and suspense the more painful. Then perhaps, whilst we are thus pondering and hesitating, some event occurs, or some fresh complication of circumstance arises, over which we have no control; and this renders impracticable all courses but one, so that we may now take this one course with a feeling of relief. It is not only that the tension of suspense is relaxed; the burden of responsibility is also lightened. And it is significant that this sense of relief is often experienced even when the one course to which we are constrained is a course which involves a greater amount of labour or of suffering. Indeed, the very hesitation of a pious and conscientious man sometimes springs from the fact that he is afraid, on the one hand, of shirking duty through choosing a path of greater ease, and afraid, on the other hand, of "tempting Providence" through choosing a path of difficulty or danger to which God is not calling him. And so, when the easier of two courses is rendered practically impossible, a godly man may well experience a feeling of relief. He knows that he cannot be tempting Providence, when Providence itself is shutting him up to the course of danger, difficulty, or suffering. Having been in painful perplexity as to his true path, he is relieved to find his way "hedged up" for him, even though it be "with thorns." And, being thus set free from the responsibility of choosing his own course, he casts himself with all the more confidence on that God who has, so to speak, taken upon Himself the responsibility of choosing it for him. A task which is manifestly of divine appointment brings with it the tacit proffer and assurance of divine assistance.

It is further to be noted that a man may sometimes be practically constrained, not by circumstances from without, but by his own affections, conscience, or character. Two alternatives may theoretically lie before him; but, of these two, one may be so utterly repugnant to his own nature as to be practically excluded from his choice. It might be physically possible for a son to murder his own father; and yet filial affection might make such an act a moral impossibility. Thus also, in a crisis of commercial difficulty, a man of thorough integrity may feel that he is shut up to the endurance of misfortune, when the only way of escape is the way of immorality and dishonour. And so it happens that, whilst to one man there may appear to be a number of courses open, another man in similar circumstances feels that to him there is only one course open, all the others being so repugnant to his moral nature that he cannot even look at them as possible. And this sense of constraint brings with it a great relief from the suspense of hesitancy and the pressure of temptation.

When Jesus said to the twelve, " Will ye also go away?" the answer of Peter was, " Lord, to whom shall we go?" Theoretically, there were the two alternatives before the apostle—either to go, or to stay. But, of these two alternatives, one was so intolerable as to lie outside the region of practical choice. It was not as if he had before him two paths, both leading in the same direction and to the same destination, causing him perplexity as to which was the better road. No: he had before him a path which was manifestly a good one; and to quit this path would be to go out upon a trackless waste where he would be only likely to lose his way. To go away from Jesus! The very thought was enough for Peter; for to whom could he go? And, in the midst of the conflict which is now being waged in our own day between Christianity and infidelity, it is no small relief to feel that our own spiritual nature and experience constrain us to abide in the faith. There are those who tell us that historical criticism and scientific truth are rapidly making Christian faith impossible. They ply us with arguments which tend to shake belief in any inspiration of the Bible; they insist on the incredibility of miracle; they present the scientific doctrine of evolution and development in such a form as to give a mythical look to the incarnation and even the sinlessness of Jesus; and they regard all thought as being so absolutely a function of the brain that they dismiss the doctrine of immortality as a baseless dream. Now, if we were to do nothing but listen to such arguments, if we were to hold our judgment regarding Christianity in suspense until we could see our way through all the difficulties suggested by infidelity, we might simply plunge ourselves into painful perplexity. But this is a practical world; and the question between Christ and unbelief is a practical question. Nor is this a question on which an attitude of pure scepticism and suspended judgment is resultless. To accept Christ as our Teacher, Saviour, and Lord has its serious issues; to reject Christ and His gospel has its serious issues; and an attitude of indecision, as between Christ and infidelity, is also fraught with its own serious issues. If a man is hungry, and two different kinds of food are offered him, he does not necessarily mend matters by refusing to partake of either! This may or may not be the wiser course, but it certainly has its own results. And if, of the two kinds of food, the one is bread, which in his own experience has heretofore satisfied his hunger and given him strength, whilst the other is an unpalatable-looking mess from which he instinctively turns away, he would surely be a foolish man if he refused to eat at all until he had answered the arguments which seek to persuade him that the nourishing power of bread is a delusion, or that the bread with which he is familiar is not free from adulteration.

We know what Christ is to us, and what He can do for us. He reveals God as our Father; He draws us to penitence; He assures us of pardon; He inspires us with trust, patience, and love; He strengthens us for duty; He gives us the hope of heaven. If we leave Him, whither shall we betake ourselves? To Atheism, with its universe of whirling atoms ungoverned by any mind? Or to Pantheism, with its vague, unknowable force, and its religion of "cosmic emotion" and lyric poetry? Or to the Religion of Humanity, which directs us to worship the human race, and to look for our only immortality in the influence which may survive our death? Shall we give up bread for a stone? Shall we give up that to which our soul responds, and take that from which our soul shrinks back with instinctive repugnance? No: there are some alternatives which we cannot choose. And thus, amid the perplexities of modern thought, it is a relief to feel that the spiritual instincts and necessities of our nature constrain us to keep clinging to Jesus, as the Christ of God, the Revealer of the Father, the Saviour of the world.

SERVANT-FRIENDS.

[Read at a Devotional Meeting held in connection with the Cheshire Congregational Union, at Middlewich, April 6th, 1886, and reprinted from *Sun and Shield*, May 1st, 1886.]

YOU are met here this evening to stimulate one another in the service of Christ, to pray together for more power and grace to serve Him, and to ask God's blessing, especially on the Christian work which by your united efforts you are endeavouring to do in this county. It is a serious thought for all of us, that we might perhaps be more truly successful in our work for Christ if we were more thoroughly devoted to His service, and if we had more sympathy both with the aims and the methods of our Lord. And it might stimulate and help us greatly if we were to realize more fully that, as disciples of Christ, we are called upon to be at once His servants and His friends. "Henceforth," He said, "I call you not servants; for the servant knoweth not what his lord doeth; but I have called you friends: for all things that I have heard of my Father, I have made known unto you." This, of course, does not mean that, up to a certain point, the disciples had been simply His servants, and that then they altogether ceased to be servants, and became simply His friends. No: Christ's relation to us as our Master is an abiding relation. "Ye call me Master and Lord; and ye say well: for so I am." And Christ speaks as a Master, even when He calls His disciples friends. "Ye are my friends, if ye do whatsoever I *command* you." *We* do not usually speak of commanding our friends: but Christ's friends are to manifest their friendship in obedience. We must, therefore, unite the two ideas of an obedient, faithful servant, and a loving, sympathetic friend, in order to reach the complete ideal of the Christian's relation to Christ.

Now, in our ordinary human relationships there are sometimes to be found instances in which these two elements are more or less blended, and which therefore furnish some analogy to this peculiar relation of the "servant-friend." Thus, an employer may take one of his servants into confidence, revealing to him the secrets of his business, explaining to him the ends he has in view and the means by which he hopes to reach them, and sometimes even going away for a season and leaving the management of the business in his hands. Such a "confidential servant," as we call him, may be none the less—but rather all the more—scrupulous in carrying out his master's wishes and plans. The trust reposed in him naturally deepens his loyalty; whilst the insight which he obtains into his master's business enables him to co-operate more intelligently and efficiently for the furtherance of his master's interests. But perhaps a somewhat closer analogy is to be found in the case of *the family-servant who has lived in the same household for many years—* whose warm attachment and keen sympathy have given the insight which only love *can* give—who has been the tender nurse at many a sick-bed, and has shown reverential sympathy in many a trial—who has gradually been taken into deeper and fuller confidence —who can anticipate wishes before they are expressed —and whose loyal devotion would follow the family even into poverty and shame. This one of the most striking and pathetic of all human relationships—the blending of respect and familiarity, of scrupulous obedience and loyal sympathy—is beautiful to look upon. And this may furnish some analogy to the ideal relation of the Christian to Christ. Now, might we not perhaps have more true success in our Christian work if we were to cherish within our hearts more of the spirit of this special relationship of the servant-friend?

There is a tendency in some Christians to speak of Christ with a kind of familiarity which seems to be deficient in reverence. They dwell on the tenderness of their relation to Christ until there is some danger of their forgetting His supreme claims and His absolute authority. And perhaps they even begin to presume on His gentleness, so as to become negligent and careless in the doing of His will. Now, we ought never to forget that our loving Saviour is our Divine Master. A confidential servant has no right, because of the dignity of his position, to neglect his master's interests or to presume on his master's forbearance; rather is he in honour bound to a deeper fidelity. Though friends, we are servants still. "We must all be made manifest before the judgment-seat of Christ." The Master will "reckon" with His servants according to the "talents" which He has entrusted to their keeping—whether they be talents of faculty, of money, or of influence. Let us, then, take care lest we substitute sentiment for service. Perhaps our work might be more successful if there were more of it—more actual expenditure of energy and time and money in the cause of Christ. May not the fault with some of us lie here,—that we have not enough of the spirit of conscientious and obedient service?

But now, on the other hand, let us remember that we are not servants only, but friends also. Our Lord clothes for us the firm, rugged rock of Duty with the sweet flowers of Affection. Our service ought not to be a mere mechanical obedience, however scrupulous. It ought to be a service of intelligent and appreciative sympathy. Christ has given us some insight into His own motives and plans. He gives us His spirit to make us sharers of His own life. "We know what our Lord doeth." We know both His object and His method. We know that His object is the redemption of mankind, the rescue of souls from sin and death, the establishment of the reign of righteousness and peace. We know also something of His method—the method of holy, meek, loving patience—the method of the Cross. And so, when He summons us to be co-workers with Himself towards His grand object, we ought to work not only as servants who wear His livery, but also as friends who exemplify His spirit. Christ's disciples are in the world as His representatives, and, so to speak, His confidential agents. They are to work for His kingdom therefore, "in His name," as those who have been commissioned by Him to promote His cause, according to the spirit of His methods. Hence the promise, "Whatsoever ye shall ask the Father, *in My name*, He will give it you." We are not to ask God for anything we please, and then to suppose that the mere addition of the words "in the name of Christ" will act as a kind of magical formula, securing a favourable answer to our requests. No: we are actually to ask "in the name of Christ"— as His representatives and servant-friends—as organs of His spirit: we are to ask for what will better enable us to carry on *His* work. Now, can we say that the objects which we have in view are always Christ's objects,—that our supreme desire is to be instrumental in promoting the kingdom of God? If we would pray in His name, let us work in His name. But may it not be that, when we pray for success in our Christian work, we are sometimes praying that our own special methods may succeed, rather than that we may be led into a fuller appreciation and use of Christ's methods? Is it not the case, alas! that the work which the church has done in the world has too often been as the work of mere servants who were ready to adopt almost *any* methods of promoting their Master's interests, rather than as the work of friends who were anxious to adopt only such methods as were in harmony with their Master's spirit? If we are servant-friends who "know what our Lord doeth," let us seek and pray that we may carry out His purposes in His own ways. To exemplify the spirit of Christ in our work for Christ is one of the most important parts of our Christian service. And the spirit of Christ is the spirit of reverence, of faith, of love, and of patience. Christ's kingdom is "not of this world," and the grand instruments for its promotion are spiritual truth, spiritual life, and spiritual character. Might we not, some of us, be more successful in promoting it if we trusted less in mere organization and more in spiritual forces? Might we not be more successful in the long run if we were less impatient for immediate results, and more willing to carry on a steady, patient work of such kind and quality as would be indicative of fuller sympathy with the mind of Christ?

Some of you may remember reading how, in the month of October last, a little girl stood in the midst of a great crowd of people at the mouth of New York harbour, and, by simply touching a button, shattered an island of rock which had lain as an obstruction in the channel. Now, to any one who was not in the secret, that would have seemed a very strange and sudden event. But we know that it was not so strange or so sudden as it looked. For who was that little girl? She was the daughter of an engineer; and for ten long years men had been at work on that rock—away down sixty feet beneath low-water mark —patiently cutting tunnel after tunnel—four miles of tunnels—and filling ever so many holes with gunpowder and dynamite, until the nine acres of rock were like a huge honeycomb filled with 140 tons of explosive material. Then, at the end of all this labour, an electric wire had been laid between the shore and the island; and all that the engineer's daughter had now to do was just to touch the button which brought the electric spark into contact with the gunpowder and dynamite. Thus, by the touch of that girl's finger a huge rock, which had lain there for millenniums, was in a moment shattered into thousands of fragments. But what would have been the use of her touch, and what would have been the use of the electric spark, but for those ten years of steady, careful, plodding labour which had gone before? And is it not the case that, in the spiritual world also, crises of individual conversion and religious revival are often preceded by periods of preparatory work? Christ Himself came "in the fulness of the times"; and this means that there had been ages of preparation for His advent. The sudden manifestations of the Day of Pentecost were preceded by the workshop in Nazareth, the ministry in Galilee, the death on Calvary. And how often does the conversion of the sinner stand connected, even more perhaps than he himself knows, with religious influences put forth upon him in former years? May it not be that we are sometimes too eager to have the honour and glory of putting the manifest and finishing touch to some spiritual work, instead of being content to labour on industriously, steadily, and perhaps obscurely, in our Christian service? It is not given to every one to touch the electric button, but we may all of us lend a hand in the tunnelling of the rock.

Thus, then, if we are seeking to accomplish our Master's objects, according to our Master's commands, we may possibly be doing a really successful work for Him, even although it may be some time before our success is apparent. But, on the other hand, we must not forget that perhaps our work might be *even manifestly* more successful than it is, if by simple faith and more earnest prayer we were to lay hold of and utilize those spiritual forces which are within our reach. In the natural world man achieves his greatest triumphs, not by his own physical strength, but by utilizing the physical forces which lie all around him in nature. What could that little girl have done, in her own strength, towards removing the island of rock? Or how could those men who tunnelled the rock have removed it out of the channel by their own strength? It was by the use and the combination of certain forces in nature that the thing was done. And even so, in all our work for the promotion of Christ's kingdom in the world, we shall be successful in proportion as we make use of spiritual and divine forces. It is by the touch of faith and the prayer of faith that we are able to make the best use of these forces. "If," said Christ, "ye have faith as a grain of mustard seed, ye shall say unto this mountain, Remove hence to yonder place; and it shall remove." A metaphor, no doubt; but a metaphor on the lips of Christ is no mere ornament of rhetoric. A simple faith in God—expressing itself in the prayer of faith and the labour of faith—brings to a man a strength that is not his own. Let us, then, seek as the servant-friends of Christ to carry on His work after His own methods, so that, by faith and prayer and a fuller reception of His spirit, we may make larger use of spiritual forces, and become more and more the willing instruments of a divine energy.

LAW, MIRACLE, AND PRAYER.

A PARABLE FOR THE TIMES.

[Reprinted from *The Congregationalist*, February, 1877; subsequently abridged by the author.]

Two children—brother and sister—were once crossing the ocean in a steamship. The captain was a relative, and showed them much kindness. They had never been on board a steamer before. The great engines attracted much of their attention. They used to stand in a safe place, and look down into the engine-house, and watch the huge, smooth, regular movements of this colossal thing that propelled the ship. They had asked some of the sailors whether it did not rest during the night; and the sailors told them that it kept moving on, in just the same way, all the time they were sleeping.

Now, sometimes these two children used to discuss the question whether this engine could be stopped, and whether their friend the captain had any power over its movements. The little girl, who had great faith in the captain, was sure that he could stop the machine whenever he pleased. She argued that the engine must have been set a-going when the ship started, although they had not seen it done. Besides, she had asked some of the sailors; and they had told her that the captain could stop the engine, and that, indeed, once or twice—not often, but once or twice—they had seen him stop it, even on the voyage. So she, for her part, believed the sailors.

But the boy, who was a little sceptic in his way, was not so sure about it. He did not know when or how the engine had been set a-going; perhaps the captain had nothing to do with that: the machinery had always been moving, since *they* knew anything about it; that at any moment, in the middle of the voyage, whilst the fires were all burning, and the great machine was in full motion, the captain could suddenly stop it—this was difficult to believe. Besides, even if he were able, somehow or other, to stop the machinery, it did not follow that he *had* ever interfered with its regular movements. True, a few sailors said they had seen him do so; but even they said they had only seen this once or twice; and perhaps the sailors were mistaken, or perhaps they were even "telling a story."

Thus, then, the little boy and girl used to argue the matter; only, of course, in their own childish fashion and language. One day the boy was playing on deck with a large, bright-coloured ball, when suddenly it bounded over the side of the ship and fell into the sea. He was in great trouble about this, and ran at once to tell his sister, who happened at the moment to be sitting on the captain's knee. "Oh, captain!" she said, looking up beseechingly into his face, "stop the engines and get the ball!" But the captain, stroking her hair, smiled, and said, "What! stop that great machine and this great ship for *that?* No; little boys must be more careful of their balls!" He looked and spoke so kindly, that the little girl did not lose her faith in him; but, for all that, she thought it strange that a friend so kind and good to children did not stop the ship, when her brother was so vexed about losing his beautiful ball. As for the boy, he was now quite confirmed in his opinion that the captain either could not stop the engines in mid-ocean, or at least never had done it, and never would do it—whatever a few sailors might say.

One day, however—not long after—as they were both standing together near the captain, and looking down into the engine-house, they heard a sudden shriek, and then a cry, "Man overboard!" Then, in a moment, they saw the captain give a sign; and then they heard the cry, "Stop her!"—and then, in another moment, the great engine seemed somehow to get a sudden check, and began, as it were, to pant, and to move slowly, as if it were out of breath; and then presently it came to a standstill—and the ship too. And, meanwhile, some one had thrown a life-buoy to the poor sailor who had fallen overboard; and presently he caught it; and then they drew him in by the rope, and he was saved. Whereupon the captain suddenly gave another sign, and the huge engine began once more to move, and in a very little time was moving at its former speed. Only a few minutes had passed altogether, and there was the machine working away again with the old ponderous regularity of movement, just as if it had never been and could not be interfered with! Then the little boy saw, not only that the captain could at once stop the engine when he pleased, but also that he did stop it, *whenever he thought there was sufficient reason.*

A few days afterwards, as the little girl was standing with a large doll in her arms, looking down into the engine-house, the doll slipped out of her arms and fell into the midst of the machinery—she could not tell where—away out of her sight. She began to cry; but she thought of her friend the captain, and was for rushing off at once to ask him to get her doll for her. But her brother, who had now (with his way of it) become quite a little philosopher, stopped her. "What is the use," said he, " of going to the captain? Very likely your doll is all crushed to pieces by this time. Besides, the captain would have to stop the engines in order to get it; and do you think a doll lost is like a man overboard? You shouldn't bother the captain about such things!" But the little girl was not to be hindered. She knew the captain was kind, and she had great faith in what he could do. "Well, he won't be angry with me," she said, "for asking him. He will be sorry that I've lost my doll. He may perhaps be able to get it for me. I need not ask him to stop the engines; perhaps he may be able to get it without doing that. I cannot tell. I can at least ask him." "Very well," says the little philosopher, "you may go; but it is all of no use. I'll tell you beforehand what he will say to you: 'Little girls must just learn to be more careful of their dolls!'" But the girl persisted and went to her friend, and said, "Oh, captain! it was very careless of me, and I am so sorry; but I have let my doll fall down amongst the engines, and I don't know where it is. Do you think you could get it for me? I don't ask you to stop the engines; but, if it is possible, I wish I could have it again." And the captain was greatly pleased with the child's confidence, and he felt sorry for her loss; and so he smiled and said, "Well, well, we shall see what can be done." It was not a very definite promise; but the little girl had faith in her friend, and believed that he would do what was wise and kind. And the captain went down into the engine-room, and spent some time in looking for the doll. At length he spied it in an out-of-the-way corner, not much the worse for its fall. And the brother and sister waited, and watched the engines, and saw that they never stopped. But, after a while, the captain came back and said, "Well, here, you see, is your pretty doll; but, you know, little girls should be more careful!" Then the child kissed and thanked him, and loved him more than ever. But the boy grew jealous, and forgot all his philosophy, and thought that his sister was a "pet" of the captain's; and he began to quarrel with her, and said; "Oh, yes, he can take pains and trouble about *your* doll; but he does not at all care when I lose *my* ball!" But he was wrong once more; for, when they all came ashore at the end of the voyage, the good captain surprised him by buying for him a larger and more beautiful ball than the one he had lost at sea.

This story is merely a parable; but perhaps it may help to show how, even in front of the unchanging laws of nature, we may cling to a reasonable faith both in the historical fact of miracles and in the present power of prayer. We may be told that, if we really believe in miracles, we ought even nowadays to kneel down and pray that paralysis may be cured in a moment, or that our dead may be brought back to life. But we have simply no warrant for asking God to work such miracles merely to meet our own wishes and longings, and therefore we do not offer such prayers. *The captain may not stop the engines for a boy's ball; but, for all that, he may have stopped them to save a man from drowning.* The miracles of the Lord Jesus Christ stand in direct relation to the salvation of perishing humanity. To save mankind from spiritual death, to rescue humanity, struggling in the dark waters of atheism and sin, and to bring it into a state of faith in the heavenly Father—this we may surely regard as a worthy reason for the miraculous birth of the Son of God, for those wondrous works which "manifested forth His glory."

But it may be said: Well, you admit, at any rate, that the age of miracles is now past; and therefore it is a foolish thing to pray for material blessings.

I reply: That to pray for material blessings is not necessarily to ask for a miracle. *A captain may be so tender-hearted as to give back to a little girl her lost doll, and yet he may not need to stop the engines.* If God is my friend, He will not be angry when I lay my desires before Him. It *may* be that I am asking what He cannot wisely bestow. But, on the other hand, it *may* be that, in answer to prayer, He can and will come to my help, without working any miracle. And so I cry, "Father, if it be possible!" and there I leave it. Nor need I imagine that those who get their requests are the petted favourites of heaven. Rather let me believe that if, in response to the prayer of faith, God does not give me what I ask, *He will doubtless give me, by and by, that which is far better.*

TRANSLATIONS FROM GOETHE.

The Erl-king.

THROUGH the lone dark night and stormy blast
A father and child were riding fast;
The father's arm his boy caress'd,
The boy clung close to his father's breast.

"Why hid'st thou thy face, my boy, in fear?"
"See'st thou not, father, the Erl-king here,
  With his crown and his streaming silver hair?"
"My boy, 'tis a wreath of misty air."

"Come, dear Earth-child, come and play with me
  By the flowery shore of the Faery Sea,
  Where games never tire, nor flowers decay,
  And my mother shall dress thee in golden array!"

"O father, dear father, dost thou not hear
  How softly the Erl-king speaks in my ear?"
"Hush! hush! my child, 'tis only the sound
  Of the rustling leaves on the frosty ground!"

"My pretty Earth-child, come away with me!
  My daughters will nurse thee with love and glee;
  They will dance thee at eve round the mystic ring,
  Then lull thee to sleep with the songs they sing!"

"Look—look—father! there, in the dark, dost thou see
The Erl-king's daughters waiting for me?"
"Oh, father knows well what his own boy sees;
'Tis but the grey gleam of the old willow trees."

"I love thee, sweet child, but I cannot stay;
If thou wilt not come, I must tear thee away."
"O father! dear father! he's seizing my arm,
That wicked Erl-king has done me harm."

The father shudders—he rides fast and wild;
To his breast he strains closer the moaning child:
On—on to the courtyard swiftly he sped;
But there, in his arms, lay the dear boy—*dead!*

Wer nie sein Brod.

WHO never ate with tears his bread,
    Who never thro' the long night-hours
Hath wept in sorrow on his bed,
    He knows you not, ye Heavenly Powers!

'Tis ye who bring us into life,
    Ye let the poor man work his sin,
Then ye resign him to the knife,
    That Virtue may the victory win!

Reminder.

WILT thou far and wide be roaming?
    Lo! the good is very near:
Only learn to seize good fortune,
    Then good fortune's ever here!

The Lover's Nearness.

I THINK of thee, when the bright sunshine streams
　　　　Down on the sea;
And when the fountain in the moonlight gleams,
　　　　I think of thee.

I see thee, when far off the dust appears
　　　　Along the road,
At midnight, when the trembling traveller's fears
　　　　Some ill forebode.

I hear thee, when the waves each rocky cove
　　　　With murmurs fill.
I often go to listen in the grove,
　　　　When all is still.

I am with thee; and thou, though far away,
　　　　To me art near:
Soon will the stars peep out at close of day—
　　　　Would thou wert here!

Comfort in Tears.

"How comes it—when all else is glad—
　　　That you so gloomy keep?
One only has to see your eyes,
　　　To know they often weep."

"And may I not in secret weep
　　　Over my private grief?
The tears of sorrow flow so sweet,
　　　They bring my heart relief."

"But now your merry friends are here,
    Our hearts are opened wide;
  Come, then, whatever you have lost,
    To us that loss confide."

"Ye stir and shout, but cannot guess
    What puts me on the rack;
  Ah, no! 'tis nothing I have lost,
    But something that I lack."

"Then rouse yourself, you still are young—
    Weep not in vain desire;
  At your age men possess the strength
    And courage to acquire."

"Ah, no! I cannot *this* acquire,
    It stands away too far;
  It dwells so high, it shines so bright,
    Like yonder lovely star."

"The stars!—we do not long for stars,
    We but enjoy their light,
  And oft look up with ecstasy
    Into the glorious night."

"I too look up with ecstasy,
    Through many and many a day;
  Then let me spend my nights in tears,
    And weep my grief away!"

Sadness.

Ye are fading, pretty roses,
　You my loved one did not wear ;
Ye only bloomed for him whom sorrow
　Now hath plunged into despair!

Of those days I think with sadness,
　When I, angel, hung on thee,
Early in my garden watching
　The first bud on plant and tree.

All the sweetest fruits and blossoms
　Did I carry to thy feet ;
And my heart, in thy dear presence,
　With high hopes began to beat.

Ye are fading, pretty roses,
　You my loved one did not wear ;
Ye only bloomed for him whom sorrow
　Now hath plunged into despair!

The Wanderer's Night-Song.

Thou that from the heavens art,
　Calming all the storms of grief,
To the doubly wretched heart
　Bringing doubly sweet relief,

From this stir I fain would cease,
　What means all this joy and pain ?
Come, blessèd Peace,
　Oh come, and in my bosom reign !

A Pendant.

OVER all the hill-tops
 Broodeth Peace ;
In all the tree-tops
 The air doth cease
To stir leaf or bough ;
 The little birds all nestle silently ·
Only wait ; presently
Calm, too, art thou !

Heidenröslein.

[The Heath rose, or Scottish rose.]

A LADDIE spied, a' wat wi' dew,
 A rosebud i' the glen ;
Sae fresh and like the dawn its hue,
He ran to get a nearer view,
 His e'e it sparkled then !
  Rosebud, rosebud, rosebud red,
  Rosebud i' the glen.

The laddie said, " I'll gather thee,
 Rosebud o' the glen ! "
Said the rosebud, " I'll prick thee,
So as thou'lt aye ha'e mind o' me ;
 I'll no be pu'ed, I ken ! "
  Rosebud, rosebud, rosebud red,
  Rosebud i' the glen.
   x

The laddie pu'ed, that very morn,
  The rosebud i' the glen;
The rosebud pricked him wi' her thorn,
But frae her place she maun be torn,
  Nae cry could save her then!
    Rosebud, rosebud, rosebud red,
    Rosebud i' the glen.

TRANSLATIONS FROM SCHILLER.

The Maiden from the far Countrie.

THERE came with every opening Spring,
   Into a valley poor and bare,
Soon as the larks began to sing,
   A maiden wonderful and fair.

She was no native of the vale,
   And whence she came no shepherd knew;
For ever, as she left the dale,
   All traces of her vanished too.

She was a blessing to behold!
   To her all hearts were opened wide;
Yet no one durst be over-bold,
   Her sweetness was so dignified.

And ripest fruits and richest flowers
   She carried in her bounteous hand,
Which warmer suns and milder showers
   Had nurtured in some fairer land.

Whoever would might freely come;
   She gladly welcomed every guest;
And none who came went empty home,
   The young and old alike were blest.

But, when there came some loving pair—
  All happy in the golden hours—
To them she gave the richest share,
  Theirs was the crown of fairest flowers.

The Dividing of the Earth.

To men spake Jove on high, the bounteous giver :—
  "Take the round Earth; it shall be yours, I swear,
To you I give it—to be held for ever—
  But grudge to none his share."

At the glad word both young and old upbounded,
  All hands bestirred themselves with might and main ;
Through glen and glade the huntsman's horn resounded ;
  The farmer seized the grain ;

The merchant took the goods in which he traded ;
  The abbot chose the ruddy, generous wine ;
The bridges and the streets the king blockaded,
  And said "The tenth is mine !"

At last—long after all had been decided—
  From far away the bright-eyed Poet came ;
Alas ! he saw all earthly things divided,—
  None left for him to claim !

" Woe's me ! am I the only one remaining
  Undowered, and yet thy most devoted child ?"
Thus wailed he out to Jove his loud complaining,
  With bitter grief and wild.

" If thro' the land of dreams thou *wilt* be gliding,"
  Replied the god, "lay not the blame on me ;

Where wert thou, when the Earth was a-dividing?"
The Poet said, "With THEE!

"The beauty of Thy face mine eye was praising;
   The music of Thy heaven entranced mine ear;
Forgive a soul, that, on Thy radiance gazing,
   Hath lost the earthly here!"

"What shall I do?" cried Jove, "the world is given;
   The harvest, chase, and mart are mine no more;
Come, dwell with me in my own beauteous Heaven!
   Come when thou wilt, thou'lt find an open door!"

The Pilgrim.

SPRING-LEAVES in youth's tangled wildwood
   Were yet fresh upon the boughs,
When I left the sports of childhood,
   Wandering from my father's house;

All my heritage, forsaking,
   Lightly did I cast away,
And, my pilgrim-staff uptaking,
   Went forth gladly on my way.

For a mighty hope possessed me,
   And a vague faith filled my soul;
"Wander on," it cried, "nor rest thee
   Till thou reach the Eastern goal;

"Till thou reach a golden gateway,
   Then thy pilgrimage is done;
There the heavens and earth will straightway
   Meet, and be for ever one!"

On I journeyed—morn till even—
   Never, never rest for me!
But ever hath remained still hidden
   That which I have longed to see.

In my path lay mountain-ridges,
   Rocky clefts and rivers deep;
Over torrents built I bridges
   And o'er ravines wild and steep.

Then I reached a shining river,
   Eastward ran its silver thread,
And, with hopes that made me quiver,
   Flung myself into its bed.

Its gleaming waters quickly bore me
   Where the waves of ocean roll;
The blue expanse now lies before me,
   But—no nearer to my goal!

Ah! thither no bridge leads us mortals;
   Ah! those heavens so sweet and clear
Will never touch this Earth's dark portals,
   And our THERE is never *here!*

Punch Song.

FOUR simple elements,
   With vigour rife,
Build up the universe,
   Shape all its life.

Press the juice of the lemon
   From out of the core;

Life's innermost kernel
Is bitter and sore.

Then with sweet sugar,
Added at length,
Temper the bitter
And burning strength.

Pour sparkling water
Into the bowl,
Water encircles
Quietly the whole.

A drop of pure spirit
Now into it pour;
For to life spirit giveth
Life more and more.

Ere it evaporates
Quick drink it up!
Only whilst sparkling,
Refreshes the cup.

The Archer's Song.

WITH his bow and arrow,
Over hill and dale,
Early comes the archer,
Whilst the dawn is pale.

As the kite is sovereign,
In the air-domain;
So through glen and mountain
Doth the archer reign.

> Far as arrow reacheth,
> Wide his kingdom lies;
> And he claims as booty
> All that creeps and flies.

The Maiden's Lament.

> The black clouds lowered o'er the tossing wood,
> On the green of the shore the maiden stood;
> The billows came thundering in with might,
> And she sighed out her grief to the dark'ning night,
> Her eyes all beclouded with sadness :—
> "My heart it is withered, the world is bare,
> It can give me nothing for which I care;
> Thou Holy One, take now Thy child above!
> I have done with life—I have done with love—
> I have tasted the earthly gladness."

> "In vain flow the tears from the eyes that weep,
> No wailing awakens the dead from their sleep!
> But say what can comfort and heal the heart,
> After all the sweet pleasures of love depart,
> I will send it thee, child, from above."
> "Oh let the tears flow, though in vain I must weep,
> And my wailing awakes not the dead from his sleep!
> The sweetest relief to the sorrowing heart,
> After all the dear pleasures of love depart,
> Are the woes and the wailings of love!"

GERMAN LYRICS—MISCELLANEOUS.

Charlemagne's Voyage.

WITH his twelve peers King Charles set sail,
    For the Holy Land steer'd he;
But sudden uprose a stormy gale,
    And caught them in mid-sea.

Then outspake Roland, the hero brave:
    "I can use both sword and shield;
But against the force of the mighty wave
    Such weapons we cannot wield!"

" With my harp," said Holger, the lordly Dane,
    "I can make the sternest weep;
But Orpheus himself would strive in vain,
    To lull these winds to sleep!"

Sir Oliver gazed on his trusty blade
    That had been in many a fight;
"I care not so much for myself," he said,
    "As for *Alta Clara* bright."

Then thought the wicked Ganelon,
    And mutter'd within his breast:
"Were I but safe on shore alone,
    The devil might take the rest!"

Archbishop Turpin, sighing, prayed:
"Thy soldiers, Lord, are we;
Come, dearest Saviour, grant Thine aid,
And speed us o'er the sea!"

Count Richard the Dauntless then began:
"Ye fiends of the nether hell,
Oft have I served you like a man;
Now serve me just as well!"

Lord Naimé said: "Much counsel wise
Is given in many a matter;
But oft on shipboard good advice
Is scarce as good fresh water!"

Lord Riol the others thus addressed:
"A warrior old am I,
And I could wish my bones to rest,
Where all my fathers lie."

Then sweetly sang the young Sir Guy:
"Had I the wings of a dove,
I'd soar beyond this storm, and fly
To the arms of my lady-love!"

Outspake the noble Count Garein:
"May the gods propitious be!
For I'd rather quaff good Rhenish wine,
Than the water of the sea!"

The gay Lord Lambert echoed the wish:
"May the gods propitious be!
For I'd much rather eat good fish,
Than have good fish eat me!"

Sir Godfrey spoke with calm despair :
"I yield to the adverse Fates;
And, after all, I only share
   The doom of my trusty mates."

King Charles sat calm amid this band,
   And never a word spake he;
But steer'd the ship with steady hand
   Thro' the wild and stormy sea!
Uhland.

On the Death of a Child.

SHE came—she went—a passing guest,
   With traceless footstep light and low:
Whence?—whither?—ah! it stands confessed—
   From God—*to* God—is all we know!
Uhland.

O lieb', so lang.

OH love, and let thy love be true!
   Oh love, and let thy love be deep!
There comes an hour—there comes an hour—
   When at the grave thou'lt stand and weep!

See that thy heart doth ever glow
   With love, and ever love enshrine,
As long as any other heart
   In love responsive beats to thine.

Whoe'er to thee unlocks his soul,
   For him do all within thy power;
For him fill every day with joy,
   And give him no unhappy hour.

Oh guard thy speech with jealous care!
　Forth from thy tongue the wild word leaps;
God knows it was not meant for ill!
　But yet thy friend in secret weeps.

Oh love, and let thy love be true!
　Oh love, and let thy love be deep!
There comes an hour—there comes an hour—
　When at the grave thou'lt stand and weep!

Amid the tall, dank churchyard grass,
　Thou kneelest down with streaming eyes;
For now thou nevermore canst see
　Him who beneath in stillness lies.

Thou criest, "Smile on me, my friend,
　Forgive, forgive the wound I gave;
God knows it was not meant for ill!
　Oh see me weeping at thy grave!"

But ah! he cannot see or hear;
　He comes not to relieve thy woe;
The lips that kissed thee cannot say,
　"Friend, I forgave thee long ago!"

Yes, he forgave; yet, at the time,
　Tears ran as if they could not cease;
Sharp was the pain; 'tis over now;
　His race is run—he rests in peace.

Then love, and let thy love be true!
　Oh love, and let thy love be deep!
There comes an hour—there comes an hour—
　When at the grave thou'lt stand and weep!

Freiligrath.

Hope.

LET Winter rage and beat the ground,
    Our hands with his cold benumbing;
Let him fling his snows and ice around:
    Yet Spring is surely coming!

The mists may gather thick, and doom
    Both earth and sky to sadness;
But the sun breaks through their murky gloom,
    And wakes the world to gladness.

Howl, winds, and blow with all your might!
    You shall not find *me* mourning;
For with light footsteps, overnight,
    The Spring is swift returning.

And then, she knows not how or why,
    The green Earth wakes from her sleeping,
And she laughs up into the sunny sky,
    As if she for joy were leaping!

She decks her hair with garlands gay
    Of flowers all fresh and living;
And her brooklets sparkle adown their way,
    Like tears of glad thanksgiving.

Then hush! my soul, and be resigned,
    Though hell itself be scorning;
There yet will dawn for all mankind
    A grand and sweet May morning!

And ye, who feel keen Sorrow's frost
    Your very *hearts* benumbing,
In God's wise love still calmly trust,
    For Spring is surely coming!

Geibel.

The Heart.

Two chambers hath the heart;
    There Sorrow
And Gladness dwell apart.

Gladness in one room waketh,
    In the other
Sorrow her slumber taketh.

O Gladness, quiet keep!
    Speak softly
Lest Sorrow wake from sleep!

Herm. Neumann.

Thamire an die Rosen.

HERE my lover vowed to meet me
    Ere the roses should have blown:
That time now has come to greet me,
    Roses! and I'm here alone.

Lovely gifts from Heavenly Donor,
    Roses! spare me, spare me pain;
Also spare my shepherd's honour:
    Close, oh close your buds again!

J. N. Götz.

Mein Herz, ich will dich fragen.

My heart, I wish to ask thee
    What is this Love so sweet?
"Two souls, with one thought between them,
    Two hearts with one heart-beat!"

And tell me how Love cometh?
"She comes, and there is she!"
And say how Love departeth?
"Oh that can never be!"

And what is Love the purest?
"She that from self doth cease!"
And when is Love the deepest?
"When she most silent is!"

And when is Love the richest?
"When she most lavish proves!"
And tell me how Love talketh?
"She does not talk—she loves!"

Halm.

An Leukon.

Now, whilst it bloometh, pluck the flower;
    To-morrow's not to-day:
Learn thou to seize each passing hour;
    Time flies on wings away!

Drink! kiss! whilst now is given to thee
    The chance that may not stay!
Where wilt thou on the morrow be?
    Time flies on wings away!

Do now thy good and kindly deed;
    We oft repent delay;
My counsel is to live with speed;
    Time flies on wings away!

Gleim.

Ich sprach zur Sonne.

I ASKED the Sun: "Come, tell me, what is Love?"
  He gave no answer save his golden flame;
I asked the Flower: "Come, tell me, what is Love?"
  She gave me fragrance, but no answer came.

I asked th' Eternal: "Tell me, what is Love?
  Is it sweet trifling, or a holy task?"
And then God gave me a true darling wife,
  And what Love is, I nevermore need ask.

Emil Rittershaus.

The Book and the Leaf.

I HAVE a dear old auntie,
  And she has a quaint old book;
And in it there lies an old leaf,
  With a dry and withered look;
And the hands, too, are dry and withered,
  That plucked it in other years:
What ails the dear old auntie,
  That her eyes thus fill with tears?

Anastasius Grün.

On the Strand.

WHAT writes the wave upon the sand?
  She writes thereon her bitter woe;
  Her everlasting ebb and flow;
Her too brief stay upon the strand.

But I look out across the bay,
  And write with joyful heart and hand
  My love and hope upon the sand;
The next wave washes all away!

R. Gottschall.

Der Rosenstrauch.

THE child sleeps under the lilac trees,
The little buds swell in the soft May breeze;
Sweet are her dreams 'neath the closéd eyes,
She plays with the angels in Paradise.
      The years roll on.

The maiden stands near the lilac trees,
Around her playeth the fragrant breeze;
She presses her hand to her heaving heart—
All glowing and throbbing with love's sweet smart.
      The years roll on.

The mother kneels at the lilac trees,
Rustle the leaves in the evening breeze;
She thinks of the days that for ever are past,
And the tears to her eyes are rising fast.
      The years roll on.

Leafless and bare mourn the lilac trees;
The leaves have decayed in the Autumn breeze,
And, shaken by winds that howl and rave,
They have fallen and covered a quiet grave.
      The years roll on.
                    Ferrand.

Frisch gesungen.

  OFT in the circle of friendship,
    At rest in the fragrant dell,
  Have I sung some lively ditty,
    And all was happy and well.

And again, when shut up in sorrow,
  As in some gloomy cell,
I have once more sung my ditty,
  And all has once more been well.

And many a time it has happened,
  When into a fury I fell,
I've betaken myself to my singing,
  And all has again been well.

Then do not be ever complaining,
  Nor against thy fate rebel;
Strike up—strike up—some ditty,
  And all shall again be well!

Chamisso.

Kleines Frauenlob.

" *Woman's*" named, because *Woe* cleaveth
  To the *man* that has no wife;
" *Wife*" is named, because she weaveth
  Joy into her husband's life.

Man is *marred* until he's *married;*
  Man is *weeded* when he's *wed;*
Who *avoids* the eyes of women
  Keeps his own heart *void* and dead.

Oh! how sweet when *ladies lade us*
  With the gifts we long to see:
Bliss *unalloyed,* and love *all-loyal,*
  Like the wife who clings to me!

Rückert.

Prayer during Battle:

FATHER, I cry to Thee!
Smoke from the thundering cannon is pouring,
Lightnings flash forth from the midst of the roaring;
Ruler of battles, I cry to Thee!
    Father, oh lead Thou me!

    Father, oh lead Thou me!
To victory or to Death's dark land!
Lord, I acknowledge Thy command:
Lord, as Thou wilt, so lead Thou me;
    God, I acknowledge Thee!

    God, I acknowledge Thee!
In autumn blasts that make leaves quiver,
In battle storms that make hearts shiver,
Fountain of grace, I acknowledge Thee;
    Father, oh bless Thou me!

    Father, oh bless Thou me!
In Thy strong hand my life I lay;
Thou giv'st, and Thou canst take away:
In life, in death, oh bless Thou me!
    Father, all praise to Thee!

    Father, all praise to Thee!
Not for mere earthly goods we fight,
But in the sacred cause of Right;
So, falling or conquering, praise I Thee:
    O God, take charge of me!

O God, take charge of me!
When o'er me the thunders of death are pealing,
When from my veins the life-blood is stealing;
Oh then, my God, take charge of me!
Father, I cry to Thee!

Körner.

Encouragement.

The lark—an embodied song—on high
Trills his clear notes in the morning sky,
And carols with joy in the sunny air:
  "The world is fair!"

The flower awakes in the sweet sunshine,
And gently unlocks her fragrant shrine;
From her open cup breathe the odours rare:
  "The world is fair!"

In liquid silver ripples the stream;
Wave follows wave in the morning gleam,
And, kissing the shore, they whisper there:
  "The world is fair!"

Why stand'st thou, O man, with look distress'd,
Nursing thy grief in thy gloomy breast?
Oh, see the joy round thee everywhere!
  The world is so fair!

K. E. Ebert.

www.ingramcontent.com/pod-product-compliance
Lightning Source LLC
Chambersburg PA
CBHW020104020526
44112CB00033B/836